MW01015905

THE ANANSI READER

WITHDRAWN FROM COLLECTION VANCOUVER PUBLIC LIBRARY

THE ANANSI READER

Forty Years of Very Good Books

Edited by LYNN COADY

ANANSI

Copyright © 2007, House of Anansi Press, Inc. Copyright to each individual piece in this collection is held by the author of that piece.

All rights reserved. No part of this publication may be reproduced or transmitted in any form or by any means, electronic or mechanical, including photocopying, recording, or any information storage and retrieval system, without permission in writing from the publisher.

Published in 2007 by
House of Anansi Press Inc.
110 Spadina Avenue, Suite 801
Toronto, ON, M5V 2K4
Tel. 416-363-4343
Fax 416-363-1017
www.anansi.ca

Distributed in Canada by
HarperCollins Canada Ltd.
1995 Markham Road
Scarborough, ON, M1B 5M8
Toll free tel. 1-800-387-0117

Distributed in the United States by
Publishers Group West
1700 Fourth Street
Berkeley, CA 94710
Toll free tel. 1-800-788-3123

11 10 09 08 07   1 2 3 4 5

LIBRARY AND ARCHIVES CANADA CATALOGUING IN PUBLICATION

The Anansi reader : forty years of very good books / edited by Lynn Coady.

Includes index.
ISBN 978-0-88784-775-2 (pbk.)

1. Canadian literature (English)—20th century. 2. Canadian literature (English)—21st century. 3. House of Anansi Press. I. Coady, Lynn, 1970–
PS8251.A53 2007   C810.8'0054   C2007-903441-1

Library of Congress Control Number: 2007930190

We acknowledge for their financial support of our publishing program the Canada Council for the Arts, the Ontario Arts Council, and the Government of Canada through the Book Publishing Industry Development Program (BPIDP).

Printed and bound in Canada.

To writers and readers, past, present, and future.

CONTENTS

INTRODUCTION

Sometimes I used to think of it as wandering into a clearing in the forest with a bow and some arrows and sitting down and firing an arrow into the air... It plops in the ground. But then you fire another one and it hits a tree. You happen also by sheer coincidence to have a pot of paint and a paintbrush, so you chug over to the tree and you paint a target around where the arrow has landed. And now it's clear you've hit the bull's-eye.

I don't mean that to be derogatory, either, because to actually recognize when something has substance, when something resonates, when something has landed somewhere—it takes an eye. But the overall shape of what you're doing emerges gradually.

—Dennis Lee, in conversation, 2007

In the corner of my cramped desk, Margaret Atwood and Dennis Lee lay interwoven. This is what I do when I read two books at once, two books I'm trying to hold in my head simultaneously. I use one chunk of the first book as a page marker for the place I want held in the second book, and vice-versa. So Dennis and Margaret are lying there, holding each other's place for me.

In Lee's *Nightwatch*, I am reading his long poem, *The Death of Harold Ladoo*. In Atwood's *Second Words*, I am reading her essay on the poetry and death of John Thompson. That is to say, I'm reading an essay about a poet and a poem about a writer of prose.

Both Thompson and Ladoo were electrifying writers, unnerv-
ing personalities, and early discoveries of House of Anansi Press,
the Canadian publishing house founded by Lee and David
Godfrey in 1967. And, as you may have intuited from the above,
both writers died in a tragic and untimely manner. Harold Sonny
Ladoo, author of the novels *No Pain Like this Body* and the posthumous *Yesterdays*, was murdered in 1973 during a visit home to
Trinidad. Thompson, similarly, published two books of poetry
with Anansi—*At the Edge of the Chopping there Are No Secrets,* and
the shattering *Stilt Jack*—before his grim and mysterious death
three years later.

I don't mean to kick things off on a morbid note; it's just that
over the past few months I've had Anansi books embracing in
the way I describe above—Thompson folded into Ladoo, Lee
into Atwood and vice versa—all over my apartment. I only want
to underscore the parallel way in which these four decades'
worth of books and writers have begun—it seems to me—to call
out to each other, and reflect one another, across eras, genres,
and those infamous geographical distances that have been so celebrated, so bemoaned in our ongoing cultural conversation.
Since starting this project I've been experiencing these echoes
and reflections with increasing intensity. The furious heartbreak
of Lynn Crosbie's 2006 long poem *Liar* folds back into 1967, to
Atwood's *Circle Game*, a more circumspect, yet no less tortured
autopsy of love gone wrong. Sheila Heti's gnomic snippets in *The
Middle Stories* are strikingly of a piece with the playful vignettes
of David Godfrey's first book, *Death Goes Better with Coca-Cola*,
or the surrealist tales of Quebeçois writer Jacques Ferron. Marie-
Claire Blais' breathless *These Festive Nights* seems to nod in retrospect
to Graeme Gibson's formally trail-blazing *Five Legs*.

Admittedly, Atwood and Lee started out peas in a pod in life
as well as literature, shuffling across the dance floor at a Victoria
College freshman mixer, and they continued to shuffle around
together—creatively, at least—for years. To this day they refer-

ence one another in countless instances. In conversation, Atwood refers to her early, quasi-volunteer activities devoted to keeping Anansi afloat as "giving blood." Months later, Lee reproduces the phrase exactly, and in the same context. You can almost imagine their marathon editorial sessions, blue-pencilled pages flying, Atwood intermittently exclaiming, "Dammit, I'm giving my *blood* here, Dennis!" One way or another, it seems the phrase became lodged in Lee's consciousness—particularly in association with Anansi's foundational years. In *The Death of Harold Ladoo*, he writes of Ladoo's "three horrific childhoods," observing:

> it was *there* you first
> gave blood, now you could use it
> to write.

What metaphor could be more apt when it comes to writing and publishing? Why, after all, do we give blood? Not *bleed*, mind you. Nobody bleeds happily, or, at least, voluntarily. But to give blood is an act of faith—an act of communion. It's not fun, exactly, but it is ultimately, I think, joyous. You don't start up a publishing house on nothing but artistic and political ideals (and I mean *nothing*, and I mean *starry-eyed* ideals) without opening up a few veins. To quote Anansi poet Eli Mandel, *You think it's easy?*

Let's talk about those ideals. By "starry-eyed," I mean the kind of nationalist cultural sentiment that today is only given voice on the obscurest of blogs or most insufferable of beer commercials. And even consigned to such an utterly non-threatening no-man's-land, many of us will still sneer reflexively at such ideals. God knows I get as fed up with Canada as any other self-respecting Canadian—and the fact that I just stopped to titter at this oxymoron only goes to my complaint.

But it wasn't always like this. In the late 1960s—my god. Two young literary unknowns decided to start a joint publishing venture in the basement of a rented house. OK, so this is nothing new. They were spurred on by a shared frustration with the cultural norms of their time and place, and an antipathy toward "the establishment." Again, not exactly unheard of. But, get this: *the entire country was listening.* The entire country was on their side. Anansi was propitiously founded in Canada's Centennial Year, the year of Expo, and the house found itself riding a wave of pro-Canadian cultural fervor.

In the pages of the national media, Dennis Lee was saying things like:

> . . . Anansi was born out of a desperate anger about the fact that we've never taken this country seriously enough to fight for it.

Elsewhere, he referred to himself and Godfrey as "uber-nationalists," insisting:

> Literature is a whole dimension of being a citizen of a country, which we've generally been deprived of. . . It's a civilized act to wrestle with the mind and passions of our own time and place. And if we don't do that, we're less than civilized.

And since the creation of Anansi was news, for no reason other than—according to Atwood—"it seemed such a daring and provocative and peculiar and weird thing to do," so, then, were its authors.

Graeme Gibson found himself at loose ends after being briefly courted by McClelland and Stewart, introduced at parties as the next big thing, and then summarily dumped. A friend put him on to Dennis Lee, even though the only fiction Anansi had published to this point was Godfrey's, and the house was otherwise assumed to be shaping itself into a poetry press. Gibson headed to Lee's, manuscript in hand, where he found Dennis "up a ladder," working on his house. It was a long way from the cocktail parties at M&S, but it didn't stop Gibson's novel from garnering rapturous media attention, followed by instant bestseller status. Everyone involved in the publication of *Five Legs* was gobsmacked, and a slushpile of fiction manuscripts soon materialized. Suddenly, Anansi was the first stop for would-be writers of cutting-edge Canadian fiction. An immediate result was the birth of the Spiderline series—five first novels released simultaneously with identical covers. Matt Cohen's first novel, *Korsoniloff*, was a Spiderline edition. He is said to have hated it. When all the back copies were destroyed in a fire in '71, there were playful suggestions that Cohen had struck the match. Meanwhile, the likes of Harold Ladoo, Austin Clarke, Marian Engle, and Roch Carrier were waiting in the wings.

Anansi had already experienced success as a poetry publisher with its wildly popular reprint of Atwood's *Circle Game* in '67 ("You're mad," Atwood told Lee, when he said he was planning a print run of two thousand copies; the book has not been out of print since). Then *Five Legs* came along, and Anansi was a new force to be reckoned with in fiction. The house was no stranger to non-fiction by the time Atwood and Lee hatched the idea of publishing a sort of self-help guide to Canadian literature. Anansi's of-the-people political leanings had already led them into similar DIY forays. There was Clayton Ruby and Paul Copeland's *Law Law Law*—guess what that was about?—and Mark Satin's coyly titled *Manual for Draft-Aged Immigrants to Canada.* (This title briefly attracted the attention of the FBI and RCMP, leading to a half-assed attempt at surveillance. A man from the phone company is said to have stumbled upon the wire tap, disgustedly pointing out its shoddy workmanship to the Anansi staff.) But my favourite of these early, well-intentioned tracts—at least in terms of title—would have to be *VD: The People-to-People Disease.*

Survival: A Thematic Guide to Canadian Literature was conceived along similar lines—"Let's do a *VD* of Canadian Literature!" piped Atwood in a meeting. They thought it would sell at best

3,000 copies. It sold ten times that amount. And suddenly, as Atwood writes in her introduction to the 2004 edition, "CanLit was everybody's business."

To put it another way, the shit hit the fan. Controversy! Backbiting! Warring, or at least sniping, factions! In *Canada*! About *books*! Jim Polk, editing for Anansi and married to Atwood at the time, remembers the "fierce and agonized reviews," musing, "it seemed as if the nation at large was beginning to wake up to itself." Now we were overtly, publicly grappling with our own image and culture—we were finally, as Lee foretold, taking the country seriously enough to fight for it—wrestling with the minds and passions of our time and place. To this day, people can't stop bickering about *Survival*. In John Metcalf's meticulous essay, "A Collector's Notes on the House of Anansi," published in 2002, he touches only briefly on "Atwood's unfortunate *Survival*," which "has done incalculable damage to the idea of Canadian literature." And there he leaves it. You can almost hear the author's molars grinding.

So, depending on where you stand, Anansi either manfully forged ahead through the post-*Survival* CanLit ruins, or rode the enthusiastic momentum it had no small hand in generating into the subsequent decade. *You think it's easy?* It was not. Even during the heady period of the late 1960s and early 1970s, "easy" is not a word that applies to the care and maintenance of Anansi. Lee and Godfrey parted ways early on, and who can say if the end of the founding partnership was fractious? All anyone will tell me is that Godfrey's wife Ellen went on to write a murder mystery set in a publishing house, and the killer bears an unmistakable resemblance to Lee.

Lee himself left around the time *Survival* debuted, perhaps as a means of securing his own survival, or at least that of his poetry and mental well-being. Here's a taste of the mood he was in, from *Sibelius Park*:

shitwork in a cold basement, moody
triumphs of the mind
hassling printers hassling banks
and the grim dungeon with friends

After Lee, Anansi moved out of the cold basement and continued to be more-or-less run by committee, with Shirley
Gibson—who had assisted with the promotion of her then-hus-
band Graeme's novel—taking over the management role from
Lee. The resident saviour however, was by all accounts Ann
Wall. She and her husband Byron had moved to Rochdale
College in the 1960s to avoid the American draft, and there they
met Lee. They invested in the floundering press when things
were at their most desperate, but perhaps more importantly,
they contributed basic business sense. The aptly-named Ann
Wall—in her role as managing editor and then publisher—kept
the roof from falling in well into the 1980s.

Now only Polk, flourishing in his new role as editor, remained
of the old guard. Imagine this: Polk says that when he started at
Anansi in 1972, "the early days had already crystallized into myth."
This was only five years into the venture. But, true enough, the
core Anansi values had been well-established: to publish "fine,
iconic books" (Lee's words in *Sibelius Park*) of fiction, poetry, and
non-fiction. Even its ongoing mandate to showcase the most
exciting new French Canadian writers in translation had been
kicked off by the publication of Roch Carrier's *La Guerre, Yes Sir!*
as early as 1970—a practice that has continued throughout the
decades with authors like Jacques Ferron, Anne Hébert, Marie-
Claire Blais, and Gaétan Soucy—and thanks in no small part to
the award-winning translation work of Sheila Fischman.

So began a period when today's brightest stars were only
beginning to twinkle. A poetry manuscript by a relative unknown

named Erín Moure arrived, and by 1988, her fourth Anansi publication, *Furious*, had won the Governor General's Literary Award. The prize coincided with the sale of Anansi to Jack Stoddart of Stoddart Publishing, which marked the beginning of an entirely new era. Suddenly, Anansi was part of a group of companies. Although Stoddart reportedly had the best intentions, there were some raised eyebrows amongst the old-guard idealists. When Ryerson Press was sold to Americans in 1970, this act provoked a storm of protest. Graeme Gibson climbed up onto the statue of Egerton Ryerson, wrapped it in the U.S. flag, and led the crowd in a caustic chorus of "I'm a Yankee Doodle Dandy." The eighties weren't like that, is my point. Most people were happy to see Anansi still kicking up dust.

Still, certain parties looked askance. "Stoddart was seen as the big bad wolf," remembers Michael Davis, who was brought in from Irwin to act as publisher. "People had a certain image of Anansi," he recalls, and in their minds, the Stoddart Publishing Group wasn't where the independent brainchild of two radical 1960s intellectuals belonged. It was a tricky situation for Davis. He had worked at Macmillan—the house that had offered to buy out Dennis Lee for a single, smart-ass dollar back when Anansi was starting up. "There was a certain amount of sneering on the part of the larger presses around that time," he admits. Now, here he was, being sneered at by the true believers of Canadian literature. But Davis was well aware of what Anansi had accomplished since the late 1960s. Dennis Lee et al had made the kind of editorial decisions that had defined and shaped the culture. "I'm a publishing apparatchik," Davis freely admits. He knew that if the house's reputation and relevance were to remain intact, he was going to need help.

To that end, Davis assembled an editorial board of academics, critics, and writers—many of whom were all three at once. There was David Arnason, Janice Kulyk Keefer, Esta Spalding, Gordon Johnston, Pamela Banting, and—for good measure—

Jim Polk. The rationale was that not only were these people in tune with what made good literature, they were also—through their work on university campuses—frequenting the places where the newest young writers and readers were most likely to be. It was a strategy that would eventually snag them the upstart likes of Ken Babstock, Lynn Crosbie, and Stephen Heighton.

The board also proved invaluable to the education of a twenty-four-year-old editorial assistant named Martha Sharpe, later to become publisher. Today, Sharpe insists she learned everything she needed to know about books and editing from sitting in on those meetings. "We had these great brains coming in once or twice a year, watching closely what was going on, [and] caring deeply." The board had no tangible stake in the house itself—they were not shareholders or marketers or publicists; their only concern was whether or not the books under discussion were in keeping with the good name of Anansi. Counter to expectation, both Sharpe and Davis use the word "pure" when they talk about the way editorial decisions were made under Stoddart.

But let's hear it one more time: *You think it's easy?* Every once in a while, Jack Stoddart thought he'd found the perfect title for Anansi. For example, there was the time he signed up Slobodan Milošević's wife. There were the threats of mass resignation from the board. And there was, finally, the bankruptcy of Stoddart Publishing and General Distribution Services.

It happened in 2002, just when things at Anansi were really starting to hum. Lisa Moore's *Open* was a dark-horse nominee for the Giller Prize that year, and this was just one of the nominations that had begun rolling in under Sharpe, who had become publisher in 1998. Before his departure, Davis had secured rights to publish the CBC Massey Lectures, and they had become some of the house's best sellers. And with a renewed commitment to showcasing the best new poets, Anansi's poetry roster was every bit as robust as it had been under Lee. (In order to distinguish itself, Anansi proffered an advance of $500—generous for poetry—to every poet, as well as a "nice lunch" and the promise of French flaps on the books. "We just thought it was a nice thing to do," Davis recalls. "Poets *love* French flaps.")

In short, anyone could see that Anansi was approaching full bloom as Stoddart was being disbanded. It could not be left to wither on the vine; you'd have to be *crazy*. Philanthropist and celebrated Canadian poetry-lover Scott Griffin was not that. He bought and saved the press in the nick of time.

Fast forward five years to 2007, because here is where things really get exciting. The energy, success, and quality generated by the house these past five years is inescapably reminiscent of the headiest of Anansi's early days. The difference is, whereas in the 1960s the very fact of a successful small press was an achievement to be lauded, the Anansi of today has evolved into another creature entirely—one distinct on the Canadian publishing landscape. Anansi can no longer be rightly called a "small" press, for one thing. It is a successful *independent* press, and the fact that the house has managed to disentangle those two categories is astounding unto itself. In 2002, even with Stoddart disintegrating all around it, Anansi was awarded Small Publisher of the Year by the Canadian Bookseller's Association. But five years later, after an unprecedented domination of the awards lists in 2006, including two Giller nominations and six Governor General's Literary Awards finalists, it shrugged off its small press status and walked away with Publisher of the Year (and Editor of the Year for Lynn Henry, Anansi's publisher since Sharpe's departure in 2005). Until now, Publisher of the Year had been a category tacitly reserved for the "big boys"—houses owned, for the most part, by foreign multinationals. Somewhere, Dave Godfrey—always the more "uber" of Anansi's founding uber-nationalists—must have been chuckling. Maybe Egerton Ryerson smiled to himself in the great beyond.

Under Sarah MacLachlan, the house's new president, and publisher Lynn Henry, Anansi has entered a new phase of evolu-

tion. The always-popular CBC Massey Lectures have erupted—
with the publication of titles by Thomas King, Ronald Wright,
and Stephen Lewis—into out-and-out blockbusters. The new
generation of Anansi fiction and poetry talent—people like
Babstock, Crosbie, Moore, Heti, Michael Winter, Rawi Hage,
Peter Behrens, Bill Gaston, and Gil Adamson—seems every bit
as era-defining as the founding crop. Moreover, in the past three
years Anansi has successfully brought these very good books
into the international market, selling rights around the world,
and in turn brought international luminaries like A. L. Kennedy,
Jim Harrison, and Simon Armitage to Canadian readers.

Now roll ahead a few months, to me in the Anansi offices,
trying not to geek out completely in front of MacLachlan and
Henry, who have just asked me to do this book. Here's how it
felt: as if that kid you went to high school with, the one who
wore Vulcan ears to school every day no matter how many
times he was beaten up for it, had been contacted by William
Shatner and Leonard Nimoy to curate the Gene Rodenberry
Museum of All Things Trek. Am I making myself understood? I
was precisely the CanLit nerd for the job, is what I'm saying. I
practically used to dress up as Milton Acorn for Halloween. There
was nothing else to say but thank you, which I'll say again now.

Thank you, Sarah MacLachlan, Lynn Henry, Margaret Atwood,
Graeme Gibson, Dennis Lee, Jim Polk, Michael Davis, Martha
Sharpe, Ken Babstock, and Laura Repas.

Thank you, readers, writers, and blood donors all.

Lynn Coady
Toronto, 2007

THE
FIRST DECADE

—

1967-1977

1 A SAMPLING OF THE POETRY

MARGARET ATWOOD
Excerpts from *Circle Game* (1967)

The City Planners

Cruising these residential Sunday streets
in dry August sunlight:
what offends us is
the sanities:
the houses in pedantic rows, the planted
sanitary trees, assert
levelness of surface like a rebuke
to the dent in our car door.
No shouting here, or
shatter of glass; nothing more abrupt
than the rational whine of a power mower
cutting a straight swath in the discouraged grass.

But though the driveways neatly
sidestep hysteria
by being even, the roofs all display
the same slant of avoidance to the hot sky,
certain things;
the smell of spilled oil a faint

sickness lingering in the garages,
a splash of paint on brick surprising as a bruise,
a plastic hose poised in a vicious
coil; even the too-fixed stare of the wide windows

give momentary access to
the landscape behind or under
the future cracks in the plaster

when the houses, capsized, will slide
obliquely into the clay seas, gradual as glaciers
that right now nobody notices.

That is where the City Planners
with the insane faces of political conspirators
are scattered over unsurveyed
territories, concealed from each other,
each in his own private blizzard;

guessing directions, they sketch
transitory lines rigid as wooden borders
on a wall in the white vanishing air

tracing the panic of suburb
order in a bland madness of snows.

A Meal

We sit at a clean table
eating thoughts from clean plates

and see, there is my heart
germfree, and transparent as glass

and there is my brain, pure
as cold water in the china
bowl of my skull

and you are talking
with words that fall spare
on the ear like the metallic clink
of knife and fork.

Safety by all means;
so we eat and drink
remotely, so we pick
the abstract bone

but something is hiding
somewhere
in the scrubbed bare
cupboard of my body
flattening itself
against a shelf
and feeding
on other people's leavings

a furtive insect, sly and primitive
the necessary cockroach
in the flesh
that nests in dust.

It will sidle out
when the lights have all gone off
in this bright room

(and you can't
crush it in the dark then
my friend or search it out
with your mind's hands that smell
of insecticide and careful soap)

In spite of our famines
it keeps itself alive

: how it gorges on a few
unintentional
spilled crumbs of love

ALLEN GINSBERG
An excerpt from *Airplane Dreams* (1968)

History of the Jewish Socialist Party in America

In a meeting hall, a small room or foyer of private house downstairs on street storefront level—we're inside—me, and my friend,
a square FBI agent who is arresting us all, but wants more information so doesn't take us in but lets us continue our activity,
which is all internal regulation of the party which now has very
few members anyway, being, as the FBI boy knows to his chagrin,
much more concerned with psychic regulation of the idealism
of its members than any activity relating to the US Govt—in
fact we are completely unconcerned with the US Govt. and far
from spying on it we welcome spies in our midst in the hope
they be converted and learn something about us—since the
internal structure of the party is a mystery still unresolved even
to us—a fact which embarrasses the FBI fellow further since he
guesses our general crazy goodwill and devotion to some mysterious politics of complete integrity, so extreme that the policy
of the party is really dedicated to discovering what the policy is
and who the leaders really are—we being willing to share the
info with anyone—even the US Govt—with complete faith that
with such an open policy no harm can befall anyone, even jail or
execution is further opportunity for study, revelation, or martyr-
dom to the Mystery of Idealistic Socialism and a further chapter
of the Jewish S. Party's profound activity in America—no less

profound because limited to a small group which pursue the basic study, for the intensity of their dedication.

Thus we are having a meeting in the foyer—as Aunt Rose's tho smaller 1930—& the FBI man, with tie askew & coat over arm, sweating in summer heat, pistol in one hand & other on telephone, is undecided what to do, so I advise him, after a nervous walk in the plaza, to trust us & wait awhile till something definite develops. He seems to agree, nodding his head, tho worried we'll all escape, vanish, and he'll lose his job & be fired by his intemperate boss a cruel Faggot named J. Edgar Hoover.

The subject of tonite's meeting was announced by President Berg last week to be a speech—manifesto of policy—by an old & trusted member Dr. Hershman—who arrived earlier very disturbed, took over the meeting—and announced—"The Subject of my Announcement will be the Follows—please take note and understand why I am announcing it so that anybody who does not wish to be further implicated may leave the room: *Why I killed President Berg and Member Hoffman.*" This throws everybody into turmoil—there are only 5 or 6 members & all realize they will be held as accomplices—but maybe he had good reason, so why leave & betray his mad trust?—It's an apocalyptic party full of necessary mistakes. The FBI man is thrown into a crisis of nerves— He is ready to telephone to arrest us all, but wants to hear why they killed Berg & Hoffman—But also afraid he might be implicated, since he too is (tho spy) a member of this small Socialist Party which long ago agreed to be mutually responsible & share all guilt. If the FBI man waits he might wind up in jail with all of us, if he don't wait he'll never fulfill his mission to find out what the Mystery of the Party is and arrest us on basic evidence of conspiracy—Arrest now for mere murder means little but regular cop crime to the FBI not a political triumph. I advise him to hold his horses and stick with us, we all want to find out.

Horowitz is in the chair, talking furiously: "Comrades, Berg was a traitor to the Party, he wanted to end the Party & had legal power to dissolve it—I realized the danger, so did he, he invited me to address you on the subject & he also invited me to take the necessary action on the subject—an action which hadn't occurred before because a similar situation had not arisen.—

"And here is the can of Napthaline with which I killed him—gagged him & poisoned his soda water with it, & made him drink, and his co-conspirator Hoffman—I'm going to burn the Evidence—in the Fireplace right now—"

He opens the (Ether type) Napthaline can in the floor of fireplace & lights it—it burns & gives off dull blue flame & great fumes of wierd gas—everybody coughs—I sniff & realize you can get high on it, so I want to stick around & not call firemen or cops—

"Let it burn" we all yell—the FBI man rushes outside but I rush him back in—"Smell it & get high maybe we'll all get the Answer that way. Don't give up the Ship."

The girls are nearly fainting, the can is burning in the fireplace, fumes dizzy us, one girl faints in chair, her Jewish girlfriend rubs her hands & fans her, the FBI man is sweating, Horowitz is sniffing furiously—the room is in turmoil—we will all be arrested for murder—"Destroy the Evidence & let's get high" shouts the killer—on this scene of evident excitement, a new chapter of the history of Jewish socialism nears its end & the Dream concludes prematurely.

JOE ROSENBLATT

An excerpt from *Winter of the Luna Moth* (1968)

Annie Mamba
or The Evolution of a PIG

Annie Mamba loveth boys & girls
effeminate males are her pidgins
deep in her heart she's a virgin.
Sweet 19. Mamba split with parentulas
exchanged 60 grand serpentarium
for shab solarium in the suburbs
there to contemplate a fallen navel.
Afterwards came the girls: quick taxi hacks:
butches the size of Soviet tankers
then weed, speed & pops of horses
with He & She, who in reality
was Ace Laius: labour columnist
for the Daily Helium . . . a real gas!
What a smashing scene
Mamba in Alice Land losing gravity
& beyond theology: CANCELLATION.
She dug to lay her analyst
". . . after hours baby, after hours . . ."
Gentle Mamba: every cat after her asp.
She had it on for Hippies
don't mean a diaphragm,

Every hirsute was her playmate. Cheap bunny girl.
If I had a Centennial dollar for every crab she grabbed
I'd be a jumping millionaire.

Who could love Mamba?
Why that would be like falling in love with cancer
though for Mamba I have a certain fondness.
like snakes
I believe Annie evolved from something personal
an Egg.
Two suicides for Mamba, wow
Narcissus hung herself
Taurus went to Dreamland.
The bureaucracy of Love is cruel
around the pubic regions.

GEORGE BOWERING

Excerpts from *The Gangs of Cosmos* (1969)

Dobbin
   —*for Mike Ondaatje*

We found dead animals in our sagebrush hills,
every day it seems now, deer, heads of
unimaginable elk. Or rattlesnake killed
by some kids we likely knew, upside down,
wrong coloured in the burnt couchgrass.
But my first dead horse. It was something
like mother, something gone wrong at home his
opened & scattered body was tethered,
the old shit surrounded his tufted hair
& his skin, the oil gone, just twisted
leather without eyeballs. A horse, as if
someone had lost him, obeying the rope
thru his open-air starving.
I was then, then, no longer another one
of the animals come to look, this
was no humus like the others, this
was death, not merely dead; that rope
may now hang from some rotted fence.
Words Like Our Daily Bread

Today at a place you might know about
called Saltery Bay
I found clear shallow water
unlike anything I've seen in the East
with discarded oyster shells
as a base
or floor.

& also that I'd lockt myself
out of my car.
I said God damn it
that crystal clear water I could always look into it
& those fine blue & white shells.

The gulls fly away.

Tonight I saw a baseball game
sitting in the bleachers in the night
with an old Swede
who won three golf balls
& there was a bunch of kids, moving.

Denver 6, Vancouver 4.
None of the light bulbs were out
& there were three clear home runs.

In between I was reading
Le president by Georges Simenon
when I lookt up to see some land for sale
so pretty
I wanted to buy it.

That's not quite clear.
I was moving in a car or boat
south on 101.
    The gulls fly away
when the boat hits the pilings.

Harbour Beginnings and That Other Gleam

She has it in her power
(continually or not)
to give me back my face
when she will.
But this world (I constructed it
from whole cloth)
is a world of bargain.
That is, I have my part to do,
continual tailor, to ply this needle
(yes, relentless metaphor)
or this manly implement, to seek
its well-known place. It is often in
the dark.
Then a halo of her excitement
settles around my neck, & there by her
term magic,
my face, shining. She has told me
it does. then.

MICHAEL ONDAATJE

Excerpts from *The Collected Works of Billy the Kid* (1970)

(page 15)

After shooting Gregory
this is what happened

I'd shot him well and careful
made it explode under his heart
so it wouldnt last long and
was about to walk away
when this chicken paddles out to him
and as he was falling hops on his neck
digs the beak into his throat
straightens legs and heaves
a red and blue vein out

Meanwhile he fell
and the chicken walked away

still tugging at the vein
till it was 12 yards long
as if it held that body like a kite
Gregory's last words being

get away from me yer stupid chicken

The barn I stayed in for a week then was at the edge of a farm and had been deserted it seemed for several years, though built of stone and good wood. The cold dark grey of the place made my eyes become used to soft light and I burned out my fever there. It was twenty yards long, about ten yards wide. Above me was another similar sized room but the floors were unsafe for me to walk on. However I heard birds and the odd animal scrape their feet, the rotten wood magnifying the sound so they entered my dreams and nightmares.

But it was the colour and light of the place that made me stay there, not my fever. It became a calm week. It was the colour and the light. The colour a grey with remnants of brown—for instance those rust brown pipes and metal objects that before had held bridles or pails, that slid to machine uses; the thirty or so grey cans in one corner of the room, their ellipses, from where I sat, setting up patterns in the dark.

When I had arrived I opened two windows and a door and the sun poured blocks and angles in, lighting up the floor's skin of feathers and dust and old grain. The windows looked out onto fields and plants grew at the door, me killing them gradually with my urine. Wind came in wet and brought in birds who flew to the other end of the room to get their aim to fly out again. An old tap hung from the roof, the same colour as the walls, so once I knocked myself out on it.

For that week then I made a bed of the table there and lay out my fever, whatever it was. I began to block my mind of all thought. Just sensed the room and learnt what my body could do, what it could survive, what colours it liked best, what songs I sang best.

There were animals who did not move out and accepted me as a larger breed. I ate the old grain with them, drank from a constant puddle about twenty yards away from the barn. I saw no human and heard no human voice, learned to squat the best way when shitting, used leaves for wiping, never ate flesh or touched another animal's flesh, never entered his boundary. We were all aware and allowed each other. The fly who sat on my arm, after his inquiry, just went away, ate his disease and kept it in him. When I walked I avoided the cobwebs who had places to grow to, who had stories to finish. The flies caught in those acrobat nets were the only murder I saw.

And in the barn next to us there was another granary, separated by just a thick wood door. In it a hundred or so rats, thick rats, eating and eating the foot deep pile of grain abandoned now and fermenting so that at the end of my week, after a heavy rain storm burst the power in those seeds and brought drunkenness into the minds of those rats, they abandoned the sanity of eating the food before them and turned on each other and grotesque and awkwardly because of their size they went for each other's eyes and ribs so the yellow stomachs slid out and they came through that door and killed a chipmunk—about ten of them onto that one striped thing and the ten eating each other before they realised the chipmunk was long gone so that I, sitting on the open window with its thick sill where they couldnt reach me, filled my gun and fired again and again into their slow wheel across the room at each boommm, and reloaded and fired again and again till I went through the whole bag of bullet supplies—the noise breaking out the seal of silence in my ears, the smoke sucked out of the window as it emerged from my fist and the long twenty yard space between me and them empty but for the floating bullet lonely as an emissary across and between the wooden posts that never returned, so the rats continued to wheel and stop in the silences and eat each other, some even the bullet. Till my hand was black and the gun was hot and no other animal of any kind remained in that room but for the boy in the blue shirt sitting there coughing at the dust, rubbing the sweat of his upper lip with his left forearm.

(page 27)

His stomach was warm
remembered this when I put my hand into
a pot of luke warm tea to wash it out
dragging out the stomach to get the bullet
he wanted to see when taking tea
with Sallie Chisum in Paris Texas

With Sallie Chisum in Paris Texas
he wanted to see when taking tea
dragging out the stomach to get the bullet
a pot of luke warm tea to wash it out
remembered this when I put my hand into
his stomach was warm

(page 57)

When Charlie Bowdre married Manuela, we carried them
on our shoulders, us on horses. Took them to the Shea
Hotel, 8 rooms. Jack Shea at the desk said
Charlie—everythings on the house, we'll give you the

Bridal.

No no, says Charlie, dont bother, I'll hang onto her ears until I get used to it.

HAWHAWHAW

bill bissett

Excerpts from *Nobody Owns th Earth* (1971)

Another *100 Warrants Issued*

newsflash: 7 men enterd a Vancouver graveyard
only to disappear in a flash of white light

Whats it like o straight person
square john to be abul to shop
around say at th 3 vets or th
Army & Navy without being stoppd
harassd etc. by th Narks at every turn
yu take, hey, whats it like
to get up in th morning, gatherd,
yu nd yr friends close ones, around
th warming stove without th R.C.M.P.
crashing thru th veils within th
bardos of mistrust, Canada, etc.,
how duz it feel, yr children,
terrorized, hiding, facing jail
or what is sumtimes worse, parole,
to have a nark recognize yu so
that there is no recourse, markd
yu advocate nothing except
humanity and only th overthrow
of this state's tyranny, yu go thru

th streets on fire as an alarm
to yr friends as they get nabbd
this week of Jan 7/69 in Vancouver,
th Narks go thru th houses, ripping
apart floor boards, cupboards, children's
dolls, in a red convertible, Caesar's
computer men, bullet heads, pigs,
whats it like o yu who feel yu are
citizens of this sold-out Grandmother's
land to not have pigs vomitting at yu
all th time, to stand trial for
ovr a year, to see friends jaild
for 3 years for keeping th peace
with themselves their world etc.

      No clean white snow can cure this bummer,
no apologies, no justice, feeble pretenses
can resolve th heartache, th parted
friends and lovers, all th tears thru th
falling volcanoes, nothing can be done
now by government to assuage th grief, it is
too late Mr. and Mrs. Square John,
as yu stand by, watching yr children
burn, yu blew it, yu pricks, get
it, have yu heard a child scream
as a Mountie breaks down a door, yr
wrists bleeding, handcuffs, jeers, etc.,
for perhaps one joint, 5 mos in th
can, a years probation, yu are
perhaps 20 years old, yu are now
too old, ancient, yu wanta join us
in these timeless wails yu pricks,
yu havc allowd all this to take place
as yu support th war in Vietnam,
yu have watchd, glazd eyed as all

beauty, love, gets destroyd, yu can
go fuck yrselves, like don' cum
near me ever until yu can see
what yuve done with all our love.

Th Emergency Ward

        So as i was regaining con
sciousness alone paralysd th shrink
was skreeming at me that hed never
seen such an obvious case of a
psychologically feignd man
ifestation of an apparently
physiological injury sumone
had phond in or sumthing that
i was a paintr so he sd that
again it was obvious that i was
trying by pretending
payalysis to get out of
painting that damn it

hed make me move again if he
had to shock me into it but
doctor hes bleeding nurse
shut up yu shud know
that advanced catatonia
and bleeding are not in
compatible sorry doctor
th ambulance is getting
ready so they were undr
his ordrs he kept shouting at

me bout yu and yur
kind hel fix us alright

bunduling me off to River
view th out of city mental
hospital extremely undr
staffd for shock treatment
when as they were rollin me
onto th stretchr this
beautiful neurologist chick
staff doctor sz stop thats
an inter cerebral bleed

if i ever saw one so as
th shrink had got me
first they had to
make a deal so this

is my re entry i thot so far out
so th trip was if th neurologist
chick cud get proof of an
inter cerebral bleed then i
wud go to th neurology ward
othrwise th shrinks wud get
me with inter cerebral bleed
shock treatment sure wud kill
me alright iud go out
pretty fast i gess so befor
th operation th neurologists
came to see me askd whethr i
wantid to go ahead with th
trip to th o.r. why not i
sd what have we got to

lose maybe yr life she sd well
lets get on with it alright she sd
do yu want partial total or local
iul take total evry time i sd
playd jimi hendrix water
fall thers nothing to harm yu
at all in time to th blood gushin
out of th ventricals up there to
keep them relaxd 12 neurologists
inside my brain like fantastik
voyage woke up in th middul
of th operation gave em a poetry
reading sure was fun they
put me out again sd i mustuv
known my way round drugs
cause they sure gave me a lot
well they got proof of th inter
cerebral bleed thing rescued
me from th shrinks who

still usd to sneak up th back
stairs to get at me but th nurses
usd to kick them back down
those neurologists and th nurses
in that ward sure were good
to me usd to lift th covrs off my
head which was liquifying or sum
thing my eyeballs turning to
mush ask me if there was
very much pain strong tendr
angel eyes iud say theres

so much pain don't worry we'll
bring yu anothr shot thank yu
iud moan and now i can even
write this tho th spastik fine
print in th elbow or wherever
it is is kinda strange but ium
sure lucky and grateful
fr certain that it was an intr
cerebral bleed

DENNIS LEE
Excerpts from *Civil Elegies* (1972)

Sibelius Park

I

Walking north from his other lives in a fine rain
    through the high-rise pavilion on Walmer
lost in the vague turbulence he harbours
        Rochdale   Anansi   how many
    routine wipeouts has he performed since he was born?
                    and mostly himself;
          drifting north to the three-storey
    turrets & gables, the squiggles and arches and
    baleful asymmetric glare of the houses he loves
          Toronto gothic
walking north in the fine rain, going home through the late afternoon
    he comes to Sibelius Park.
Across that green expanse he sees
    the cars parked close, every second licence yankee, he thinks of
    the war and the young men dodging, his wife inside
      with her counsel, her second thoughts
          and the children, needing more than they can give;
and behind him, five blocks south, his other lives
    in rainy limbo till tomorrow
      Rochdale, yes   Anansi

the fine iconic books, sheepish errata
   shitwork in a cold basement, moody
triumphs of the mind
                  hassling printers   hassling banks
   and the grim dudgeon with friends—men with
deep combative egos, ridden men, they cannot sit still, they go on
                  brooding on Mao   on Gandhi
and they cannot resolve their lives but together they make up
                  emblems of a unified civilization,
      the fine iconic books;
                  he is rooted in books & in
that other place, where icons come alive among the faulty
         heroes & copouts, groping for some new tension of
      mind and life, casting the type in their own
      warm flesh
                  hassling builders   hassling banks
and he is constantly coming and going away, appalled by the force of
         wishful affirmations, he thinks of the war, he
hears himself 10 years ago affirming his faith in Christ
      in the lockers, still half-clasped in pads & a furtive
                  virgin still, flailing the
lukewarm school with rumours of God, gunning for psychic opponents
      though he could not hit his father and what broke at last was the
         holiness; and he can't go back there any more
      without hearing the livelong flourish
                  of Christ in his mouth, always he tasted His funny
taste in every arraignment but it was himself he was burying.
And the same struggle goes on and when
                  he drinks too much, or cannot sleep for his body's
      jaundiced repose he can scarcely read a word he wrote,
                  though the words are just but his work has
thc funny taste and his life pulls back and snickers when he begins.

And then Sibelius Park!
        The grass is wet, it
    gleams, across the park's wide
            vista the lanes of ornamental
    shrub come breathing and the sun is filling the
                rinsed air till the green goes luminous and it does it
                            does, it comes clear.

II

Supper is over, I sit
        holed up in my study. I have no
    answers again and I do not trust the
        simplicities, nor Sibelius Park;
                        I am not to be trusted with them.

But I rest in one thing. The play of
        dusk and atmospherics, the beautiful rites of
    synthaesthesia, are not to be believed;
            but that grisly counter-presence, the warfare in the lockers, myself
    against myself, the years of desperate affirmation and the dank
            manholes of ego which stink when they
    come free at last
            —the seamy underside of every stiff
    iconic self—which are hard   which are welcome
are no more real than that unreal man who stood and took them in;
    are no more real than the fake epiphanies,
                    though they ache to bring them down.

For they are all given, they are not
        to be believed but constantly
    they are being
            given, moment by moment, the icons and what they
    suppress, here and

here and though they are not real they have their own real
presence, like a mirror in the grass and in the
      bodies we live in we are
acceptable.

There is nothing to be afraid of.

Third Elegy

The light rides easy on people dozing at noon in Toronto, or
here it does, in the square, with the white spray hanging
upward in plumes on the face of the pool, and the kids, and the thrum of
      the traffic,
and the people come and they feel no consternation, dozing at lunch-
time; even the towers comply.
And they prevail in their placid continuance, idly unwrapping their food
day after day on the slabs by the pool, warm in the summer sun.
Day after day the light rides easy.
Nothing is important.
But once at noon I felt my body's pulse contract and
balk in the space of the square, it puckered and jammed till nothing
worked, and casting back and forth
the only resonance that held was in the Archer.
Great bronze simplicity, that muscled form
was adequate in the aimless expanse—it held, and tense and
waiting to the south I stood until the
clangor in my forearms found its outlet.
And when it came I knew that stark heraldic form is not
great art; for it is real, great art is less than its necessity.
But it held, when the monumental space of the square
went slack, it moved in sterner space.

Was shaped by earlier space and it ripples with
wrenched stress, the bronze is flexed by
blind aeonic throes
that bred and met in slow enormous impact,
and they are still at large for the force in the bronze churns
through it, and lunges beyond and also the Archer declares
that space is primal, raw, beyond control and drives toward a
living stillness, its own.
But if some man by the pool, doing his workaday
job in the city, tangled in other men's
futures with ticker-tape, hammering
type for credits or bread, or in for the day, wiped out in Long Branch
by the indelible sting of household acts of war,
or whatever; if a man strays into that
vast barbaric space it happens that he enters into
void and will go
under, or he must himself become void.

We live on occupied soil.
Across the barren Shield, immortal scrubland and our own,
where near the beginning the spasms of lava
settled to bedrock schist,
barbaric land, initial, our
own, scoured bare under
crush of the glacial recessions
and later it broke the settlers, towing them
deeper and deeper each year beneath the
gritty sprinkle of soil, till men who had worked their farms for a lifetime
could snap in a month from simple cessation of will,
though the brute surroundings went on—the flagrant changes
of maple and sumach, the water in ripples of light,
the faces of outcrop, the stillness, and up the slopes
a vast incessant green that drew the mind
beyond its tether, north, to muskeg and

stunted hackmatack, and then the whine of icy tundra north to the pole—
despotic land, inhuman yet
our *own*, where else on earth? and reaping stone
from the bush their fathers cleared, the sons gave
way and they drank all year, or went strange, or they sat and stared outside
as their cars settled back to slag and now what
races toward us on asphalt across the Shield—
by truck, by TV minds and the ore-bearing flatcars—
is torn from the land and the mute oblivion of
all those fruitless lives, it no longer
stays for us, immemorial adversary, but is shipped and
divvied abroad though wrested whole from the Shield.

Take Tom Thomson, painter; he
did his work in the Shield.
Could guide with a blindfold on. Was part of the bush. Often when night
came down in a subtle rush and the scorched scrub still
ached for miles from the fires he paddled direct through
the palpable dark, hearing only the push and
drip of the blade for hours and then very suddenly the radiance of the
renewed land broke over his canvas. So. It was his
job. But no two moments land with the same sideswipe
and Thomson, for all his savvy, is very damp and
trundled by submarine currents, pecked by the fish out
somewhere cold in the Shield and the far loons percolate
high in November and he is not painting their cry.

Small things ignite us, and the quirky particulars
flare on all sides.
A cluster of birches, in moonlight;
a jack pine, gnarled and
focusing heaven and earth—
these might fend off void.
Or under the poolside arches the sunlight, skidding on paper destroyers,

kindles a dazzle, skewing the sense. Like that. Any
combination of men and time can start the momentary
ignition. If only it were enough.
But it is two thousand years since Christ's carcass rose in a glory,
and now the shiny ascent is not for us, Thomson is
done and we cannot
malinger among the bygone acts of grace. For
many are called but none are chosen now, we are the evidence
for downward momentum, although despite our longing still restrained
within the real, as Thomson's body really did
decay and vying to praise him we
bicker about which grave the carcass fills.

New silences occur in the drone of the square's great spaces.
The light overbalances, shadows
appear, the people walk away.
But massy and knotted and still the Archer continues its space,
which violates our lives, and reminds us, and has no mercy upon us.
For a people which lays its whiskey and violent machines
on a land that is primal, and native, which takes that land in greedy
innocence but will not live it, which is not claimed by its own
and sells that land off even before it has owned it,
traducing the immemorial pacts of men and earth, free and
beyond them, exempt by miracle from the fate of the race—
that people will botch its cities, its greatest squares
will scoff at its money and stature, and prising wide
a civil space to live in, by the grace of its own invention it will
fill that space with the artifacts of death.

On Queen Street, therefore, in Long Branch, wherever the
people have come upon it, say that the
news is as bad as we thought:
we have spent the bankroll; here, in this place,
it is time to honour the void.

ELI MANDEL
Excerpts from *Crusoe* (1973)

A Cage of Oats
(To James Reaney and Jay Macpherson)

How many prisons do I count?
Here is the wall I first ran from
and here there is a second wall,
the wall I ran against to flee
the first, and here there is a cage.

Inside the cage there is a second cage.
Inside the second cage there is a third.

Inside the third
there is a bird.

A Quaker holds a box of oats
on which a Quaker holds a box.
A mirror mirrors oats
for oats are mirrors of their crops
which farmer-quaker-man will thresh
and eat to put the seeds inside
the Quaker man who holds a box.

There may be stars inside of stones
(or other stones): inside of stars
there may be burning seeds.
What boxed bird so great
it can eat
stone, man, star and seed?

Cassandra

This has nothing to do with brothels.

Sometimes it seems my daughter or my wife
or my neighbour's wife, bright-eyed,
imitates an image out of sleep. They walk
as if I had dwindled, looking past me
toward unreasonable parliaments
crouching beside senatorial hills.

I have been practising this poetry in secret.
Also I have made advances toward pregnant women.
But there have been no unusual shadows,
all the swimming pools remain clear of blood,
and by the gates the watcher has not raised his arms.

Songs from the Book of Samuel

i

the intellect does not age, the body dies
daily the mind declares its lies
about the soul, about the self
about the body and its ageless cries

now mind grows freer as the body dies
daily the body ages in its lies
about the mind, about the self
about the mind's dear sense of paradise

ii

I forgive the adulterer, I forgive the song
I forgive the straw man in my bed
I forgive the old man his lies about the bed
I forgive my armies for their arms
I forgive the generals for their boots
and the mayors for their homes
and the councillors
my mother
for her prophecies, my father
for his mistaken comfort in failure
my teachers for their religion
I forgive the girl's face in the flower
the instrumental poet hung on his strings
the colonies for the times they did not eat
I forgive the food of the armies
and the carpets under the general's feet
I forgive the poet for lying about god
I forgive god for tomorrow
I forgive the arisen prophet
the man who is a weapon

the weapon
death
the song
the singer dying in his song
even myself

PAULETTE JILES

An excerpt from *Waterloo Express* (1973)

Clocks

The clock's hands dislodge hours—
sticking them to the walls.

I never notice them until
strangers bang at the door,
newspapers replace themselves,
and my associates begin to fold their lives into tidy squares.

Now they are in my eyes, shifting
in batik patterns.
I see my life

through a clear pane of minutes and hours
like the faceted spectacles of flies,
those nitwits, their quick
garbagey lives.

AL PURDY
Excerpts from *Poems for All the Annettes* (1973)

At Roblin Lake

Did anyone plan this,
set up the co-ordinates
of experiment to bring about
an ecology of near and distant
batrachian nightingales?
—Each with a frog in his throat,
rehearsing the old springtime pap
about the glories of copulation.
If not I'd be obliged if
the accident would unhappen.
The pike and bass are admirably silent
about such things, and keep their
erotic moments a mensa et thoro
in cold water. After which I suppose
comes the non-judicial separation.
Which makes them somewhat misogynists?
In any case frogs are ignorant
about the delusion and snare women
represent—they brag and boast
epicene, while piscene culture doesn't.
This tangential backyard universe
I inhabit with sidereal aplomb,

tho troubled with midnight debate
by frog theologians, bogged
down in dialectics and original
sin of discursiveness
(the god of boredom at one remove,
discreetly subsidized on wooden plates)—
Next morning I make a shore-capture,
one frog like an emerald breathing,
hold the chill musical anti-body
a moment with breath held,

thinking of spores, spermatozoa, seed,
housed in this cold progenitor,
transmitting to some future species
what the wall said to Belshazzar.
And, wondering at myself, experiencing
for this bit of green costume jewellery
the beginnings of understanding,
the remoteness of alien love—

—*1958*

At the Quinte Hotel
(for Alan Pearson)

I am drinking
I am drinking beer with yellow flowers
in underground sunlight
and you can see that I am a sensitive man
And I notice that the bartender is a sensitive man too
so I tell him about this beer

I tell him the beer he draws
is half fart and half horse piss
and all wonderful yellow flowers
But the bartender is not quite
so sensitive as I supposed he was
the way he looks at me now
and does not appreciate my exquisite analogy
Over in one corner two guys
are quietly making love
in the brief prelude to infinity
Opposite them a peculiar fight
enables the drinkers to lay aside
their comic books and watch with interest
as I watch with interest
A wiry little man slugs another guy
then tracks him bleeding into the toilet
and slugs him to the floor again
with ugly red flowers on the tile
three minutes later he roosters over
to the table where his drunk friend sits
with another friend and slugs both
of 'em ass over electric kettle
so I have to walk around
on my way for a piss
Now I am a sensitive man
so I say to him mildly as hell
"You shouldn'ta knocked over the good beer
with them beautiful flowers in it"

So he says to me "Come on"
so I Come On
like a rabbit with weak kidneys I guess
like a yellow streak charging
on flower power I suppose

& knock the shit outa him & sit on him
(he is just a little guy)
and say reprovingly
"Violence will get you nowhere this time chum
Now you take me
I am a sensitive man
and would you believe I write poems?"
But I could see the doubt in his upside down face
in fact in all the faces
"What kinda poems?"
"Flower poems"
"So tell us a poem"
I got off the little guy but reluctantly
for he was comfortable
and told them this poem
They crowded around me with tears
in their eyes and wrung my hands feelingly
for my pockets for
it was a heart-warming moment for Literature
and moved by the demonstrable effect
of great Art and the brotherhood of people I remarked
"the poem oughta be worth some beer"
It was a mistake of terminology
for silence came
and it was brought home to me in the tavern
that poems will not really buy beer or flowers
or a goddam thing
and I was sad
for I am a sensitive man

—1964

PATRICK LANE

Excerpts from *Beware the Months of Fire* (1974)

Passing into Storm

Know him for a white man.
He walks sideways into wind
allowing the left of him

to forget what the right
knows as cold. His ears
turn into death what

his eyes can't see. All day
he walks away from the sun
passing into storm. Do not

mistake him for the howl you hear
or the track you think you
follow. Finding a white man

in snow is to look for the dead.
He has been burned by the wind.
He has left too much

flesh on winter's white metal
to leave his colour as a sign.
Cold white. Cold flesh. He leans

into wind sideways; kills without
mercy anything to the left of him
coming like madness in the snow.

Mountain Oysters

Kneeling in the sheep-shit
he picked up the biggest of the new rams,
brushed the tail aside,
slit the bag,
tucked the knackers in his mouth
and clipped the cords off clean—

the ram   stiff
with a single wild scream

as the tar went on
and he spit the balls in a bowl.

That's how we used to do it
when I was a boy.
It's no more gawdam painful
than any other way
and you can't have rams fightin,
slammin it up every nanny...

and enjoyed them with him,
cutting delicately
into the deep-fried testicles.

Mountain oysters make you strong

he said
while out in the field
the rams stood holding their pain,
legs fluttering like blue hands
of old tired men.

2 DAVID GODFREY
An excerpt from the novel
Death Goes Better with Coca-Cola (1967)

Mud Lake: If Any

Death too, I think at times, is just another one of our match box toys.

I am now, as the lecturing surgeons say, preparing the electrodes for insertion. I am now, into the alien elements, inserting myself. My colleague, gentle Nye, will observe the reactions of the patient, if any. If any?

The duck boat has been swamped, almost suddenly. We are clinging to its metal sides. Cold; somewhat reassuring. Beyond us and around us, when we have recovered from the shock, from a frightened awareness of chill waters to which we submit not, there appears one of those dinky visions the times are wont to grant us. The Sporting Goods Department at Simpson's, struck by flood, floats toward shore: six wicker goose decoys, a worn pair of oars, one green Alpine tent, eight hand-carved mallards with their neck-wrapped anchors, two Arctic down sleeping bags, a box of Cheerios, my ragged lambswool vest, a soggy blue duffel bag, Nye's insulated pants and jacket of cross-hatched nylon, a spare pair of sole-up rubber boots. Lo, the affluent surface of things.

The waves are gentle. The water not too cold—for mid-September near Flin Flon. Shore less than a mile off. We can push it in thirty minutes, *je me dis*. We bob beside the camou-flage-green boat, two anchored heads, and observe one another. A perfect layout of decoys, *je me dis*, if one wanted to call down some passing, strange flock of honking department stores, a migrating flock of Sears-Roebucks, Batons, Fitchs, Saks, Morgans, Simpsons, Magnins.

Except who then would be the hunters? What high-ball could lure down such monsters? Nye and I are both submerged to our shoulders. The guns, the ammunition, the camp stove, all things of solidity, are already at the bottom of Mud Lake. Amidst this absurdity of floating paraphernalia, buoyed by their still water-proof lace of feathers, float the one single redeeming object, our afternoon's booty of mallards and coots and buffleheads.

It has been, so far, an unusual voyage but not bizarre.

Relying upon childhood memories of a far more southerly portion of Manitoba, I had blind-guided Nye, a fellow trumpet player and sojourner in Iowa, a veteran of African campaigns, on a long, long trip up beyond the 55th parallel, beyond Snow Lake, beyond the cessation of roads, to the inlet of Little Herbe Lake, to a perfect, marshy river mouth, untrampled by even one other hunter, and as fat with ducks as is a Christmas cake with sweet rinds. It was almost too good a spot, the kind one should visit once and then leave, letting its memory remain to alter and modify your impression of later places both mediocre and uncommon.

So we did only visit it once. It was no regular trip up Little Herbe, and we had progressed as much by intuition as by map-knowledge. We came back down below the 55th (and thus south of the early season), to wait for our one afternoon of regular-season hunting. Off a rock ledge, in deep, clean water we did get some pike; and we thought we might get some Canadas. At nightfall we could hear them, high, high overhead.

Down off the road from Flin Flon to the Pas, we found a suit-ably ugly lake, with a harsh, muddy, cat-tail shore, and spent the morning getting our gear through the two hundred yards of shore mud and crossing the lake. Shooting opened at noon; we had a good afternoon, and set off back across the lake.

I'm not sure why the boat was so loaded. Whether we were afraid of theft or had developed a possible plan of spending the night on the far shore and then driving night and day back to Iowa. But loaded it was. I was scanning the shore with Nye's monocular, looking for a break in the shore mud, when I realized that the waves we had been moving through had slowly been attacking us, gently but progressively spilling over the bow, sloshing into the bottom of the boat beneath its mask of gear. I moved back as soon as I could get my legs untangled, but it was too late. We had made our mistake.

I must have scrambled, because the monocular never showed up, but I don't remember being frightened. Nye responded to some pre-imagined plan and freed the motor before we swamped. I stated that we were in trouble, but I was only thinking of wet-clothes trouble, not of the *aglaecean*, hungry water-monsters with which in childhood old trappers frightened me. No mile-long pike troubled me.

I watched our bobbing gear spread out and move ridiculously towards shore, and that expressed our destination. Never leave the boat. We would hang on, and kick behind its stern—our camouflaged, water-heavy, turtle board. But first we had to rock as much water out as possible, and it was on the recoil from one of these foundationless heaves, pushing against the elements that melt away, that I hit the Leacock bottom of that muddy, ugly lake. It oozed beneath me, an ooze of treacle and slushy cement. Which did frighten me. I thought of sinking-sand. And I laughed, rather loudly. Once I had my footing.

Nye turned full-face to me. And I saw, laughing, thinking really only of Lake Wissanotti, that Nye was truly frightened. The *aglaecean* were taking teeth-sharp bites at him. I remembered then, back in Iowa, his wife bending across to warn me that

Nye's response to penicillin was lost in the war, that for him pneumonia could have no sure cure. And he had his hip boots on still, ready for the shore mud, not for this quick calamity. Or say that the German mine was finally tripped beneath his ambulance still rambling across the Sahara, and, wounded and thirst-wracked, he could see the whole muddy lake as no other than a tongue-split mirage.

"Hey, hey," I said. "Bottom. It's the old muddy bottom. Get out the bread-balls and we can bob for suckers."

A mile from shore, we were only neck-deep from bottom. And he laughed too, letting go. Welcoming the mud.

We became surface-floaters again. Collected some of our decoys and protective clothing. Spread by the waves, and soggy, it had lost some of its absurdity; still we let much of it go. We turned down the chance to practice an enforced economy; we dried the gear in the sun and by a fire and slept dry.

Nye knew his Thoreau better than I. "Minks and muskrats," he mumbled. "We go from the desperate city into the desperate country and console ourselves with the bravery of minks and muskrats."

In the early morning, long before sunrise, there was a single shot.

"Poachers," said Nye, mocking my Englishness.

"Somebody who really lives here," said I. "Probably that old Indian who bummed the smokes. Potting a fat hen for Sunday dinner." Said I from my Arctic down, mocking something else, something to do with my own sense of most questionable survival. Was it not my true ancestor who had fired the single shot?

It is one of the strangenesses of youth that you can treat a specific chance of death with no more care than you'd give to your old Dinky Toy, that one-inch, green-camouflaged, British Army troop lorry.

3 MARK SATIN

An excerpt from the nonfiction book
Manual for Draft-Age Immigrants to Canada (1968)

Preface: Words from Canadians

"WE ARE HAPPY TO WELCOME YOU"
by VINCENT KELLY, L.L.B., *Barrister and Solicitor*

Even though circumstance and not choice has made Canada your haven, we are happy to welcome you. Those of us providing service to the Anti-Draft Programme assume that your opposition to the war in Vietnam stems from principle and therefore you are likely to become outstanding citizens.

Be forewarned that this opinion is not shared by Canadians generally. Our society is no less conservative, no less enthusiastic about containing Communism than yours.

If we had not burdened ourselves with participation as the Western representative on the International Control Commission (ICC), we would now be undoubtedly another Uncle Tom ally in South Vietnam.

Legally, too, our societies are similar. We adhere to most of the Anglo-Saxon precepts of natural justice but have no entrenched Bill of Rights. As a result, significant differences arise in connection with right to counsel and admission of illegally obtained evidence, to cite two instances.

But if you do enter our country legally and abide here peaceably the likelihood of deportation is remote. Deportation is probable if you become involved in criminal offences involving moral turpitude.

Entry is a straight-forward administrative matter. I am confident that the average young American could fulfill our legal requirements just as thousands of young English, Italian, French, and other foreign nationals do each year.

Introduction

THIS IS YOUR HANDBOOK

Slowly at first, and now in growing numbers, from Maine to Alabama to California, from ghettos, suburbs and schools, young Americans are coming to Canada to resist the draft. There is no draft in Canada. The last time they tried it was World War Two, when tens of thousands of Canadians refused to register. Faded "Oppose Conscription" signs can still be seen along the Toronto waterfront. The mayor of Montreal was jailed for urging Canadians to resist—and was re-elected from jail. No one expects a draft again.

It's a different country, Canada.

This is a handbook for draft resisters who have chosen to immigrate to Canada. Read it carefully, from cover to cover, and you will know how. It was written by Canada's major anti-draft programmes and their lawyers. Part One goes through the immigration process step by step. If you are still unclear, or face special difficulties that are not covered here, make sure to write. Or come in as a visitor and get help and advice.

Immigration is not the best choice for everyone and this pamphlet does not take sides. Four other alternatives are open to draft-age Americans: deferment, Conscientious Objector status, jail or the armed forces. The groups listed in Chapter 24 can help you choose among these alternatives or fight the Selective Service system as long as possible. Canada is not an easy way out; in many cases it means cutting yourself off from parents and friends. But there are many reasons draft resisters have chosen Canada—as many reasons as Americans. What these Americans are like is described at the end of Part Two.

Canada has not "opened its borders" to young Americans. There is no political asylum. But an American's possible military obligations are not a factor in the decision to permit him to enter and remain. FBI agents on official business are barred from Canada. Most other Americans are welcome, unless they fall into one of the "prohibited classes" (see Chapter 16).

On April 12, 1967, General Mark Clark asked the Canadian Embassy in Washington to help return all the "Draft Dodgers." He was told that it would not be possible. Canada's extradition treaty with the U.S. lists the extraditable offenses one by one (see Appendix A); resisting the draft is not among them, nor is desertion. Americans can enter Canada as immigrants, visitors or students (see Chapters 2–4) at any point in their induction proceedings.

You do not leave civilization behind when you cross the border. (In fact, many Canadians would claim that you enter it.) Part Two will tell you about Canada. We have not tried to sell you on Canada—our chapter on climate is chilling—but the truth is that Canada is a nice place to be.

There is little discrimination by Canadians against draft resisters, and there is a surprising amount of sympathy. Most Americans lead the same lives in Canada they would have led in the U.S. Americans who immigrate are not just rejecting one society; they are adopting another. Is it really freer? Most draft resisters—and most Canadians—think so.

It cannot be overstressed that draft resisters will probably never be able to return to the U.S. without risking arrest. This applies even to family emergencies. When a draft resister's father died last summer, two FBI agents showed up at the funeral.

Draft resisters have had and should continue to have only normal difficulties immigrating. Probably any young American can get in if he is really determined, though all will need adequate information and many may need personal counselling. We cannot emphasize too much that people should send us their questions or visit before they immigrate (see Chapter 25). This applies to all except those with a minimum of two years' skilled job experience and a B.A. Even these people should check with us by phone before applying at the border. DO NOT ATTEMPT TO APPLY AT THE BORDER BEFORE CHECKING WITH US.

Finally, the toughest problem a draft resister faces is not how to immigrate but whether he really wants to. And only you can answer that. For yourself.

That's what Nuremberg was all about.

· · ·

FBI agents have told some parents that their sons can be returned. This is not true. Rumours have been circulated by U.S. authorities because there is no other way the government can keep young Americans from coming. One AP wire had it that 71 "fugitive warrants" had been issued for young Americans in Canada. The story implied that the warrants were valid in Canada. They were not; they cannot be. Unfortunately, some Canadian consulates are staffed partly by Americans and partly by Canadians who have been "Americanized." Draft-age Americans are often refused legitimate information and given incorrect versions of the law by these self-appointed recruitment officers. For example, some officials are telling young Americans that they can only apply throught the consulates. Americans are very seldom told that they can apply at the border or from within Canada. One young New Yorker was told simply that "Canada doesn't want draft dodgers." It is a violation of Canadian law for an immigration or consulate official to give you false information to deter you from coming to Canada. Canadians' anti-draft groups would appreciate receiving a notarized statement of such incidents. So would the Department of Immigration in Ottawa.

Public officials, amateur draft counsellors, lawyers who do not specialize in draft work, and, unfortunately, the "underground" press are notorious sources of misinformation. Read this handbook again and again, and contact a Canadian anti-draft programme.

From *Part Two: Canada*

Your son, as he was growing up, has been learning a lot of living skills—common sense, initiative and self-reliance—that you thought he was never going to acquire. When he is in situation where the chips are down he uses these skills. Many times I've heard a boy say, "If my mother could see me now, she wouldn't believe it," as he goes through all the business of getting status as an immigrant, getting a job, and accepting responsibility for himself. And, even though most of the job he must do himself, he has friends here who will help as much as they can.

It's important that you not worry too much because right now, while he is here in Canada trying to make a new life for himself, he needs your support. Sometimes when we are worried ourselves it is hard to give the kids we love the support they need. You may think that he is wrong to be here but you can still be proud to know he has the guts to do what he thinks is right. Perhaps, the way you brought him up, he can't bear to see dripping napalm on little Vietnamese babies.

Another thing, even if he has to stay here in Canada he isn't going to be lost to you forever. Our countries are much more the same than they are different. It will be very easy for you to visit here and you will be very welcome. Your son will be a respected citizen who really belongs, not a fugitive. Canada isn't a northern wilderness. The climate in Toronto is very like that of New York. But Canada is growing faster and this often increases opportunities. It might even be quite a good place for your grand-children to grow up.

Those of us here who are interested in your sons know that our support is not the same thing as your support. So please write let-ters, maybe bake a few cookies or send him a warm scarf against the northern winds, and come for a nice visit after he gets settled.

"CHRISTIANS ARE CALLED FIRST TO LOVE RATHER THAN JUDGE" by the REV. ROY G. DE MARSH, Secretary, Board of Colleges, United Church of Canada

From early childhood I recall stories of my maternal forebears who renounced their New England home and at great personal sacrifice came to live in Canada. History labels them United Empire Loyalists. The name implies fidelity to higher ideals than personal or family fortune, or the unquestioned support of the colony which aspired to sovereign nationhood through revo-lution. Freedom of dissent, whatever the cost, is a basic ingredient of the history of both Canada and the United States. In vastly more complex and tragic circumstances today, Canada is again receiving a procession of people of a new generation who, in dissent from the Vietnam war policy of their nation, have made the often agonizing decision to leave the U.S.A., perhaps forever. In this informational guide no attempt is made to promote or discourage, to defend or attack the basis of the decision, or the ideals which are implied in making so painful a choice. The fact of that decision, and the value and autonomy of the person is accepted without question and the booklet focuses most help-fully on the consequent procedures and provisions.

As a minister of the Church in the receiving country and having often said that Christians are called first to love rather than judge those who are in need, I find here a valuable example. Hopefully I urge all Canadians to reach out in the same spirit of this booklet, with concern and assistance to all facing the difficult transition to a new life. Some will need temporary accommodation or financial assistance, and help in finding employment. Many will suffer loneliness being away from family and friends. All will need friendship and acceptance.

4 GRAEME GIBSON

An excerpt from the novel *Five Legs* (1969)

There was a boy
A very strange enchanted boy
They say he travelled very far, very far
Over dum dee-dah
Dah dee dah-dah

Glancing with his wry smile at the wryly-smiling self above the basin, carefully rolls his crisp blue sleeves. Not a bad shirt after all. Dee dumm dah-dah. But it isn't quite the same. Rubbing his fingers on his beard he stares more closely. Critically, I don't look too bad. Hah. Not an unhandsome face although I couldn't rely on it to see me through. A face of character. Yes, behind that face lies a man who is interesting to know. Ironic. Snorting briefly through his nose he wryly smiles again. A quizzical smile, objective irony. That's it. Hmmm. He takes the razor from its shelf, blows briskly to clear the hundreds of tiny cutting edges, bangs it on his hand and plugs it in. Jeez! This noise will waken my head again. So enjoyed this summer here with you. Certainly seemed appreciative with her golden thighs and sun-bleached hair. Sweet thing. And I'm really looking forward to working on Teahouse with. Would you mind awfully Doctor Crackell? I just can't reach right up the back. Would I mind sweet thing in this dark green summer's fancy heat, would I mind? The razor pushes folds of skin along his cheek. Baby oil and iodine heavy in the sun and I smoothed it in small circles on her back. Aah Doctor Crackell! That's nice. Crescents of youthful flesh, her ears revealed by tangled hair. And my hands seemed strangely rough.

Pleasantly conscious of my stolen summer's drink and that beautiful pale doe of a girl at the cash desk casting her eyes at me, I browsed among the conjuring books. Tapping the side of my foot with the old invisible cane. Tap-tap. Good grief but there are lots of books. Who writes them all? And in all colours. Tap. Nothing like a haircut and a shoe-shine to liberate the social man. And whistling lightly. When I look up, casually, she'll be watching you bet; and the warm quick flush will reveal her. Hah! Can't keep her eyes off you, you sly young fox. Just easily raise the old head and throw a wry and enigmatic smile in her direction. Ready? Now! Well hello there. It's Susan. All crisp and pretty in her starched sun-dress. How are you this fine afternoon and why aren't you in the warmth of the garden? Hmmm. I see. Well perhaps you'll join me for a drink on this hot thirsty day. Dah dee dah-dah. The light was shining on her face and her dress rustled sharply as we marched out past those almond eyes. Ah-ha! A nod of my head and the cheerful goodbye.

The terrible noise this razor makes outside my head reemphasizes the necessity of water. Lots of water before I sleep. Oh boy. Dilute the poisons of a night like that. Jeez! There was nothing for it but go down and meet her when the play had ended. Closing his eyes he massages them with a careful hand. And the razor snarls. Stinking parties with her friends are like an entry to another world, across a frigging ocean to an unreal world. Watching themselves in the mirrored walls they moved in vague and frantic forms: they twittered about me like bats in a desperate dream. Shrill with laughter above it all, the actors removed their make-up while we watched until tired and greasy their faces appeared; they sat in undershirts or robes with flaccid skin pale in fluorescent glare. Pushing the razor into the top of his throat, he tries to catch the last remaining whiskers. My name was called but the voice was carried away in the crowd and my face too, was there on the wall. Dark and nervously drawn. And because I once danced with useless joy and absurdly flowed out and overlapped my world. It is only drink that saves me.

Once again the summer street's hot afternoon with air contained by stores on every side. Carefully on the hot pavement we went to the light click-clack of her heels. With dignity. A trim pony beside me on the window's bright and jumbled face. Then in through the side door with sudden darkness on the eyes. Click-clack. And coolness, blessed coolness as blinking you wait for Bert with buttons tarnished by the air-conditioned air. The tray of frosted glasses on his hand. Back again Mister Crackell, you weren't gone long. Then with languorous and familiar ease the drinks were ordered, cigarettes were lit and easily we settled in to talk. Really nice and cool Doctor Crackell. I don't come in here very often.

You don't? Well goodness gracious me my dear you really should. Yes indeed. You really should. A womb away from home as it were. Ha-ha.

Well Martin doesn't like it very much. He says he prefers the taverns to a bar. I don't know why. I think this is very nice, don't you? It's not so dark when you get used to it. I couldn't come in alone though. And anyway men are always waiting for girls in bars. I remember once in Detroit... You heard the lady. Coldly staring from my dangerous eyes; my pale hands resting on the table's top. You heard the lady, so bust off. Right away fella and play your games with someone else. Hah! Then lunging at me with strangled rage and I'd drop to my knee like a shot and out with the right arm, pow with straightened fingers driving under his breastbone! Arrgh! And the poor bastard's writhing on the floor. Make the others pause as well. Jesus mack, his voice astonished, you've killed him! He can't breathe. Then I'd loosen his belt and set him right. Oh Doctor Crackell. Thank you, thank you

Doctor Crackell. Surprising speed for a man my age and size but it's the thought-out move that triumphs every time. Smooth pads of his fingers on the now-shaved face and his cool and calculating smile. Now I think you should stop this Doctor business, and call me Lucan. Think quickly, clearly and then the execution with finesse. Pow! Wonder if I could. Self-discipline and the rigorous control of movement should do the trick. Jeez! A worker's bony fist against my nose and mouth. Squash! The pain of it wow and I'm blinded by my tears and blood. At his mercy. Oh boy, it's best to run like hell. If possible. But a man has responsibilities, inescapable commitments. Certainly wouldn't want to get hurt though. Winding the cord securely about the razor he returns it to the shelf, brings down Old Spice and liberally smoothes it stinging on his face. Nevertheless, self-control and. Could do the trick.

5 RAY SMITH

An excerpt from the novel *Cape Breton is the Thought-Control Centre of Canada* (1969)

A Centennial Project

Why don't we go away?
  Why?
  Why not?
  Because.
  If we went away things would be different.
  No. Things would be the same. Change starts inside.
  No. Change can start outside.
  Possibly.
  Then, can we go away?
  No. Perhaps. All right. It doesn't matter.

So you believe in Canada and you're worried about American economic domination? But you can't understand international finance? What you do know is that a landlord can give a tenant thirty days to get out, eh? And the tenant can stay longer if he has a lease, but you don't recall having signed a lease with the Americans?

So you're saying to yourself: 'What can I do? What can I do? I can't influence Bay Street...what can I do?...'

Well...uhhh...thought of blowing the Peace Bridge?

The Americans are loathe to fight without a divine cause. Assume we provide this by electing an N.D.P. Government, stirring ourselves up with Anti-American slogans like: 'Give me liberty or give me death!' or (the most divine of all) passing legislation that is prejudicial to American money.

With their divine cause, the Americans would destroy our Armed Forces in one week. (This makes a fine game; you can play it out on a map.) Canada will have ceased to exist as a free nation. Now: *Think of the fun you'd have in the Resistance!* It's a great subject for daydreaming: Be the first kid on your block to gun down a Yankee Imperialist.

A virgin named Judy, an attractive girl in her early twenties, is so curious about sexual intercourse that, despite certain misgivings, she goes to a party determined to find a man willing to do the deed. She wears an alluring but tasteful dress, has her hair done, and bescents herself with a flattering perfume.

At the party are certain men of her own age whom Judy knows and finds attractive; and certain men of her own age whom she doesn't know and finds attractive. All realize that Judy is a virgin and that she wishes to experience intercourse. Each feels he would like to help her. At the party are other girls, but they do not figure in the story, being all the same as Judy.

The party progresses pleasantly enough. The guests dance and sing and drink enough alcohol to feel light-headed, but not enough to become maudlin, violent, or unconscious. A good time is had by all.

The end of the party nears, and Judy has not yet been offered help. Desperate, she decides to make the proposal herself. In no time at all, the men are seated about her discussing the problem with her. This goes on for several hours until the men pass out and Judy walks home alone. On a dark and lonely street, she is pulled into an alleyway and raped by a stranger who leaves her with her clothes torn, her body sore and bleeding, and her eyes streaming tears.

A week later, her virginity restored in a Venus-wise bath, she goes through the same events. Judy is a happy girl, for she leads a sane, healthy, and well-balanced life.

Consider the Poles. They have built a nation which, if not great and powerful, is at least distinct.

Of course, the Poles have their own language, and they have been around for a thousand years. But they have survived despite the attentions paid them by their neighbours, the Russians and the Germans.

Analogies are never perfect, but the Poles do have what we want. Consider the Poles; consider the price they have paid and paid and paid.

Wit: Did you hear about the Canadian Pacifist who became a Canadian Nationalist?

Self: No; why did he do that?

Wit: Because he wanted to take advantage of the economical Red, White, and Blue fares.

Recently a friend conned me into explaining my interest in compiled fiction, an example of which you are now reading.

'Hey, that's great,' he said. 'That really sounds interesting.'

'I'm interested in it,' I replied, razoring out the distinction.

'But I hope you aren't expecting to sell any of these compilations. The publishers won't touch anything as new as that.'

'Well, that's their business, isn't it? I mean, if they figure it's not for their magazine or it's lousy or something, they reject it. It's a basic condition. If you want to demand they publish your stuff, the best and fastest way is to buy the magazine, fire the editor, and hire a yes-man.'

'I didn't mean....'

'I know what you meant; but, in fact, the technique isn't new at all. I got it from Ezra Pound and he got it from some French poets. Other precedents might be Francis Bacon's essays, the Book of Proverbs...the whole *Bible*....'

'But....'

My friend babbled on. He talks a lot about writing but, so far as I know, doesn't do any.

You can't see up through the mist (up through the high timber where the air is clean and good) but you know the dawn is already gleaming on the snow peaks; soon it will reach down here and burn away the mist and then it will be too late. Where the hell is that bloody supply column? You hunch forward between the rock and the tree and peer into the gloom. The armoured-car escort will appear...there: when it gets...there Mackie and Joe will heave the cocktails and when the flame breaks Campbell will open up with the Bren...Christ, you hope you get some arms out of this because if you don't you'll have to pack it up soon... Christ, it's cold, your joints can't take much more of...a growl from down around the bend...a diesel growl....

Do you love me?

Yes. I love you. You're my wife.

Why did you say, You're my wife?

Uhh....

You said it because you think just because I'm your wife you have to love me when really it has nothing to do with it.

Perhaps. It's more complicated than that.

It's always more complicated. Why can't it be simple? You always say things are too complicated when what you really mean is you don't want to talk to me. Why can't things be simple?

They are. I love you. As simple as that. So simple there's no point talking about it.

Complicated, too, I suppose.

So complicated that to talk about it would always oversimplify it. It's the same with everything.

Then what. . . . Oh! You're impossible to talk to.

You know that isn't true.

Yes.

So. . . .

Then what is important?

Doing.

Doing what?

Mmmmm. . . .

Ohhhh. . . .

Toronto is a truly despicable city.

6 MARIAN ENGEL
An excerpt from the novel *The Honeyman Festival* (1970)

Honeyman. The name if she let it still causing sharp shooting sparks in the abdomen. Honeyman.

The great lolling length; body, as though partially disjointed, a lay figure, beside her; "Broke up," he said, from riding broncos, and scarred, certainly from the accident-prone days before she knew him, before she was born. The strange softness of the old-young drying skin, loose, a little loose, beginning to be liver-marked, but not pouchy. Exotic to her.

She sat, startled by waves of emotion. Years since she weakened last for him, though she had never stopped talking to him in her head, saying, "See, Honeyman?" when she did what she was proud of, or what he would like, or resisted him. And more often when she tried perversely to summon up his flesh it would be the firmer flesh of Norman burrowed into her that came to mind. And she loved Norman and the children, they were more to her, more hers, more real, more possible.

Only he was fifty-five to her twenty, and he knew a lot, and taught her some of it, it went in and stayed there and changed her in a direction she was thankful for. Friends murmured "father-figure" and she denied it, but he was, of course; a father chosen instead of imposed, who knew the things she wanted to know and taught her them.

What he gave me by knowing me. And I at twenty still wrapped in the cruel child's integument of innocence, insisting, demanding. Why didn't he throw me out or wring my sweet neck?

He was a kind man, he had patience, and children almost her age. When she lay beside him in bed and drew the heathen blanket of southern Ontario guilt around her, he turned to her, he comforted her, he talked to her, taught her what she was.

A strange man, long-headed, the grey hair curling high on the immense forehead, the nose falling straight to flared nostrils, the long upper lip, the wide, twisted thick-lipped mouth. Shooting sparks. A head on a grand scale, big-planed; and a body to match, bellyless, loose-jointed, Western and mythic in walk.

He was from Nebraska, the son of a wealthy cooper and a Christian Scientist. He had been sent to Princeton when he wanted to go further west. He left the university to take his kid's romanticism to California. Before he was twenty he arrived in Hollywood broken-backed. His father staked him to a second education in what he called "the pic-chahs."

Telling his story, leaving out the stress, the terrible passions of young-ness, lounging through it as if it were easy—he made everything look easy, even youth, Honeyman. He made it look easy to live, as if living were some road you strode along and not the puritan hurdle-course she had been taught to believe m.

And suddenly, because she knew him, it was easy: she had a flat in Paris when nobody had a flat in Paris, and jobs in films when nobody could break into films; when because of his terrifying American casualness and abruptness nobody could make contact with him, she could. People looked at her enviously and asked why she was special. Even she, for a while, wondered why she was special. "You're not, kid," he said, "but I like you." She wondered at that, too, until she grew old enough to realise that if love is an accident, liking is a kind of miracle.

He liked her, he tried to make something of her. He liked the way she looked, he said, the long legs, the big bosom, the way her lower lip stuck out. But he was not young anymore, he told her that all she had to do was to be herself, and forgot that at her age even he had not discovered what to be that was himself; he was breaking horses and had a background in Middle English. By the time she met him, he was as fixed and formed, it seemed to her, as she must seem to her upstairs hippies, a finished creation, no longer floundering in flux. Jesus; he thought the thing to do with Minn at twenty was teach her how to be unselfconscious, and put her in his movies, it was that simple. And she went through terrors and uncertainties, wilting queasily before cameras, until they discovered that neither she nor God had dreamed she would become an actress.

Then he loosened his grip on her without dropping her. The liking continued. There were other jobs she could do, on the sets, in the studios. She picked up good French easily with the grammatical backing of years of drill-mistresses and *Cours Moyen*. Forty-two university term-papers had given her fluency in writing. She had been taught at home to make lists, to finish things. She had energy. She did not lose him.

In addition, he liked to eat with her. There were gilt and flashy ladies he took to the Tour d'Argent, and Minn whom he took all over France snuffling out truffled pâtés and full-bodied wines and...

Honeyman. Years. Like some dreadful addiction, waiting for him as for a fix. Later, fighting him. "You're growing out of me," he said blandly, woundingly, almost relieved.

Honeyman. How fortunate to have...

To have been sent to the cooking-school? To have spent the summer in Italy?

Always alone in the flat in the rue Dragon. That was the arrangement, no visitors. Alone, knowing no one, waiting for him. Seeing no one for months when he was away, except the son, Cal, the rootless one, run away from another school and hiding out with a passel of rootless friends, destroying things, destroying himself.

Honeyman. My friends were marrying. How could they, not yet having turned into themselves? I waited. Finally, it was finished with him. Between sixty and twenty-five there is no democracy, I pushed for equality, I fought him fiercely, he married again.

The feeling, then: as if one's body is plaster, and flakes are falling, falling and one is finally to become the rusted, chipped maquette of a Giacometti.

She was not as young as she looked; she had money, she had class; she left her husband for him. She was in his circle. She had the villa for him to retire to. He was right.

After Norman and I got married I had cards printed, "Minn N. Burge," I dragged him down to Cannes, wrote on the inner fold, "Passons par Cannes et je me demande si c'est possible vous voir avant de partir pour l'Angleterre, Minn..." the name very large and determined. They were ladies and gentlemen: they telephoned at once, they sent their chauffeur to our ghastly hotel.

Minn heaving with nerves, swelling, sweating, her breasts pushing out in anguish, and Norman shrinking with embarrassment. Getting through the first Dubonnet without spilling. Honeyman his bland best, using his public manner. Minn knowing that. The blind intimacy pulled down. Liking the woman more.

On the way to the bathroom she faced Minn, Guinévre; she said, smiling, "So you have forgiven me!" Up close, she had crows' feet and a sense of humour. She had been a famous actress. The realisation that she was exactly right for Honeyman irked and ached.

In the salon (beams, and heavy English chairs and pottery from Moustiers), Honeyman and Norman were engrossed in each other. Norman was asking Honeyman about Fitzgerald, and Honeyman was telling beautiful stories about Fitzgerald. "I never knew you knew Fitzgerald," Minn said, and they went on without looking at her.

They left politely at five, good children, turning down the offer of a chauffeur in favour of a walk. Honeyman wrote them a cheque and made them promise to buy a *batterie de cuisine* at the store behind the Opera in Paris, which they did.

She seldom thought of him now, except perhaps when she snatched the *bain-marie* away from them in the sandbox. But she carried him always inside her like a stone, like a calcified embryo. And wondered if any power on earth could have made her into a Guinèvre when he failed to.

So tonight we celebrate the public Honeyman, she thought. The man who disclaimed artistry at the Cinémathèque, and year after year, with the greatest respect for technique and for form, turned out the best-made crap of the period.

And thought, too, of herself pasted on a peeling Italian wall, all but unrecognizable, a banner labeled OGGI over her cleavage.

7 AUSTIN CLARKE

An excerpt from the story collection *When He Was Young and Free He Used to Wear Silks* (1971)

Waiting For The Postman To Knock

"That poor girl, Enid! The whole week Enid lay down in she bed, waiting for the postman to knock. The sheets and the blanket which the Jewish woman she was working for give she for Christmas last Christmas was wrap over she head, and she was in pain from head to foot. Enid wet her pillow, I tell you, with tears of blood. She had just been discharge from the General Hospital, but she was still weaky-weaky and poorly. And not a dollar to her name! I ain't telling you no lie. This is a true, true story! Two times for the whole week she manage to get outta bed, to rub she arms and legs with some Canadian Healing Oil which she mother had send up for her last year. Enid was so sick that she was barely able to wash she face and hands. When she move in the bed the pain, child, the pain increase a little more. And water was coming outta Enid eyes like Niagara Falls self.

"Winter. Child, snow was outside like if somebody had paint the whole world white. And sadness dwelling inside Enid bedroom. Enid cry and cry and all the time she crying she cussing sheself that she ever was foolish enough to say she emigrading to this terrible place call Canada. Not a blind soul to make a cup o' tea or coffee, for she; nobody to run to the corner store to buy a bottle of ginger ale, a pack o' chewing gum, not even mensing pads, then! Is so Enid lonely in this big country. You could imagine what it was for Enid, because even when she was strong and in good health she always uses to say how hard it is for a black woman living by sheself in this damn country. I hear with my own ears one day, as Enid curse God and Canada, and say, "Be-Jesus Christ, it isn't no bed of roses for a black woman living in this blasted country." Enid wait and wait for the postman to knock, and whilst she waiting, she decide to write a letter to the landlord. But the exertion nearly kill she. Anyhow, lissen to the letter Enid write:

46 Asquith Avenue, Toronto 5, Ontario.
18 December 1969.

Dear Mr Landlord,
  I am a sick woman. I barely crept out of my room yesterday to go to the bank to see what happened to that check I wrote for you. Well, I can tell you, Mr Landlord, that I don't understand how my money could dissappear so fast from that Royal Bank. The woman behind the desk looked at my card, and she told me I have two dollars to my name. One dollar and eighty cents to be exact. I know I still owing you the rent, but I am not going to run, for as I say, I am a sick lady. I only told you that to tell you this. This morning before I even crawl out of bed, somebody was knocking down my door. I didn't even open my eyes yet, nor say a word to God for sparing my life at night. But I open the door. When I open the door, facing me is a man from Beneficial Finance Company of Canada. He come for cash. The next few minutes it is the postman. Registered letter. The Bell Telephone people start writing me threatening letters. I owe them nineteen dollars, nineteen stinking dollars and they hounding me as if I am a Mafia-woman. The Hydro people called up on the same phone and threaten me that they going cut off my electricity. I do my cooking by electricity, Mr Landlord. I live by electricity. Electricity lights up this little room that I renting from you, when the nights come. If those Hydro people does cut off the electricity

as they threaten to do, how am I going to see? And on top of all that, you now come telling me that I must vacate your premises? Well, Mr Landlord, you listen to me now, sir. I am only telling you a few of the things that happens to black people in this country to let you know that it isn't no honeymoon living in this place. I came into this country as a decent middle class person back in Barbados. I did not pay any racketeer to get me here illegal. And I did not come into this country on no underground railroad, neither. I came in legal. And I came in clean. And I came as a landed immigrant. It is written down on my passport. So I am saying this to you, to let you know that it is only in Canada that I am known as a labourer, or a working woman, as it is called in this country, because back home I never lifted a straw in the way of work, for my parents were rich people. We had servants back home. And if I wanted a glass of water, our maid brought it to me. I have spent the last five years up in Forest Hill working off my sweat for a lady by the name of Silverstein. And the sad thing is that I do not have anything today in my hour of sickness to show as a testimony to that hard work. So you can't treat me as if I am any DP-person. I am a human being. And I am not writing this to you as if I do not like work. I know I have to work for my living in this country. But it is the conditions that I am talking about. And I want you to know too that I not writing this to you to beg you for nothing. I was not hiding from you, Mr Landlord. I was not hoarding up my money on the Royal Bank, and telling you that I broke when you come for your rent. I was flat on my back in the Toronto General Hospital bed. Six weeks run into seven, and I was still there sprawled out in something called a semi-private. My temperature was all up in the hundreds, and I was roasted up night and day. All my savings I had to pay out in Blue Cross, Red Cross, PSI, doctor bills and I don't know what. So because of all these troubles that I face in your country, I am asking you now, as a human being, to let me live in this room a next month until I can get my hands on a piece of change. Somebody told me of a job up in Cooksville, which as you know is not close to Toronto, if you don't have a motor car. And the moment I pacify these pains, I intend to go up to Cooksville. I am not a lazy person. I *never was. Christmas is just round the corner. I have gifts to buy and send back home. And today, on this cold-winter-day, I do not even have a dime to buy a postcard with, to send for my mother for Christmas, in Barbados. And you come telling me about vacate?*

Respectfully yours,
Miss Enid Scantlebury.

"Child, that is the letter Enid write to the landlord-man. God, that girl have heart and she have guts to do a thing like that.

"Well, the very next day, a special-delivery letter come back from the landlord-man. It say:

THE CROWN TRUST CO, INCORPORATED
19 December 1969
Miss E. Scantlebury
46 Asquith Avenue
Toronto 5, Ontario

Dear Miss Scantlebury,
    We are in receipt of your most recent letter dated December 18. We regret to inform you that due to the heavy arrears of your rent, we find it impossible to extend your tenancy of the room at the above-mentioned address.
    We urge you not correspond further with us on this matter.
                         Yours faithfully,
                         (Signed) THE CROWN TRUST CO, INC.

P.S. Please note that our proper title is not "Mr Landlord," but the Crown Trust Co, Incorporated, c/o Mortgage Department.

"As you can expect, Enid gone mad now. Mad, mad, mad as hell! Everything turning out wrong, and the pain working now from in her shoulder-blade all through her right side. And you know what women in the Wessindies does say when a young healthy woman start to get them kind o' pains! Enid tell me she start thinking bout home, bout Mammy, which is what she calls her mother, bout her boyfriend, and she sorry as hell that she didn' send for him when he did first ask to come up and married she. Well, thinking bout the devil, brain! A letter push under the door, from guess-who? Lonnie! Lonnie write to Enid and say how things back home really bad with him. Look, I going to read the whole letter, cause it is something to hear:

Haggatt Hall
Bridgetown
Barbados
The West Indies
16th December 1969

Darling Sweetheart Enid,
 This is Lonnie. I writing you because Christmas soon here, and things down here still rough rough with me in Barbados. The sugar cane crop season was a real bastard, and the estates been laying off men left and right like flies. Furthermore, a piece of sickness had me flat on my backside last month, and I had to give up the little picking a fellow by the name of Boulee from up in Christ Church parish had get for me. It was a real part-time job. I work for three days. Things real rough as I said, down here in this island, although we have independence and things like that. We have a Hilton hotel here as you know, and now people talking about building another big fancy hotel call the Holiday Inn. Both of them places build on Gravesend Beach where the sailors from the Boer War is buried. And where me and you used to go and bathe on a bank holiday and on Sunday mornings. Men walking about in Bridgetown like ants, unemploy. You have to be a craftsman to get a job these days. And as you know I am not no blasted craftsman, because I think that things like carpenters and masons is low jobs for a man in my position. Christmas soon come,

and I would like to go to church five o'clock Christmas morning, at
the Cathedral, because the news is that the new black bishop going to
preach there. But I do not have my Christmas suit yet. The one I wear
to the airport to wish you goodbye when you were leaving do not look
good anymore. I buy a piece of cloth some time back, dark with a pin
stripe, from Cave Shepherd store, about three months pass, when
things was selling out. But Cuthbert the tailor fellow, since he come
back down from up in the States and Northamerica and places like
that, he now charging everybody a hell of a lot of money to make a
suit and he adding on something he picked up up there in the States
called "sales tax" and "luxuries tax." And nobody down here don't
know what Cuthbert really mean by those two terms. But if you don't
pay them, you can't touch your own suit when it finish made, if it
made at all. So, darling love, Enid, I beseeching you, to please send a
little something for me for Christmas. I want that suit bad bad out of
Cuthbert hand, because I have not been near to a church since that
Sunday when Trevour was christen.

Your loving man, Lonnie.

"Child, there is a kind o' Wessindian man who just *loves* to live
offa women. And Enid is such a kind-hearted person that she
would give a sinner the dress offa her back. But Lonnie? Well, he
is something else, a diff'rent story altogether!

"Enid say she know now, long-time, that Lonnie is the wrong
man for she. Enid cry and cry and cry. She there flat on her back,
trying to catch her strength and a man write her all the way
from Barbados asking for money. When she read Lonnie letter,
she tell me, she could only crawl outta her sick bed, stumble in
the bathroom and look at her face in the mirror whilst she was
crying. Child, you does read these things in certain magazines,
but you *never never* think that life is really like this! Well, Enid
wipe her face and dust some powder on her face, and try to
smile, cause it looked like whatever the hell she do, is only mis-
ery and sufferation coming her way.

"Well, not that Enid didn' love Lonnie, at least once upon a time that was the case, as Enid tell me. But getting that letter from Lonnie, the man she had in mind to marry, threw her back, poor soul, right on another letter she had receive from Mammy some time back, before she went in the hospital. This is what Mammy write Enid, part of it:

I have received the few cents that you posted to me in March gone, this year. And I have been reposing myself down at the front window that you used to sit down at, and sing those lovely refrains you learned at the Fontabelle Christian Mission Church, waiting for the postman to ring his bicycle bell and then knock. Every time I see the postman pass across on his three-speed bicycle, my heart gives a leap and tears come to my eyes, because I know you have not send me anything. You have not remembered me. Nothing. Your own child, Trevour, have been sick every day for two weeks. Lonnie does not come around and even say, Take that, to the child, meaning a five-cents piece. All he does come round for is to ask, Enid send the thing? Child, you are my only child, but I have to tell you that I don't see the wisdom in you worrying out yourself behind a man like Lonnie. Lonnie not good. Lonnie, since you left here for Canada, have been running behind everything wearing a skirt. Lonnie does not even remember to take Trevour to Gravesend Beach for a seabath, even although the place full-up with tourists and hotels and foreigners. Not even on a first Sunday, then. Lonnie come round for Trevour the day after you left, to take Trevour to the Race Pasture. Trevour came back in here nine o'clock in the middle of the night. Nine o'clock. You know that I puts Trevour to bed, every single night, at six o'clock. Nine o'clock in the hands of a police who says that Trevour was loss. Trevour, my only grand-child, loss in Barbados? The police say they only guess and by luck, they find out who owns Trevour. Is that the man you sending money-order after money-order to? Lonnie walks about here telling everybody that he have a woman up in Canada supporting him. He tells people that. But I am only your mother, and you don't have to support me. And I am not even going to ask you for a cent. I will not lowrate myself to that, to ask you, who I bringed in this world, to put yourself out and send me one farthing. I brought you in this world. I send you to school. I didn't have the money in those times to send you to high school and Queens College, so I did the next best thing; I send you to learn needle-work at the best dressmaker in the island, Miss Wharton, and you learned with her till you became the best dress-maker in Westbury Village. I turned round and joined you in St Mary's Church, and you have sang more than one solo, at Easter and Christmas in the choir. And you sang so pretty one Christmas morning, that even the white man from England who used to be the sextant in those days, had to shed a tear in my presence and to my face after the service, and say, "Mother Scantlebury, your daughter may be poor, but she have the voice of an angel." That is the kind of mother I was to you. If I were really a woman of means, if I had the wherewithal, do you think you would be any blasted needle-worker today. I would have send you to Queens College or St Winifreds, and make sure that today you would be back here in Barbados where you belong, and you would be a high school mistress, or a doctor or a lawyer, anything but being in that cold ungodly place, Canada, working for white people and servanting after people who don't know how to treat you as a human being. For no matter how poor we were you know that we always had a maid to bring you a cup of tea if you wanted one. And I want you to know now, and remember it, that after your father walked through that door, that sad Saturday night, you was only a babe in arms. You must always remember that. And you will understand what a struggle it was to raise you, and I accomplished that, through thick and thin. I am not going to beg you now, for nothing. I am not going to be another Lonnie. Even if you have come out of my womb, I am not going to lowrate myself in front of you. But I am going to warn you this last time. If you don't intend to get a message through some of the decent friends you have down in Westbury Road, that your child Trevour spend this coming Christmas in a Almshouse cot, and that I had to spend it in the Poor House, you hads better get up from off your backside fast, and send down some real cash down here, real soon.

I had to get Freddie the civil service fellow to write this letter to you for me. I didn't post it before now, because I was still waiting to see if just in case the postman was going to ring his bicycle and stop at the house and hand me a letter from you. But seven days pass and I have not heard one word. Freddie was just on his way back from lunch, and I ask him to please finish off the letter, adding these few lines that you are reading now, and post it when he get in the Public Buildings. Freddie turned into a very nice gentleman these days. I wish that Freddie and you had made up your two minds and get married. And Freddie is nodding his head now, in my presence as he writes this. He is a man of wisdom. A civil servant. But it was through you, and he agrees with me, that you allowed him to get married to Pats who had a child from him three years ago. They are living together now in a lovely stone bungalow in a new subdivision. He is a Brother in the Christian Mission Church. And Enid, child, you should hear him testify on a Sunday night. It would make your heart bleed. Freddie is what I call a perfect gentleman. I do not know why you didn't follow my advice. Today, Freddie would have been my son-in-law. But I am leaving you in the hands of the Lord. I hope He talks to you. And I hope that the reaches of these few lines would find you in a more perfect state of good health than they leave me, feeling real rotten concerning your child, Trevour, and number two, in regards to Lonnie.

> With love and affection,
> Your Mother
> (and from Freddie)

8 HAROLD SONNY LADOO
An excerpt from the novel *No Pain Like This Body* (1972)

A drum was beating. It kept on beating. Well. It kept on beating and beating and beating and beating. . . . The rain began to drizzle. Ma heard the rain drizzling. Then the rain came down real hard and the lightning danced and the thunder shook up Tola. Then the wind came out from the sky and began to pull the trees and shake the house. But the drum was still beating. She held the flambeau in her hand. The wind was trying to out the light. When the drumming almost reached the house, Ma called, "Ay!"

"Oy!" Nanny answered.

Ma was happy. She listened to the drum. It beated faster and faster. She heard the drum beating inside her chest. It was beating fast and hard and fast and hard; just beating inside her chest and in the sky.

Nanna, Nanny, Balraj and Sunaree walked inside the house. They were soaked all over as if they had fallen inside the river. The drum was tied around Nanny's neck; it was brown as a brown cow. Ma went out into the yard to meet them, then she carried them inside the kitchen. She took out rice and dal. They ate.

When the food was finished, they washed their hands with rainwater that fell from the thatched roof. The water felt like ice. Balraj was trying to wash his whole hand. He leaned over; almost over the drain. There was a flash of lightning at the same time. He jumped up and fell down inside the canal. Nanna and Nanny rushed into the drain and took him out. They carried him to the rainwater barrel. He had a good bath at the back of the house. They brought him into the kitchen.

"How Rama feelin?" Nanny asked Ma.

"He sick wid fever."

"He sick bad?"

"Me eh know," Ma said. "But all you coud go and see him inside. He sleepin wid Panday."

Nanna and Nanny went into the bedroom to see Rama. He was asleep, but he was breathing hard hard. Panday was asleep too. They walked back to the kitchen, and Nanny said to Ma, "Rama have bad fever."

And Ma: "Me husban in de rumshop. He not care notten about dese chirens. But by de grace of God dese same chirens goin to come man and woman in dis same Tola."

"But Rama have to see a docta," Nanny said.

And Nanna put on a worried look. "I goin by dat rumshop to see me son-in-law. He have to come home and help me say some prayers for dis chile."

"Oright," Nanny said.

Nanna walked out of the kitchen into the drizzle and the night.

About an hour after Nanna left, Nanny started to beat the drum. The rain was falling, making its own music. Sunaree was playing the flute. Nanny's fingers were long and bony. They touched the goat's skin as if they were accustomed to it. She beated the drum slow slow. Sunaree played the flute good; her fingers touched the holes in the bamboo flute as if they were made for them. The music of the flute was sweeter than sugar; than life even. Ma was dancing. Balraj was watching. The kitchen was full of music and sadness: music from the sky and the earth, but sadness from the earth alone. And their spirits were growing and floating in the air like silkcotton flowers.

Nanny started a song. Her eyes were dark and sad. She sang a part and Ma repeated it. Ma sang a line, and she repeated it. So it went on and on. The song was in Hindi. The sky God was listening, because the drum was beating like cake over Tola; like honey. It was beating and beating and beating; beating only to keep them awake like bats; it was beating only to keep them happy and sad, happy and sad; it was beating for the black night that was choking Tola, and the rain that was pounding the earth; the drum was beating in the sky and it was beating on the earth; it was beating, and even the great sky God could not stop it from beating, because it was beating and beating and beating just as the heavens roll.

Suddenly it ended. Nanny said to Ma, "You have good chirens. God go help dem one day. Wid all dis blackness choking Tola from all sides, it hard for dem later on."

"God go help dem," Ma said with great sadness in her voice.

Nanny beated the drum again. This time she beated for the tadpoles, the scorpions and the night birds; she beated not only for the living things of Tola; she beated a tune for all that lives and moves upon the face of the earth. She beated and she knew that the great sky God was watching with his big big eyes.

A large cockroach with long wings flew *flut* over the light. It settled *taps* on the earthen wall. It was wet; it came from the rain to shelter near the light. Nanny took the brown hand drum and crushed it *crachak!* Then Sunaree took the flute and crushed it; crushed it to nothingness.

The rain continued to fall. Fall really heavy, as if the rice-land was going to overflow and cover the whole house. Ma, Nanny, Balraj and Sunaree stood inside the kitchen. White sprays jumped over the wall and soaked them. The wind was strong; it was as if big big winds were leaving from far away and blowing over Tola and the whole of the island; blowing with such force and temper; blowing with the intention of crippling even the trees, blowing just to cause trouble and hate. Ma kept lighting the flambeau. Each time she did, the strange winds outed it. Rain began to fall through the holes in the roof, soaking their heads. Some of the needle grass was blown off the roof by the wind. Rain poured through the holes more and more. Inside the kitchen, the floor was getting slippery; almost too slippery to stand. There were small holes in the earthen floor. They were filling up with water. Ma kept lighting the flambeau; it was no use.

"Like Pa send dat wind," Balraj said.

"De wind and de rain too strong for de flambeau," Nanny said.

They couldn't stand any more, so they squatted. Nanny held the drum in her lap. Cold water from the rotten rafters kept falling on their heads. Falling and running down their faces. There were crickets too inside the kitchen; by the tens, jumping crazily. Balraj and Sunaree were afraid of them. Ma pulled out a strip of tarpaulin from behind the machan, it was cold, with holes all over; but it smelt like something to eat. She gave it to Balraj and Sunaree to cover their heads. Now the water was flowing on the earthen floor; just flowing as a river flows. It was getting colder and colder.

"Ay Ma!" Panday screamed from inside the house.

Ma and Nanny ran inside the house. Water was seeping through the needle grass on the roof and wetting Rama. Ma and Nanny grabbed the ricebags and skidded them along the earthen floor. They looked up. The roof was leaking in many places.

"Rama sick. He can't get wet. Wot we goin to do?" Ma asked.

"Put Rama inside de ricebox," Nanny advised.

Balraj and Sunaree were in the bedroom helping Ma and Nanny out.

"All you help put Rama in dat ricebox," Ma said.

"Oright," Balraj replied.

Ma and Nanny grabbed one side of the ricebags; Balraj, Sunaree and Panday held the other end. They carried Rama out of the bedroom. Rama was crying, so they rested him down near the bedroom door. Then they picked him up again and carried him by the ricebox.

There was no time to ask Rama why he was crying. The roof was leaking more and more. They had to put Rama inside the ricebox quickly, because he was sick. Ma said to Balraj, "Open dat ricebox fast. We have to put Rama in dat box right now."

"Oright."

The ricebox was six feet long and four feet wide. Balraj opened the lid. He went inside. Ma held the light over the box. The unground rice in the box was wet; Balraj levelled it out with his hands. When the box was prepared, he came out.

They lifted Rama slowly; they lifted him as if he was dead. Balraj climbed back into the box. He took the light from Ma and placed it inside the box. With the flambeau inside it, the ricebox looked like a big rottening pumpkin. Then Balraj climbed out of the box. Rama and the light were shut into the box.

"I feelin cold," Panday said.

The rain sang and the thunder shouted and the lightning danced.

Ma picked up Panday. Her back was resting against the wall. She stared at the light inside the box, trying to see Rama. Nanny made a step forward. She slipped. She was falling with her head over the drum. Nanny prevented the fall by grabbing hold of the wall. The rain was falling heavier now. Brown water almost covered the floor. Outside, the thunder and the rain were shouting at Tola, and the sky God was listening; listening real good. Ma and Nanny began to speak in Hindi. Balraj, Sunaree and Panday couldn't understand too well, but they knew what Ma and Nanny were talking about: they were talking about the rain and life; the rain and the thunder; the rain and the wind; the rain and the darkness; the rain and the past, and about the rain and the future; and about life and death.

There were small cracks in the earthen wall. Red ants started to come out of the cracks. First a few, then many. They started to sting. Real hard. It was as if fire was burning their skins. They moved from against the wall, but the ants were still stinging them, ants were in their clothes and their hair. They leaned against the ricebox; against the cold cedar board. Sunaree got a scrape in her back with a nail. She started to cry.

Rama was coughing and crying inside the ricebox; crying and coughing as if he was going to die. The water from the roof was still falling upon the box.

"Balraj!"

"Yeh Ma."

"Son take de cutlass from de kichen. Go cut some fig leafs and bring dem and cover de roof. Rama feelin cold. He not sappose to get wet all de time."

"Oright."

The place was dark. Balraj went in the kitchen and got the cutlass. He went by the banana patch to the southern side of the house. He couldn't see to cross the drain. He waited for the lightning; as it flashed, he jumped over the drain. Balraj felt the wet leaves with one hand and he chopped them off the banana trunk with the other.

When he came back with the leaves, he saw that they were badly torn by the wind. He handed them to Ma and Nanny, and went back for some more. Ma and Nanny held the leaves over their heads. Crickets were jumping all over the place. Sunaree and Panday kept rubbing their feet against each other, trying to kill the crickets like.

Rama was crying and getting on inside the box; he was saying how he was getting wet.

The light was shut inside the box, because when Balraj had closed the lid, he closed the light in. Ma gave her leaves to Nanny. She went into the kitchen and made another flambeau. She came back and handed the light to Nanny. It was as if Ma didn't want to have anything to do with the light.

Balraj brought the banana leaves. This time he was more careful; they were not torn by the wind. Balraj handed the leaves to Ma. He climbed up on the ricebox. He stood on the lid, and Ma handed him the leaves. He began to push the leaves between the rafters and the needle grass. But he couldn't fit the leaves properly, because the roof was too high. Nanny got a potato crate and handed it to Balraj. He took it and placed it on top of the rice-box. He stood on the crate in order to reach the roof easily. Balraj was working real fast. The water began to fall on the ricebox less and less. He was trying hard to cover the roof, but . . .

"O God!" he shouted.

Balraj jumped down from the ricebox. He fell on the ground and started to scream, bawling as if the life was coming out of him, getting on as if he was quarrelling with the wind and the rain. Ma and Nanny thought he saw an evil spirit; they began talking in Hindi right away, saying prayers and this kind of thing. Balraj was rolling in the water, keeping his hands high in the air. The rain was pouring and pouring and pouring down on Tola. Lightning flashed. Balraj told Ma and Nanny that his hands were on fire. The water came down from the roof and fell on the ricebox *drip drip drip*. Something fell from the roof *tats*; it fell harder than the water.

Ma and Nanny moved closer to the ricebox with the flam-beau. There were three of them. Full grown. Deadly. Moving fast. Faster. Running on the ricebox. They were black like rub-ber. The long legs were hurrying. Tails in the air. Moving faster and faster. Fire stingers. The scorpions. Little but deadly; they kept running and running.

"Move fast!" Ma shouted.

Sunaree shifted.

The scorpions were running down the sides of the ricebox. Nanny crushed one with the drum. Ma burnt another with the flambeau; it smelt bad. Some more fell on the ricebox. The scorpions were running down the sides of the box too fast. They couldn't kill all of them. Ma took the flambeau and started to smoke them off the ricebox. She didn't want them to go inside the box, because Rama was still inside the box. And the scorpions were running crazily all over the place; just running with their tails in the air. Some of them went underneath the box. Others just crawled on the earth in the muddy water. Some went into the cracks of the earthen wall. A large black scorpion was climbing on Sunaree's right foot. She jumped up, and it fell in the water again. She took the flute and pounded it to death; pounded it just as the rain was pounding the house, and the wind was pounding the light.

Balraj was still bawling and rolling in the water. Rama too was screaming from inside the ricebox; screaming and saying how the scorpions were stinging him.

9 WAYLAND DREW
An excerpt from the novel *The Wabeno Feast* (1973)

I had finished my evening meal, and had drawn from my supplies some mild tea, of which I had had the foresight to bring a small quantity, for I could not stomach the raw and noxious stuff which passes for tea among these people, when I heard above the breaking of the waves and above the talk and rollicking of the men, a sound such as I had never heard, except in my darkest dreams. Like the moan of an animal it started low, undistinguished from the water coughing along the shores, and I could not have foretold whether it was a cry of pleasure or of agony, or, as so it proved to be, both and neither. It rose, and with it rose the hair on my neck and arms, while all conversation ceased about our fire and men hung suspended in attitudes of spooning food to their mouths or touching a coal to their tobacco. It rose, and spiralled in intensity and pitch, strengthening and quickening with every undulation and full of rage, or terror, but of submission also—a horrible submission—which above all chilled my blood. I thought of Gustave in that moment, erect on his bit of sinking bark and cursing heaven with both fists; so it was that a man should die, cursing death with all the last of his life, and not in this long pallid and futile howl from which all life had been sucked like substance from a cowl of fungus. Yet it rose quavering to a continuing shriek beyond the lungs of man or woman to support; and when I believed that I must shriek myself to blot it out, it ceased. In the silence it echoed in my mind, and it was some moments before I let go my pent-up breath, and moved my tongue in a dry mouth.

"There are Indians," I said, "on the island next to this."

A canoe was quickly launched. In the twilight we rounded the end of our island and approached the next, drawing close to the beach where their canoes lay, and from this vantage point I saw the tents which had previously been hidden. They also were arranged with a symmetry uncommon in Indian encampments— a precision, indeed, almost military. We did not touch, but swung broadside off the beach, and one of our men who spoke Ojibway hailed the tents asking what was amiss and if we could assist them, for we had heard a screaming. At this three men emerged from the central and largest lodge, and two from another. I had seen no savages their equal. Not only were they statuesque in bearing and haughty in demeanour, but although featured like Indians their skin bore an ambivalent pallor, neither white nor dusky. Their dress and decoration also distinguished them from others of their tribe. These wore buckskins bleached until they rivalled in brilliance the sheerest linen, and all their hands and arms up to their elbows were dyed by what appeared in that distance and falling darkness to be greased ochre. They moved warily towards us, and from them came one of remarkable height and slenderness of frame. He it was who answered our spokesman, telling him (so our man reported) that they needed no assistance, and that if we had heard a crying it must have been the wind, or the circling gulls. His voice was high, and he spoke both slyly and arrogantly, as if he did not expect to be believed and cared little if he was not.

We turned away with the merest of civilities. When I looked back I saw that the five had been joined by some six or eight others, all men, and all clothed in the same uncommon manner. They stood indolently, laughing among themselves.

"Wabeno!" said our translator, and spat into the lake. He showed a great reluctance to speak further, grimacing and waving his hand toward the Indians' tents; yet I saw fear in his expression also, and a mingling of respect.

"'There is a wabeno encamped next door with all his party," he told the others when we had again reached the fire, "and I daresay from the screaming that you will see a *wabeno wekoon-dewin* if you care to watch, at the time of the morning star." I pressed him further. He had lived long among the Indians in the *pays d'en haut* and knew much of their customs; and reluctantly he told me that this wabeno is the most powerful of their shamans, but whether his influence be curative or pernicious he knew not, although he thought the latter. The wabeno, he said, would use any means to cure disease or to quench an unrequited love, and those who placed themselves in his influence and used his potions on themselves or on others must submit entirely their will to his, for the remedies might grow extreme. When he had spoken my informant spat several times into the fire as if to rid himself of a sour taste. It was good, he added, that the power of the wabeno had declined, and that such sorceries as he practiced so as to conjure an overturn of nature grew less common as the Company's influence spread.

By evening the lake had calmed and the night spread high and cool. Before it was fully dark most men retired, anticipating an early start. At last only Elborn and I remained beside the fire. "Now, MacKay," he said, shifting closer in the smoke, "these mummeries our friend has spoken of...I confess I am not adverse to seeing something of them for myself. Judging from his remarks, the opportunity will not soon present itself again."

I remarked as dryly as possible that his interest did not surprise me.

"Oh indeed yes, I admit it freely, and note that you also have not retired. I therefore presume some little curiosity on your part? I propose, MacKay, that we cross the island and see what entertainment the savages have planned." So saying, he rose, extinguished his pipe, and set off down the beach. I followed, assuring myself that as an officer of the Company I could do worse than to learn the customs of the natives, for even the most outlandish ceremonies might find their place in the uses of our trade.

Throughout the night Elborn and I shivered on wet rocks opposite the Indian encampment, and were rewarded with neither light, nor sound, nor movement. The island was clearly visible and distinct from the others in the light of stars, for the night was clear. Had I not brought my glass and been able with it to descry their canoes still where I had seen them, I would have thought the Indians had quitted that place at dusk, so profound was the silence. At times loons called; once there was a crackling on the far shore, as of some large animal. At three, Elborn touched my arm and pointed to the east. Whether the sky had lightened there, presaging dawn, I cannot say; but there hung a multitude of stars above that eastern shore, and one far brighter than the rest, like a miniscule sun. "Venus," Elborn whispered. "The morning star."

As if his voice had been a signal, figures appeared on the island opposite, but so silent still and so obscured by shadow and murky background that I scarcely distinguished them until they reached the heights and stood outlined against the sky. There they remained in what appeared an irregular ring—perhaps a dozen or fourteen in all. At first they made no sound; but then began a faint and slow drumming which increased in volume and tempo until it reached its climax. At that instant a fire sprang to life and quickly spread. It revealed on the one side a half-circle of men with folded arms, facing eastward, and on the other the wabeno himself, rising with his arms outspread as if for warmth. Light from the dancing flames glowed on his bared chest and face. These were of the hue I have described, more grey than brown, and in the firelight a most lurid and unhealthy tone, not unlike the skin of a drowned man. Despite the chill he wore a breech-clout only, secured about his loins. Strips of ochre radiated from the centre of his face and chest. About him there hung a most baleful and malevolent intensity which caused me to catch my breath and start up from where I had been lounging.

He rose to his full height and strained backwards towards the east with upraised arms until the light of Venus struck his face, and in that arch he remained while the drumming commenced again; whereupon his body shuddered to the new rhythm. For several moments he writhed in this position, uttering cries to match the wilder gesticulations of his arms and torso, which with the increasing tempos of the drums fast became a desolate and demonic wail sent heavenward through upraised fists. At its conclusion his hands opened and he again sank to his knees before the fire which he had called into being.

The other Indians now relaxed the crescent line they had kept throughout this brief performance, and moved forward— some to heap dry wood upon the fire, some to fix for the cooking stakes on which dripping chunks of meat had been impaled. What we witnessed now could have been the scene in any encampment we have passed since leaving Montreal, except that there were neither women, nor dogs, nor children to give it a domesticity. My glass showed the wabeno crouched alone beside the fire. Even in the most convivial of his followers' exchanges I detected an alertness and anticipation altogether foreign to other Indians. It was like a knife edge in their voices which probed across the water; it glittered in their eyes which roved over the company, and the roasting meat, and into the darkness beyond the island. But the foremost difference between this scene and others similar lay not in the participants but in the fire. Never have I seen such a blaze among the Indians, who for the most part liked small and smoldering cook fires dwindling towards extinction. This, by contrast, was already a conflagration. Flames leapt from it to scorch boughs twenty feet above, and sparks and embers soared as high again, lighting such an area that Elborn and I, fearing we might be seen, crouched behind the boulders. The spitted meat was drawn back as the fire grew, and already some had been wrenched from its stakes and eaten with much gusto and laughter, although to my glass the center was raw and stringy, and the blanched skin repugnant.

"Bear, no doubt," said Elborn, watching with narrowed eyes and his ever-present, intolerable smile. "A bear eager for death, which has swum to their island through a day of storms. Ah, think how in their extremity they must have welcomed that bear, MacKay!"

My stomach revolted at his insinuation. "I presume," I replied, "they have carried their own food here, for who would venture upon Superior improperly victualled?"

"Who indeed?" smiled Elborn. "Ah, you are right, of course; I daresay they have brought their food with them, as you suggest."

Even through this exchange the fire had grown larger and now commanded half the plateau where it was built. On its fringes the Indians ate, and brought forth fresh meat from a carcass beyond the firelight, and burst into rapid, impromptu dances towards the fire and back, as if they would soon embrace it. Most had now shed their clothes except for moccasins and loincloths, and their bodies gleamed with sweat and with the grease they rubbed on their chests and shoulders. The shaman had now commenced a clockwise movement around the fire, a dance slow and ragged at first as some joined, some bent to feed the fire or tend the meat, and others fell away like men drunk on heat; but relentlessly this circling grew and so contained them all at last in a round itself composed of turnings and smaller circles as men sought to escape the fearsome heat by exposing another side of their bodies, turning as if they themselves had been spitted into place for roasting. Throughout, the master of the dance remained impassive, closer to the flames than all the rest, and when at last several at once reached the limit of their endurance and spun away whooping with pain and nursing scorched flesh, the drumbeats throbbed to a crescendo and the wabeno continued and quickened his contortions almost onto the fire itself, writhing like a lean snake the while, and for a time this lone dancing continued amidst the very flames until I swore the man must be consumed. Yet he emerged, his loin cloth in smoking ribbons and his face flickering with mingled pain and pleasure which was horrible to look upon.

The flames grew; the meat sputtered and dripped, was consumed and instantly replaced, and the drumming again increased its tempo, urging another man to follow the wabeno's example, and another, and yet another until the fire appeared to vomit bodies; and although none moved with the litheness of the tall man, yet some displayed a readiness to expose themselves equal to his, and a fortitude among the flames which I would not have credited. The cause of their colour thus became apparent—ash-white from the scars of burns, and as one by one the loincloths were burned off or dispensed with I saw that in some cases their very manhoods had been seared away.

This revelation, more than any other, touched me to the roots of my being. Singly, through my glass, I searched the faces of these revellers and found there neither explanation nor hint, and was left to conclude that the intensity of this playful competition led some to that ultimate test, whereby manhood itself was sacrificed; but to what end, or to what god or goddess, that I could not tell. The inferno, the drumbeats which still increased, the wanton swaying of these dancers, all acted upon my senses until I supposed I beheld a dream, a nightmare wherein fiends of neither sex made their mockery of both.

At the height of the dance, the fire suddenly spread swiftly through the island in undulating runnels and rivulets, seizing its own liquid life, and for some moments I watched uncomprehending, bedevilled by what I had seen and what I saw. Their bodies gleaming red with grease and burns, the revellers had seized great brands and, holding them aloft, moved outward through the forest to the fringes of the island, keeping the rhythm of the drums and punctuating the night with such cries and wailings as the damned in torment might have uttered. The island's shape was soon pricked out by these flailing torches. Only the wabeno himself kept beside the fire, rigid as if entranced, his head thrown back, his teeth exposed, his fists clenched at his groin. For some moments he remained thus, and then the drumming ceased, the cries from the island's fringe diminished. In a silence broken only by the surging of the blaze he spun snakelike towards the largest of the nearby pines and flung his hands out and up in a gesture which included it entirely. What trickery he employed I cannot say, but the tree shimmered in malefic radiance, contracted as if swept by giant hands, and burst with flame. Its boughs thrashed, its trunk cracked, spewing resin. Smoke and embers rolled upward in a wanton cataract. Howls from all the island greeted this new pyre, and in an instant a dozen other fires from torches thrust like cartridges into bark and bracken swarmed lasciviously towards it and joined with it in a general consummation.

The island blazed. So intense was the heat that we were forced to leave our vantage point for the protection of the forest, encountering others from our brigade who had been roused from sleep. Ash and embers fell everywhere on us and around us, and fearing fire on our island also, we retired with dispatch to load our canoes. Within the half-hour this was done. Behind the trees to the west the conflagration had meantime reached the peak of its ferocity and, by the time we embarked, had begun to decline.

Our file of canoes passed silent in the half-light, all eyes on that smoldering island which lifted its charred trunks and branches, horribly bejewelled, in futile supplication.

10 ANNE HÉBERT

An excerpt from the novel *Kamouraska* (1973)

My first son is born. Endless ordeal, a day and a half. They had to use forceps. And Antoine, nowhere to be seen. They found him four days later, dead drunk. All huddled up, feverish, shivering with the cold. Lying on the wet sand. In the rushes. By the river.

He swears on his son's life never to drink again. We toast the baptism with champagne just off the boat from France. Antoine goes drinking all through the house. Down in the kitchen, up in the attic. Looking for a green and yellow pumpkin, to mix up a special punch of his own.

"A party for my wife and son! Like none you've ever seen before! Ring the bells! Bang the glasses! Ding, dong! Ding, dong! You see? I've gone mad!..."

My mother-in-law goes scurrying here and there, filling the cups. Tells everyone that her grandson is quite a bawler, and that her son is twice as bad!

All's right with the world. The dead below. The living above. Little baptismal scenes. The manor, lit up, shines in the night. Like a ship out of water. Perched on a promontory. Up for repairs. All lights ablaze. And inside, swarming with life. All the townsfolk, drinking and eating their fill. In the kitchen, bursting with eels and every kind of bird. Flowing with their wine and whiskey brew.

"It's a boy! Monsieur has a son!"

The scene is such a happy one, so full of promise. Why not hold on to it, cling to it?

On the walls in the couple's room, a piece of mirror is still in place above the chest of drawers. The soot falls away in a velvety powder. Uncovers a clear, round, silver space...Look through the little porthole. See the pretty scene reflected in the stagnant water. Family portrait. Father and mother, all aflutter, bending over a newborn baby, red as can be. Mother-in-law brings over a homespun shawl, one she knitted herself.

Mother says it's too rough for her baby. Mother-in-law, offended, raps on the floor with her cane. Three good raps, loud and clear. Announcing the drama we're destined to play. Leaves in a huff.

"Theatre, that's all it is!"

Now we're on our own. For better or worse. Antoine Tassy and I, Elisabeth d'Aulnières, his wife.

Again my husband is wearing a band of white, wrapped round his forehead. Raising his arm above my head, waving his fist. To curse me. I'm holding my son in my arms. I close my eyes. Now my mother-in-law comes back. Tells us we're just a couple of puppets...Oh! The piece of mirror is breaking, smashing to bits...

One last sliver clings to the wall. Tiny triangle, all jagged around the edges. But so clear. Limpid. No, I refuse to move. I'll stand like this as long as I have to, clutching my son to my breast. I'll keep my eyes shut tight, no matter what. They'll have to pry them open to make me look. That mirror, too flawless. Its flash is sure to pierce my heart. Better to face his anger. Awful, like a wounded beast's. Antoine and his revenge. Anything, rather than see that clear, blue, childlike look of his again. That look of sad bewilderment.

"You? Elisabeth? My wife? How could you..."

His tortured voice, too soft and gentle. God, what have I done? What's the crime...

My skirts are covered with mud. My bodice, ripped apart. We're running, the two of us. So fast. Can't catch our breath. Over the wet bank. Falling in the rushes. The little puddles of greenish water splashing under our weight. The slimy seaweed, red and yellow. The sea fern, outlined on our skin...Antoine Tassy, my husband...Good heavens, if ever the servants or the folks in town...We're two wild children. Let's hold each other's hands. Kiss each other on the lips. So hard we almost smother. Let's take off all our clothes again. Run quick and hide in the little house at Paincourt that my husband uses for his own affairs...

He's throwing a kitchen knife at me. Straight for my head. I barely have time to move. The knife is stuck in the woodwork, right on a level with my throat.

He's mad. Look at him, sitting in his chair, so quiet and motionless. Or on his feet. Stiff as a heavy stump. At the window, against the light. As if the burden of immobility builds up inside him, bit by bit. Bears down on him with all its ponderous weight. And all its silence. Like an earthen jar filled up with iron pellets, one by one, right to the brim...Everyone away! Locks and seals on all that excess weight. On his petrified gaze. No other thought in mind but following the secret workings of that awesome something, forgotten, left behind almost unthinkingly to gather dust. Though everyone knows what kind of beast it is, there in the sack. What mischievous little mouse, what devilish sprite triumphant. Antoine seems so far away. But he's listening to that deadly voice within him. The underside of his noisy, brawling joy. The bitter, all-commanding voice of his despair.

I throw myself at his feet. I beg him to come to his senses. If only I could rid him of that one idea, that obsession. He looks at me but doesn't see me. Speaks in a voice calm and controlled.

"I'm going to kill myself. Kill myself. I have to kill myself. You know I have to. There's no other way. I'm going to kill myself, Elisabeth. Kill myself."

His mother says he's been like this five years now. Says to make him drink black coffee. Talk to him about other things. Keep an eye on him all the time...

At night he raves, delirious. He goes to confession. Calls the priest a dead tree. Beats his breast.

"I'm living in filth, Father. Stuck in the mire. I say the foulest things, Father. Debauched, depraved... Doing my tricks, cutting my capers. My somersaults. Squealing like the swine I am... A clown, Father. That's it, I'm a clown. Full of brandy and beer. A clown who laces his wine with whiskey. Plenty of it... Ugh! I'm falling, Father. Into a black hole. Going blind... You're a big dead tree, Father. With lots of dead branches." — "The better to hang you with, my child." — "Look, Father, I'm putting my damn fool head through the noose. Right now. Amen!"

Antoine, down on his knees, drags himself along the floor. Tries to get up. Wants to confess again, in front of the piece of mirror stuck in the wall above the chest of drawers.

"I want to see my damn fool face!"

He stares in the mirror, wide-eyed. Opens his mouth, sticks out a coated tongue. Shoots a bullet at the glass. Misses. Hole in the wall. While the one last sliver still intact, stuck on a nail, quivers. Dizzily...

I'm pregnant again. I like being pregnant. It makes me so awfully important in the house. Surprised, Antoine goes slinking about, almost unnoticed. My mother-in-law attacks her knitting with a vengeance...

Antoine is calling to me from a shed in the courtyard. He's sitting on a white wooden box. Behind him, tied to one of the beams, a thick rope, ending in a noose, swings back and forth. He struggles to his feet, mumbling.

"Are you coming, Elisabeth? I'll make the noose bigger and you can come too. Swinging from a rope. Husband and wife, hanging together, two heads in one noose. Isn't that nice? And the baby will split your belly, all by himself. No midwife to help him. He'll fall on the straw like a rock. And his very first screams will ring in our ears. Just before we get to hell, the two of us. Come on along. The rope is big enough for two, Elisabeth. You see? The bonds of marriage. A thick rope, nice and solid. A noose to strangle in together. You promised, for better or worse. Come on, come on..."

He's screaming with laughter, trying to slip the noose around my neck. I push him away and make believe I'm laughing too. A moment later he loses his balance and falls on the straw. With a great, dull thud.

Translated by Norman Shapiro

THE

SECOND DECADE

—

1977-1987

1 JOHN THOMPSON
Excerpts from the poetry collection *Stilt Jack* (1978)

XI

The fox is quick; I haven't seen him; he's quick.
The rainbow strikes one foot at my door.

The kettle lid lifts: must be fire,
it keeps.

It's too dry to plough; gulls grow in the cut corn,
owls, harriers: so many swift wings.

There's all the noise here,
it's so quiet:

the sky sleeps on the backs of cattle,
streams slow to black.

Last night I died: a tired fly woke me.
On White Mountain I heard a phrase carving the world.

XXI

I know how small a poem can be:
the point on a fish hook;

women have one word or too many:
I watch the wind;

I'd like a kestrel's eye and know
how to hang on one thread of sky;

the sun burns up my book:
it must be all lies;

I'd rather be quiet, let the sun
and the animals do their work:

I might watch, might turn my back,
be a done beer can shining stupidly

Let it be: the honed barb drowsing in iron water
will raise the great fish I'll ride

(dream upon dream, still the sun warms my ink
and the flies buzzing to life in my window)

to that heaven (absurd) sharp fish hook,
small poem, small offering.

XXIV

Always the light: a strange moon,
and the green I don't understand;

knives set in order; somewhere else,
eyes looking back against a terrible space:

a meeting in a garden, hands, knees, feet
in the dirt: animals; the flies feeding;

what comes from this? Pour wine on it:
have you read all your blood?

No prophecy in the furrow: only the print of bare feet,
anxious for what grows;

nothing? One small leaf is a heart:
a leaf we divide, dividing us.

Lift up the soily stones,
feel the burn of lime,

a handful of seeds, a handful of earth,
silence in thunder on the tongue:

a long waiting without stars,
ending in snow.

2 ROCH CARRIER

An excerpt from the story collection
The Hockey Sweater and Other Stories (1979)

The Hockey Sweater

The winters of my childhood were long, long seasons. We lived in three places—the school, the church and the skating-rink—but our real life was on the skating-rink. Real battles were won on the skating-rink. Real strength appeared on the skating-rink. The real leaders showed themselves on the skating-rink. School was a sort of punishment. Parents always want to punish children and school is their most natural way of punishing us. However, school was also a quiet place where we could prepare for the next hockey game, lay out our next strategies. As for church, we found there the tranquility of God: there we forgot school and dreamed about the next hockey game. Through our daydreams it might happen that we would recite a prayer: we would ask God to help us play as well as Maurice Richard.

We all wore the same uniform as he, the red, white and blue uniform of the Montreal Canadiens, the best hockey team in the world; we all combed our hair in the same style as Maurice Richard, and to keep it in place we used a sort of glue—a great deal of glue. We laced our skates like Maurice Richard, we taped our sticks like Maurice Richard. We cut all his pictures out of the papers. Truly, we knew everything about him.

On the ice, when the referee blew his whistle the two teams would rush at the puck; we were five Maurice Richards taking it away from five other Maurice Richards; we were ten players, all of us wearing with the same blazing enthusiasm the uniform of the Montreal Canadiens. On our backs, we all wore the famous number 9.

One day, my Montreal Canadiens sweater had become too small; then it got torn and had holes in it. My mother said: 'If you wear that old sweater people are going to think we're poor!' Then she did what she did whenever we needed new clothes. She started to leaf through the catalogue the Eaton company sent us in the mail every year. My mother was proud. She didn't want to buy our clothes at the general store; the only things that were good enough for us were the latest styles from Eaton's catalogue. My mother didn't like the order forms included with the catalogue; they were written in English and she didn't understand a word of it. To order my hockey sweater, she did as she usually did; she took out her writing paper and wrote in her gentle schoolteacher's hand: 'Cher Monsieur Eaton, Would you be kind enough to send me a Canadiens sweater for my son who is ten years old and a little too tall for his age and Docteur Robitaille thinks he's a little too thin? I'm sending you three dollars and please send me what's left if there's anything left. I hope your wrapping will be better than last time.'

Monsieur Eaton was quick to answer my mother's letter. Two weeks later we received the sweater. That day I had one of the greatest disappointments of my life! I would even say that on that day I experienced a very great sorrow. Instead of the red, white and blue Montreal Canadiens sweater, Monsieur Eaton had sent us a blue and white sweater with a maple leaf on the front— the sweater of the Toronto Maple Leafs. I'd always worn the red, white and blue Montreal Canadiens sweater; all my friends wore the red, white and blue sweater; never had anyone in my village ever worn the Toronto sweater, never had we even seen a Toronto Maple Leafs sweater. Besides, the Toronto team was regularly trounced by the triumphant Canadiens. With tears in my eyes, I found the strength to say:

'I'll never wear that uniform.'

'My boy, first you're going to try it on! If you make up your mind about things before you try, my boy, you won't go very far in this life.'

My mother had pulled the blue and white Toronto Maple Leafs sweater over my shoulders and already my arms were inside the sleeves. She pulled the sweater down and carefully smoothed all the creases in the abominable maple leaf on which, right in the middle of my chest, were written the words, 'Toronto Maple Leafs.' I wept.

'I'll never wear it.'

'Why not? This sweater fits you...like a glove.'

'Maurice Richard would never put it on his back.'

'You aren't Maurice Richard. Anyway, it isn't what's on your back that counts, it's what you've got inside your head.'

'You'll never put it in my head to wear a Toronto Maple Leafs sweater.'

My mother sighed in despair and explained to me:

'If you don't keep this sweater which fits you perfectly I'll have to write to Monsieur Eaton and explain that you don't want to wear the Toronto sweater. Monsieur Eaton's an *Anglais*; he'll be insulted because he likes the Maple Leafs. And if he's insulted do you think he'll be in a hurry to answer us? Spring will be here and you won't have played a single game, just because you didn't want to wear that perfectly nice blue sweater.'

So I was obliged to wear the Maple Leafs sweater. When I arrived on the rink, all the Maurice Richards in red, white and blue came up, one by one, to take a look. When the referee blew his whistle I went to take my usual position. The captain came and warned me I'd be better to stay on the forward line. A few minutes later the second line was called; I jumped onto the ice. The Maple Leafs sweater weighed on my shoulders like a mountain. The captain came and told me to wait; he'd need me later, on defense. By the third period I still hadn't played; one of the defensemen was hit in the nose with a stick and it was bleeding. I jumped on the ice: my moment had come! The referee blew his whistle; he gave me a penalty. He claimed I'd jumped on the ice when there were already five players. That was too much! It was unfair! It was persecution! It was because of my blue sweater! I struck my stick against the ice so hard it broke. Relieved, I bent down to pick up the debris. As I straightened up I saw the young vicar, on skates, before me.

'My child,' he said, 'just because you're wearing a new Toronto Maple Leafs sweater unlike the others, it doesn't mean you're going to make the laws around here. A proper young man doesn't lose his temper. Now take off your skates and go to the church and ask God to forgive you.'

Wearing my Maple Leafs sweater I went to the church, where I prayed to God; I asked him to send, as quickly as possible, moths that would eat up my Toronto Maple Leafs sweater.

Translated by Sheila Fischman

3 KRISTJANA GUNNARS
Excerpts from *Wake-Pick Poems* (1981)

Wakepick IX

if i wind the yarnreel
into forty-four thread wheels
into eleven-wheeled skeins
seven days for every thread
i won't be reconciled

even in the end
when we kick out the window
tumble down the snow
let the fresh air in
i won't breathe it

even if the chimney opens to the north
fill it with cloth
don't let the heat get out
i won't be reconciled

even if the crowned sparrows fly in
black-throated, black-breasted
& chirp like untidy lovers
with straw & feathers in their beaks

or if butterfly moths flutter
reminding me of loss
i won't look
won't light the hearth

& even if the harmless moth lands on my knee
i won't smile

Wakepick XVI

my life is an oath on knitting
socks, half-socks, sea-mittens & sweaters
then slaughtering ends

i knit a man's foot ready for winter
knit for Christmas
on a half-slept night
knit a long wake
a dark living room

while the wool lasts
i knit when i sit
knit when i walk between houses

i knit my life into laurel & reed
into loving wool plant
i draw out bad spirits with needles
like fleas & lice that keep in health

thrips fly out thunder
storms on the hills
under a purple dungeon sky
over a sulphur-tuft ground

& i knit in the dark
long half-slept oaths

Wakepick XVII

i've wanted better
martin & pigeon
better swift, better owl
than i've been given

i've placed bearberry twigs in the beds
i've smoked salves in a pipe
i've eaten crushed bearberry stones
to destroy

i've wanted evil more than sufferance
wanted to knit faster
a sweater a day
six sweaters in a week
two socks a day

wanted to bring a sock from card
to spinning wheel to knitting needle
to foot in one day
i've wanted everything fast

wanted scythe-shaped wings
to fly over the village & fjord
wanted instant change
to destroy the persecution of lovers
the cutting of a pine

growing from my old lover's coffin

4 RACHEL WYATT
An excerpt from the story collection *Foreign Bodies* (1982)

3.

Dozing off, Ernesta wandered into the Wild Wood, confident that Camrose would be waiting there. Often she went to sleep with his arms round her and his body close. She had never gone in for substitution in their love-making, Ned was always Ned. In any case, Robert Redford probably had unearthly and marvellous sex techniques that would make the two of them seem like animals mating in the straw. But when she wanted comfort and understanding, she did conjure Camrose. And now when he began to chant spells to her in his lovely voice, a bell rang. Bells must be answered. Bells rule O.K.

She could see the shape of the policeman through the screened door, and that explained why the handrail was on the wrong side of the stairs, and the hall carpet that hadn't been there yesterday. It was this film set they had walked into. Take one hundred and thirty. Policeman and lady. It was simpler to invite him in than to have the door kicked down and the house surrounded by armoured cars and men in combat gear. So she said to him, "Please come in."

The policeman sat down in the kitchen and took his cap off. He was a red man, red hair, ruddy face, and a round head that appeared to be stuck on to his collar like a doll's head. "We're still a bit confused about what happened today."

"Should we get in touch with the Grangers?" Ernesta asked. The Grangers had left their address neatly typed, stuck to the door of the fridge with two plastic magnets in the shape of cats: Prof. and Mrs. E.M. Granger, Hotel de France, 739 rue Alain, Paris, 75001.

"If we could see the other guy. Just a few questions."

"Would you like some lemonade?"

"Sure. Anything. Water even. It's thirsty weather. So where is he?"

"My husband's in bed."

"The other one."

"I don't know. He very kindly left us food in the house. We've never seen him before. He's a friend of the Grangers."

"So he says. You want to watch those guys," the policeman went on, taking mouthfuls of lemonade. "I've got nothing against them. Can't have in my job. Not here, in this city. But they get up to all kinds of tricks."

"Not more than any other people."

"You're jumping on me again. Listen. We know how to deal with them. Just last week we're called in to talk to a little boy who's afraid to go out. Turns out he's taken some candy from this Pakistani guy's store and the Pakistani sees him and grabs hold of him by the throat and tells him if he catches him at it again he's going to cut him into little tiny pieces."

"What did you do?"

"We took hold of the Pakistani by the throat and told him if he so much as touches the kid we'll cut him into tiny pieces."

"But . . ."

"Just kidding, Mrs. Bolster. My little joke, eh? No. We got them together. The kid and the shopkeeper, and we sit down and talk with them."

"Did it work? Does the little boy go out now?"

"No. He's afraid of cops as well, his mother says. He'll get over it."

Ernesta narrowed her eyes and the policeman became a tiny, distant speck. "I'm very tired," she said. She brushed her hand over the solid surface of the table, it was worn at the edges and full of knife marks. Sheets of pastry could be rolled out on it. She would have time now to make apple strudel with lots of fruit in it, raisins and cinnamon and splinters of pine. "It must get very cold here in the winter."

The policeman put his glass down and grinned at her. "You better believe it. And the stupidity of people. It can be the worst day of the winter. Warnings on the radio all day long. So what do they do? They get in their cars and drive about in it. And who ends up digging them out? We do. Dead sometimes. Nothing to see but an aerial sticking out of a snowdrift. You'd think they'd learn. But every year it's the same."

"We have heavy snow in Yorkshire, too."

"But there's good things as well. Skiing, if you like skiing. I like to go to my brother's farm up Collingwood way. Got a skidoo. Listen, I better be off. You let me know when that guy comes back."

"I know something about police work. I have a job in the Mayor's office at home."

So they talked about that, and about the differences between armed and unarmed guardians, and about his early life and how his parents had christened him Romeo but he had made sure from being about five years old that everybody called him Ron because what kind of name was Romeo in this country. Goodnight Officer Cattoni, who could have stayed talking there till morning.

As soon as she lay down, Ernesta fell into a heavy sleep and when she woke thought she must have slept the clock round. But only three hours had passed. The hot night had turned into a hot morning. In England the day had begun. The milkman had called at Woodley Cottage by now, and had left milk and eggs for Jack. Buses had started running across the end of the lane to town. And the Mayor was putting his socks on, getting dressed for Church. It felt like breakfast time, like bacon and toast and coffee and some of the strawberry jam left from last year.

Ned turned in his sleep and pulled at her jacket but she moved away and got out of bed again and went into the kitchen.

Monroe was sitting there, his hands pressed together in front of him and in his eyes a faraway look as though he could see his homeland or a thousand years ago. "Ah, Mrs. Bolster. Good morning. For you it's breakfast time. Milk? Three kinds of pie?"

"Milk. I think milk would be nice. I'll help myself, Monroe.'"

She opened the fridge and saw that the top shelf was full of cans of milk labelled "homo."

"A special kind of milk?"

"No, dear lady. It means merely that the cream has been blended in with the rest, homogenized, to make it all the same. You will find this a most homogenized country indeed." He laughed at his little joke and took the carton from her and poured milk into two large glasses and carried them into the living room. She sank down into those same cushions and Monroe sat on the floor not far away from her. Then he raised his glass and said, "Strangers in a strange land."

"What part of India are you from?"

"Karachi, which is not India but Pakistan."

"I'm sorry. I should have known."

"Why should you have known?"

"Because where I live there are a lot of people from Pakistan. In England. In Yorkshire."

"Yorkshire. Yes. My family, two cousins and their wives are in Yorkshire. The people there are very kind, after some time."

"How long have you been here?" Ernesta asked. She looked at the milk and wished it was alcohol that might get rid of this garden party kind of chat.

"Four years."

"And do you like it here?"

"I am not married," he replied.

"Ah."

"And in times of much unemployment like this one, we are not popular here. So that I am reduced to house-minding. But hoping before long to get a job at the new Institute."

"Where my husband will be working?"

"Yes."

"And how long did the Grangers..."

"Tomorrow or at least the day after, my new place will be vacant. Then I will be gone. Tomorrow I will show you the meat in the freezer which I have bought."

"We must pay you for that, Monroe."

"The bill is inside the fridge."

The picture on the wall opposite Ernesta seemed to be shades of yellow painted into a concentric ring; or was it a series of faces within faces within faces?

Monroe said, "That is called 'Tiger,' but it is not exactly the outline of a tiger."

"Thank you. Without my glasses..."

"You are lucky to have two ways of seeing."

"Tiger!"

"Where I live, we do not sell toy tigers for children to play with. Or make them into pictures for entertainment."

"No, I suppose not."

"More milk, Mrs. Bolster?"

"I don't think so, thank you."

"You have no need to worry about fatness. You are a woman of too much character for that. For you, no creams and coloured lotions, or rolls in your hair."

"Well, perhaps a little one then."

He returned very quietly with the milk, and had brought pie as well, and they sat there together, him with the sheet wound round him, eating and smiling at each other like children at a midnight feast, the grown-ups all asleep and unaware. She giggled to herself at the thought of writing to Mary about it: *And on Sunday morning, early...*

She tugged at the pajama jacket to make sure it was covering her thighs and said, "It was so unexpected, finding you here."

"Finding?" he queried. "Were you looking for me?"

She ate the last bite of her pie and said, "That's just a way of speaking. Not accurate."

"And usually you are accurate?"

His eyes were brown but very dark and now he stared at her as though looking through her head. She had to turn away. She had to say, "My husband and I have been looking forward to this Sabbatical."

Monroe put his plate down and shuffled across to her. "If you would allow me to read your hand. I am not an expert but have some skill and may see some of the things that are written there."

He held her hand in his and traced some of the lines with his finger, murmuring, only half aloud, "Childhood in a sad house... Decision to marry... This or that... Children... Two... With one much conflict... Much to come..."

Ernesta found herself murmuring responses, "My father died... mother a widow... Well—I chose security... She started it, Sandra did. Nothing I said was ever right..."

"And did you want to come here, Mrs. Bolster?"

The question was asked so gently that it took her by surprise and her eyes filled with tears. She tried to smile and then laugh but the tears came anyway and she had to get her hand back in order to find something to wipe her face on. He took the lace cover from the coffee table and gave it to her and although it was full of holes and prickly it served as a hanky. When she put it to her face, though, the tears came again. Monroe stood up and put his hand on her shoulder and said, "I didn't mean to make you cry. It will be all right, Mrs. Bolster. All right. In your life I see some changes, many changes. New love. Not all bad things."

She reached up and put her hand over his and tried to say thank you, but the only words that came out were, "Don't go, Monroe. Please don't go."

But his hand slipped out from under hers and she heard him whisper 'goodnight' and he was not there. She dried her face and looked around the room at the empty glasses and plates and the tiger picture and the Grangers in their silver frame and the curtain hanging down; her new home.

5 MARGARET ATWOOD
An excerpt from the essay collection *Second Words* (1982)

On Being a "Woman Writer":
Paradoxes and Dilemmas

I approach this article with a good deal of reluctance. Once having promised to do it, in fact, I've been procrastinating to such
an extent that my own aversion is probably the first subject I
should attempt to deal with. Some of my reservations have to do
with the questionable value of writers, male or female, becoming directly involved in political movements of any sort: their
involvement may be good for the movement, but it has yet to be
demonstrated that it's good for the writer. The rest concern my
sense of the enormous complexity not only of the relationships
between Man and Woman, but also of those between those other
abstract intangibles, Art and Life, Form and Content, Writer and
Critic, etcetera.

Judging from conversations I've had with many other woman
writers in this country, my qualms are not unique. I can think of
only one writer I know who has any formal connection with
any of the diverse organizations usually lumped together under
the titles of Women's Liberation or the Women's Movement.
There are several who have gone out of their way to disavow
even any fellow-feeling; but the usual attitude is one of grudging
admiration, tempered with envy: the younger generation, they
feel, has it a hell of a lot better than they did. Most writers old

enough to have a career of any length behind them grew up when it was still assumed that a woman's place was in the home and nowhere else, and that anyone who took time off for an individual selfish activity like writing was either neurotic or wicked or both, derelict in her duties to a man, child, aged relatives or whoever else was supposed to justify her existence on earth. I've heard stories of writers so consumed by guilt over what they had been taught to feel was their abnormality that they did their writing at night, secretly, so no one would accuse them of failing as housewives, as "women." These writers accomplished what they did by themselves, often at great personal expense; in order to write at all, they had to defy other women's as well as men's ideas of what was proper, and it's not finally all that comforting to have a phalanx of women—some younger and relatively unscathed, others from their own generation, the bunch that was collecting china, changing diapers and sneering at any female with intellectual pretensions twenty or even ten years ago—come breezing up now to tell them they were right all along. It's like being judged innocent after you've been hanged: the satisfaction, if any, is grim. There's a great temptation to say to Womens' Lib, "Where were you when I really needed you?" or "It's too late for me now." And you can see, too, that it would be fairly galling for these writers, if they have any respect for historical accuracy, which most do, to be hailed as products, spokeswomen, or advocates of the Women's Movement. When they were undergoing their often drastic formative years there *was* no Women's Movement. No matter that a lot of what they say can be taken by the theorists of the Movement as supporting evidence, useful analysis, and so forth: their own inspiration was not theoretical, it came from wherever all writing comes from. Call it experience and imagination. These writers, if they are honest, don't want to be wrongly identified as the children of a movement that did not give birth to them. Being adopted is not the same as being born.

A third area of reservation is undoubtedly a fear of the development of a one-dimensional Feminist Criticism, a way of approaching literature produced by women that would award points according to conformity or non-conformity to an ideological position. A feminist criticism is, in fact, already emerging. I've read at least one review, and I'm sure there have been and will be more, in which a novelist was criticized for not having made her heroine's life different, even though that life was more typical of the average woman's life in this society than the reviewer's "liberated" version would have been. Perhaps Women's Lib reviewers will start demanding that heroines resolve their difficulties with husband, kids, or themselves by stomping out to join a consciousness raising group, which will be no more satisfactory from the point of view of literature than the legendary Socialist Realist romance with one's tractor. However, a feminist criticism need not necessarily be one-dimensional. And—small comfort—no matter how narrow, purblind and stupid such a criticism in its lowest manifestations may be, it cannot possibly be *more* narrow, purblind and stupid than some of the non-feminist critical attitudes and styles that have preceded it.

There's a fourth possible factor, a less noble one: the often observed phenomenon of the member of a despised social group who manages to transcend the limitations imposed on the group, at least enough to become "successful." For such a person the impulse—whether obeyed or not—is to disassociate him/herself from the group and to side with its implicit opponents. Thus the Black millionaire who deplores the Panthers, the rich *Québecois* who is anti-Separatist, the North American immigrant who changes his name to an "English" one; thus, alas, the Canadian writer who makes it, sort of, in New York, and spends many magazine pages decrying provincial dull Canadian writers; and thus the women with successful careers who say *"I've* never had any problems, I don't know what they're talking about." Such a woman tends to regard herself, and to be treated by her male colleagues, as a sort of honorary man. It's the rest of them who are inept, brainless, tearful, self-defeating: not her. "You think like a man," she is told, with admiration and unconscious put-down. For both men and women, it's just too much of a strain to fit together the traditionally incompatible notions of "woman" and "good at something." And if you *are* good at something, why carry with you the stigma attached to that dismal category you've gone to such lengths to escape from? The only reason for rocking the boat is if you're still chained to the oars. Not everyone reacts like this, but this factor may explain some of the more hysterical opposition to Women's Lib on the part of a few woman writers, even though they may have benefitted from the Movement in the form of increased sales and more serious attention.

A couple of ironies remain; perhaps they are even paradoxes. One is that, in the development of modern Western civilization, writing was the first of the arts, before painting, music, composing, and sculpting, which it was possible for women to practice; and it was the fourth of the job categories, after prostitution, domestic service and the stage, and before wide-scale factory work, nursing, secretarial work, telephone operating and school teaching, at which it was possible for them to make any money. The reason for both is the same: writing as a physical activity is private. You do it by yourself, on your own time; no teachers or employers are involved, you don't have to apprentice in a studio or work with musicians. Your only business arrangements are with your publisher, and these can be conducted through the mails; your real "employers" can be deceived, if you choose, by the adoption of an assumed (male) name; witness the Brontës and George Eliot. But the private and individual nature of writing may also account for the low incidence of direct involvement by woman writers in the Movement now. If you are a writer, prejudice against women will affect you *as a writer* not directly but indirectly. You won't suffer from wage discrimination, because you aren't paid any wages; you won't be hired last and fired first, because you aren't hired or fired anyway. You have relatively little to complain of, and, absorbed in your own work as you are likely to be, you will find it quite easy to shut your eyes to what goes on at the spool factory, or even at the university. *Paradox:* reason for involvement then equals reason for non-involvement now.

Another paradox goes like this. As writers, woman writers are like other writers. They have the same professional concerns, they have to deal with the same contracts and publishing procedures, they have the same need for solitude to work and the same concern that their work be accurately evaluated by reviewers. There is nothing "male" or "female" about these conditions; they are just attributes of the activity known as writing. As biological specimens and as citizens, however, women are like other women: subject to the same discriminatory laws, encountering the same demeaning attitudes, burdened with the same good reasons for not walking through the park alone after dark. They too have bodies, the capacity to bear children; they eat, sleep and bleed, just like everyone else. In bookstores and publishers' offices and among groups of other writers, a woman writer may get the impression that she is "special;" but in the eyes of the law, in the loan office or bank, in the hospital and on the street she's just another woman. She doesn't get to wear a sign to the grocery store saying "Respect me, I'm a Woman Writer." No matter how good she may feel about herself, strangers who aren't aware of her shelf-full of nifty volumes with cover blurbs saying how gifted she is will still regard her as a nit.

We all have ways of filtering out aspects of our experience we would rather not think about. Woman writers can keep as much as possible to the "writing" end of their life, avoiding the less desirable aspects of the "woman" end. Or they can divide themselves in two, thinking of themselves as two different people: a "writer" and a "woman." Time after time, I've had interviewers talk to me about my writing for a while, then ask me, "As a woman, what do you think about—for instance—the Women's

Movement," as if I could think two sets of thoughts about the same thing, one set as a writer or person, the other as a woman. But no one comes apart this easily; categories like Woman, White, Canadian, Writer are only ways of looking at a thing, and the thing itself is whole, entire and indivisible. *Paradox*: Woman and Writer are separate categories; but in any individual woman writer, they are inseparable.

6 JACQUES FERRON

An excerpt from the story collection *Selected Tales* (1984)

The Archangel of the Suburb

The archangel Zag was not in Heaven at the time of the famous battle between Lucifer and Saint Michael; he was on Earth. When word of it reached him, he concluded that he had been most inspired to make this trip and decided to extend his stay. So it was that until quite recently he still dwelt among us, in a shack along Chambly Road, near the marsh which then served as boundary and garbage dump for the parishes of Saint-Hubert and Saint-Antoine-de-Longueuil. To the profane he was an old anarchist, a retired vagabond, one of those likeable outlaws who are the very charm of the suburbs. As for the clerics, they did not even suspect he was there. Zag avoided them, was distrustful of them as of the devil. With the exception of one, Brother Benoit of the Coteau-Rouge Franciscans, who often came to see him and whom he received with pleasure. Brother Benoit would bring holy pictures and religious trinkets, which Zag, out of regard for him and also as a precaution against the police, who can always make things difficult for a tramp, used to decorate his hut. But that was as far as he would go. He had said to Brother Benoit: "Why do you try to convert me? I don't try to make an angel out of you." He would not tolerate the mention of good or evil, of Heaven or Hell; to him these distinctions were distasteful. So Brother Benoit had ceased to preach at him, continuing nevertheless to visit him, out of pure loving-kindness, good Franciscan that he was.

Now Zag, who in spite of everything was no earthling, set out one morning bright and early along Chambly Road in the direction of Longueuil. At the first crossroads he turned left and found himself on the Coteau-Rouge road, heading for Saint-Josaphat. In actual fact he was not too sure where he was going. He zigzagged along as if drunk; at times his feet would leave the ground; he continued in this fashion for quite some distance. Apart from his flying, he looked for all the world like a wino. Meanwhile it was getting later, the suburb was waking up, three or four clandestine cocks crowded in defiance of the municipal regulations, and people began to gather at the street corners to wait for the yellow bus of their misfortune, people still exhausted from the previous day's work. And that same rattle-trap bus was now heading straight for Zag, who leapt up into the air and clear over it. The driver, flabbergasted, drove right past the next stop, cursed by those he had forgotten. Their protests brought the archangel back to his senses. He felt ashamed of himself, and returned to his shack in low spirits. But the next morning he was again excited, light-headed as a bird on the eve of migration. This time he went off across the fields and following the marsh, soon found himself near the Franciscan monastery. It was warm and pleasant. He stretched out on the grass. In the distance he could see the pink and grey haze of the city, the arches of the bridge and the summit of Mount Royal. However, a bush was blocking his view. Zag said to it: "Cast off thy leaves." The bush obeyed so promptly that a hen, perched among the foliage, was stripped of her feathers at the same time. This hen stared at Zag in dumb amazement, and he, equally surprised, stared back at the naked fowl. They finally came to their senses, the hen protesting, the archangel laughing; and the louder the one laughed the angrier the other became. When Zag had laughed his fill, he said: "Don't fret, old dear, I'll soon fix that. Only I can't promise to put your feathers back exactly where you had them; I might make a mistake and put one of the tail-feathers on the wing or one from the neck on the tail." But the hen demanded to be feathered as before.

"In that case," said Zag, "go fetch me some dry chips of wood." The hen brought them to him.

"Now an iron rod." She brought that too.

"And last of all," said Zag, "go into the monastery kitchen; there you'll find some matches."

The hen went into the monastery kitchen, found the matches and brought them. Then Zag grabbed hold of her, skewered her, lit a fire and roasted her. Brother Benoit, who happened to be in the monastery kitchen, meditating on a pot of chick-peas and herring, for it was a Friday, had had his appetite whetted and had followed the naked fowl.

"Ah! Brother Benoit," cried Zag, "You couldn't have come at a better moment! I have a theological problem to put to you."

Brother Benoit stretched out on the grass.

"What advice would you give to an archangel in exile on Earth, who was beginning to lose his sense of gravity and jump in the air like a harum scarum?" asked Zag.

Brother Benoit answered, "There is only one thing for him to do: go back to Heaven."

"That's all very well," said Zag, "but it so happens that this arch-angel was absent at the time of the Lucifer-Saint Michael match; how can he be sure he would have been on the latter's side?"

Brother Benoit asked, "While this archangel was on Earth, did he seek out the company of the proud and the mighty, of aldermen and other potentates?"

"No," replied Zag. And as he spoke he handed Brother Benoit a chicken leg. The fasting Franciscan took a bite and found it to his liking. In his satisfaction he declared: "Let him go to Heaven!"

"Then farewell, my friend," said the archangel Zag. And the beggar's garment, the wino's rags fell among the leaves of the bush and the feathers of the late hen. Brother Benoit ran to the monastery and to his Father Superior he related the wondrous story.

"What is that?" asked the Father Superior.

"A chicken bone."

"And what day of the week is it, Brother?"

"Friday," poor Benoit had to admit.

And thus it was that a great miracle ended in a confession. An angel, even an archangel, cannot spend time on Earth without falling into some mischief.

Translated by Betty Bednarski

7 CHRISTOPHER DEWDNEY
Excerpts from the prose-poetry collection
The Immaculate Perception (1986)

Insect Mimicry as a Thin Point

In the eyespots of giant moths predators see other predators fearful to them. The opening wings of the moth blossom into an hallucination of danger.

A reptile has had its profile painted by selective evolution on the wing-tips of the Atlas moth. This image is the index fear of a particular insectivore. A racial terror developed in the genetically sensitized emulsion of the moth's wings.

Incidental that the image of the reptile is translated into the genetic coding of another species. Not incidental that a perception beyond vision, an aperture opened by ancestral fear, becomes a slow invisible mirror held by the moth during the indelible cosmetics of its transformation.

Images of flowers, foliage, bark & animals are transferred between species, a commodity exchange of survival.
We are in-formed.

In background mimicry the forest sees itself. A mean foliage abstracted as only bilateral symmetry can. Whenever a representation is translated through the genetic aperture of survival into the vanishing point of the plane of symmetry, which is UNA, to materialize again as a generation of the plane of symmetry, we can call this representation a thin point. A thin point is a privileged view onto the immanent structure of reality & for this reason is a very efficient subject for visual flooding.

An image which has passed through the plane of symmetry is only one example of a chin point. There are other occurrences reached through very different mechanisms & mediums.

For us, protection from predators is an incidental function of mimicry.

Edge Features

Our vision relies on discontinuity & change. It seems the majority of neural processing in the striate cortex consists of an analysis of edge-features. An object is perceived by its edges, the relationship of discontinuous lines. All written languages are the abstraction and distillation of only the essential edge features necessary to perceive the form on which meaning is concomitant.

Visual Flooding

Visual flooding is a nascent propensity of vision which can be utilized with little training. It is employed in the simultaneous assimilation of large areas of movement or complex patterns by staring fixedly at a central point in the field of attention. The discipline of this process consists in not allowing the peripheral blank-out that usually develops with a 'non-conscious' stare and in refraining from any internal monologue or film-of-images during meditation. This procedure is actually a type of reflexive perceptual hypnosis where the fovea centralis, the point of attention in the retina, is slowly expanded to sensitize the entire retina. The disengagement of self-awareness during the process of visual flooding facilitates direct access to the visual cortex without conscious interpolation, like a tourist without a camera. The essence of the phenomenon is imprinted directly into the experiential reservoir of the mind.

For richness of detail natural terrain is second to none for high-speed, complex integration. Any natural tableau or process, be it an insect, flowing water, house plants or a forest, is unmatched for infinite variation & three-dimensional detail down to microscopic level. It expedites matters if the subject of visual flooding hasn't been memorized or is constantly changing. Japanese rock & moss gardens are designed with specifically this purpose in mind, the best of which override a confrontation between limited terrain & habituation.

Visual flooding with a cloud chamber, a glass apparatus filled with mist in which atomic particles leave white trails, will imprint the physics of quantum reality as direct experience. When one can exist totally between the materialization of a particle track and its decay then one can slowly expand fovea centralis until all the tracks in the cloud chamber are registered simultaneously in a harmony as self evident & resplendent as the stars.

Visual flooding can be successfully practiced on a single trace oscilloscope while it reproduces music.

Visual flooding is a basic operating skill of video games.

8 DON DOMANSKI

Excerpts from the poetry collection *Hammerstroke* (1986)

At Daybreak a Hairsbreadth Turns to Blue

you almost met her in the railyard
in the pigyard in the witch's house
you almost bumped into her on the staircase
on the doormat on the windowsill

you do want to meet her
but not like this
not with all these moons
growing out of your head
not with all these stars
pouring out of your side

you almost met her at daybreak
but at daybreak a hairsbreadth turns to blue
the Nile blue of a close call
of chance sliding down
the entire length of your body

you almost met her at noon
but at noon each second turns to red
the cherry red of a fixed grace
of delicate hands serving up
that last piece of damp air

you do want to meet her
you do want to take her in your arms
but not like this
not with all these cats
following you through the streets
not with all these letters
lying unopened in every field

you do want to meet her
but it can only be at midnight
it can only be once
it can only be forever

and when that moment comes
your mouth will be another man's mouth
your hands another man's hands
and he will tremble but not you

and he will kneel before her
he will remove his gloves and tie
he will bear the pain and joy
that an orchid feels
thick and green and luminous
but not you.

Snowbound Letter

it has snowed a lot since you were last here
the synagogue and the abattoir are covered in snow
the ships docked at the pier are white
the rapid pulse of the sailors can be heard at night
even this far inland
(like the snapping of dry twigs
in their arms and legs)

I'm not practical enough to live much longer
only a dozen more lifetimes or so
and then the freedom of insects again
the peace of being a fly for a thousand years

the window is open and it's cold in my room
but it's almost daylight and I'm listening
for the coal-train through the snow

this world separates us
with a single ache
with a button with a grassblade
it takes so little effort
to keep us apart

the neighbour's lights have just come on
they're now removing the dry leaves and earwigs
from inside their mouths

it's the wind that shapes their lives
that fills the morning glass
with sugar and water

it's the wind that allows them to live
like birds on wires
pigeons that startle each other over breakfast

I can hear the train
although it's still miles away
soon I'll be able to sleep
soon I'll be able to put up my feet
to tie up my wrists and ankles
and pull the small black hood down over my heart.

9 GEORGE GRANT
An excerpt from the nonfiction book
Technology and Justice (1986)

Faith and the Multiversity

> "*Don't let me catch anyone talking about the Universe in my
> department!*"— Lord Rutherford

I

"Faith and the multiversity" is a subject which could be tackled
from many angles, both practical and theoretical. The essence of
the issue is, however, the relation between faith and modern science. It might be maintained that there has already been enough
discussion of this over the last centuries. I do not agree. Thought
has not yet reached the core of that relation. Many Christians
turn away from the relation because they want there to be no
conflict here. Nevertheless it remains fate-filled with conflict.

It is important to be clear what is meant by the multiversity,
particularly because it is an institution which has realized itself in
Europe and North America only in the last half of this century—
although its coming to be was a slow emergence over the last
four centuries. I often meet people of my generation who went
to university in the 1930s, and who speak as if the institutions
their children or grandchildren are now attending are really the
same as those they went to. But this is simply an illusion. The

names are the same, but they are such different places that they should have different names. To say what they now are, it is necessary to describe the dominating paradigm of knowledge which rules them and determines what they are.

Different civilizations have different paradigms of knowledge, and such paradigms shape every part of the society. The principle of any paradigm in any civilization is always the relation between an aspiration of human thought and the effective conditions for its validation.

The question then becomes what is given in the modern use of the word 'science.' This is the paradigm which has slowly reached definition over the last centuries, and has since 1945 come to its apogee of determining power over our institutions. Of course, it would be folly to attempt to summarize in a paragraph the results of that brilliant progress of self-definition by philosophic scientists.

Suffice it simply to say that what is given in the modern paradigm is the project of reason to gain objective knowledge. What is meant by objective? Object means literally some thing that we have thrown over against ourselves. *Jacio* I throw, *ob* over against; therefore "the thrown against." The German word for object is *Gegenstand*—that which stands against. Reason as project, (that is, reason as thrown forth) is the summonsing of something before us and the putting of questions to it, so that it is forced to give its reasons for being the way it is as an object. Our paradigm is that we have knowledge when we represent anything to ourselves as object, and question it, so that it will give us its reasons. That summonsing and questioning requires well defined procedures. These procedures are what we call in English 'experimental research,' although what is entailed in these is more clearly given in the German word *Forschung*. Often people in the university like to use about themselves the more traditional word 'scholar,' but that word means now those who carry on 'research.' Those procedures started with such experiments as balls running down an inclined plane, but now the project of reason applies them to everything: stones, plants, human and non-human animals. Thus in North America we have divided our institutions of higher learning into faculties of natural science, social science and humanities, depending on the object which is being researched. But the project of reason is largely the same, to summons different things to questioning.

In the case of the humanities the object is the past, and these procedures are applied to the relics of the past. For example, I have lived in a department of religion in which much work was done to summons the Bible before the researchers to give them its reasons. Each department of these institutions, indeed almost each individual researcher, carries on the project of reason by approaching different objects. The limitations of the human mind in synthesizing facts necessitates the growing division of research into differing departments and further subdivisions. This paradigm of knowledge makes it therefore appropriate to speak of the multiversity.

The achievements of the modern project are of course a source of wonder. The world as object has indeed given forth its reasons, as it has been summonsed to do over the last centuries. The necessities that we now can know about stones or societies surely produce in us astonishment. These achievements are not simply practical, but also have theoretical consequences. All of us in our everyday lives are so taken up with certain practical achievements, in medicine, in production, in the making of human beings and the making of war, that we are apt to forget the sheer theoretical interest of what has been revealed about necessity in modern physics or biology.

My purpose is to discuss the relation of this paradigm of knowledge to faith. "Faith" is one of the central words of western thought which has had many meanings. What I intend by it is Simone Weil's definition: "Faith is the experience that the intelligence is enlightened by love."[1] Such a sentence, of course, simply moves one from the uncertainty of 'faith' to the even greater complexity of the word 'love.' Obviously this word has been used to cover a multitude of disparate meanings. Heidegger has used the beautiful metaphor that language is the house of being. In our epigonal times that house has become a labyrinth. Nowhere are we more in that labyrinth than when we try to sort out the relation between such words as "love," "desire," and "appetite" etc. I cannot attempt that sorting out here, but will simply express what I think is given in the word "love" in the sentence about faith.[2]

What is first intended is that love is consent to the fact that there is authentic otherness. We all start with needs, and with dependence on others to meet them. As we grow up, self-consciousness brings the tendency to make ourselves the centre, and with it the commonsense understanding that the very needs of survival depend on our own efforts. These facts push us in the direction of egocentricity. When life becomes dominated by self-serving, the reality of otherness, in its own being, almost disappears for us. In sexual life, where most of us make some contact with otherness, there is yet a tendency to lose sight of it, so that we go on wanting things from others just as we fail to recognize their authentic otherness. In all the vast permutations and combinations of sexual desire the beauty of otherness is both present and absent. Indeed, the present tendency for sexual life and family to be held apart is frightening, because for most people children have been the means whereby they were presented with unequivocal otherness. In political terms, Plato places the tyrant as the worst human being because his self-serving has gone to the farthest point. He is saying that the tyrant is mad because otherness has ceased to exist for him. I can grasp with direct recognition the theological formulation of this: "Hell is to be one's own."[3]

The old teaching was that we love otherness, not because it is other, but because it is beautiful. The beauty of others was believed to be an experience open to everyone, though in extraordinarily different forms, and at differing steps towards perfection. It was obviously capable of being turned into strange channels because of the vicissitudes of our existence. The shoe fetishist, the farmer and St. John of the Cross were on the same journey, but at different stages. The beauty of otherness is the central assumption in the statement, "Faith is the experience that the intelligence is enlightened by love."

Nevertheless, any statement about the beauty of the world is so easily doubted in our era, because it appears meaningless within the dominant language of modern science. Our uses of 'beauty' have been radically subjectivized. "Beauty is in the eye of the beholder." (But what then is beholding?) At the simplest level it is said that the sentence, "We love otherness because it is beautiful," is a tautology, because beauty is already defined as what we love. Our loves are determined by the vast varieties of necessities and chances which have constituted our desires, and these could "ideally" be explained by behavioural psychotherapists and sociologists. The fact that I call 'beautiful' the curves and lights of rock and sea in a North Atlantic bay can be explained by my particular "psyche," with its particular ancestors. I remember taking the American explorer and scientist, Stefansson, to that bay and saying: "A hard country, but beautiful." His response was to say how misleading it was to use such subjective language about terrain, and he proceeded to give me a lecture on modern geology and the modern discovery of "objectivity." In all scientific explanations we are required to eliminate the assumption of the other as itself beautiful. The platonic language which asserts that the world is beautiful and love is the appropriate response to it is believed to be based on a fundamental assumption of trust, because Plato was too early in the history of the race to have a proper scientific understanding of subjects and objects. That trust was shown to be a naive starting point by those who formulated doubt as the methodological prerequisite of an exact science.

Indeed the language of "subjects" and "objects" is one of the ways through which the beauty of the world has been obscured for us. This language was of theoretical use in the coming to be of technological science; one of its prices, however, was to obscure beauty. To state the literal meaning of "objects" yet once again: it speaks of anything which is held away from us for our questioning. Any beautiful thing can be made into an object by us and for us and we can analyze it so that it will give us its reasons as an object. But if we confine our attention to any thing as if it were simply an object, it cannot be loved as beautiful. This is well illustrated in the division between useful and non-useful criticism by professors of literature and music who explicate the texts of works of art. For example, many such explications of Shakespeare or Mozart add to our understanding of the works concerned. But one central way of dividing the useful from the non-useful among such criticisms is the recognition by the critic that his work is a means to an end, which is the further understanding of the beauty of what is being studied.

When such writing appears stultifying, it is that the critic has stood over the thing studied and therefore the thing has remained an object. Its objectivity has not been a passing means but an end. (It may be said in parenthesis that such failed works often seem to appear because the professors concerned want to share the prestige of objectivity with their colleagues from the mastering sciences.) Only as anything stands before us in some relation other than the objective can we learn of its beauty and from its beauty. To say this may seem no more than a linguistic trick upon the use of the word "objective." But this is not so. The language of "subject" and "object" can easily suffocate our recognition of the beauty of the world. In stating that the beauty of otherness is the central assumption in the aphorism "Faith is the experience that the intelligence is enlightened by love," it is necessary to bring into consciousness the sheer power of the contemporary language of "subjects" and "objects," so that the statement is not killed by that language.

Indeed the central difficulty of using the language of beauty and love, in the affirmation that one knows more about something in loving it, is that in that language beauty was known as an image of goodness itself. Yet through the modern paradigm of knowledge the conception of good has been emptied into uncertainty. The first stage of this emptying was when good came to be used simply in discourse about human ethical questions. In the last century the emptying has gone farther. "Good: has largely been replaced in our ethical discourse by the word "value." The modern emptying of "good" can indeed be seen in the emptiness of its replacement. Even its chief philosophic originator, Nietzsche, has not been able to tell us what a value is. This vagueness has resulted in the word generally being used now in the plural—our "values."

At a time when the word 'good' has been so emptied of content by the modern paradigm of knowledge, it is necessary to proceed hesitantly in trying to say what it meant in relation to our love of the beautiful. It must first be stated that what was given traditionally in the word "good" was not confined to Christians. The majority in the classical Mediterranean tradition would have so used it—Epicureanism being then a minority. A similar conception is in the Vedanta. Christianity's particular call was not to this language, but to the fact that Christ declares the price of goodness in the face of evil.

In the old language "good" means what any being is fitted for. It is a good of animals to breathe; we are not if we do not. The good of a being is what it is distinctively fitted for. Human beings are fitted to live well together in communities and to try to think openly about the nature of the whole. We are fitted for these activities because we are distinguished from the other animals in being capable of rational language. In living well together or being open to the whole in thought we are fulfilling the purpose which is given us in being human, not some other type of animal. Good is what is present in the fulfillment of our given purposes. To avoid the modern view of temporality as futurity I use a different example. A child is good, not only as a preparation, but in so far as it is at all. One loves children for what they are now. In this sense the western word "good" appears close to what the Vedanta means by the word "ananda" (bliss)—not as a feeling, but as being itself.

At the heart of the Platonic language is the affirmation—so incredible to nearly everyone at one time or another—that the ultimate cause of being is beneficence. This affirmation was made by people who, as much as anybody, were aware of suffering, war, torture, disease, starvation, madness and the cruel accidents of existing. But it was thought that these evils could only be recognized for what they were if they were seen as deprivations of good. (It must be remembered that in this account of good and evil the verb "to be" is used differently from the way it is employed in most educated modern parlance.)

Clearly this language of the given goodness of what is must be a language founded upon trust. The archetypal expositor of this language, Socrates, knew that doubt was a necessary means to philosophy. But *The Republic* makes clear that such doubt is within the overreaching assumption of trust. We start with trust in our knowledge of those things we are presented with immediately, and doubt is the means of moving to an understanding of what makes possible that trust in an educated human being. The identity of doubt and systematic thought which lies in the origin of the modern experiment was not present in Socrates' enterprise. The modern assertion that what we are is best expressed as "beings towards death" would certainly have been in Socrates' mind in what he said at the time of his execution. But it was not for him the final word about what we are. At the moment when his death was immediate he made clear that we are beings towards good. It was indeed for this reason that in the scene of his death, Socrates asserts that the absence of knowledge of good is not ignorance but madness.

NOTES

1.   S. Weil "La Pesanteur et La Grace" Plon, Paris, 1948. My translation. The greater the writer the more hesitant is the translator.

2.   Please see here the relation of what is said in the text to the Appendix at the end.

3.   The tendency of human beings to become self-engrossed has been encouraged in our era, because the distinctiveness of modern political thought has been the discover of 'individuality.' It is not my purpose here to discuss the good or evil of that 'discovery' but simply to state that one of its consequences has been to legitimize concentration on the self.

10 DAVID SHARPE
An excerpt from the nonfiction book
Rochdale: The Runaway College (1987)

The Changeling

If the new residents were a problem to the resource people, non-residents were a problem to everyone. As Rochdalians claimed floor by floor in the fall of 1968, transients discovered wide open areas on the upper floors and moved in—and out and in and out. As those areas became permanently occupied, the transients continued to wander and squat and wander again. Meanwhile, word of mouth, word of press, called out: A free college! A college so unlicensed that it offers, not freedom or license, but both. Freedom from parents, freedom from rent, freedom even from an address. Like a crowd to an accident, thousands of visitors and interim residents came from the roads and from the suburbs.

> Metro had a little school
> Its name was black as sin
> And day and night the Metro kids
> Were screaming to get in.[1]

During the winter of 1968-69, the weekends became tourist season and party time for people passing through, while the building designed for eight hundred occupants gave shelter to a thousand at the peak of the invasion. "In February," estimated a

Toronto alderman who was one of the outsiders watching askance, "as many as 3,500 young people passed through Rochdale on a week-end."[2] Some of the overflow went into rooms that were considered crash pads. One of those had bunks used around the clock by shifts of sleepers. In some cases, the residents "created split level rooms to handle twice as many guests."[3] The rest of the overflow made liberal use of lounges, hallways, closets, and even elevators, wherever they could stretch out. The 4th floor submitted photos to the *Daily* showing four of the interim residents, called 'crashers,' sleeping in the hall. The 4th floor wanted "to thank Rochdale for the new carpeting."[4]

This was "Camp Happy-Hippy," as an ad in the *Daily* put it. "No Washing No Television No Rules No Regulations/Camp Happy-Hippy is equipped with only two beds, so only the first 400 applicants will be accepted/'Guru on the premises'."[5]

As if the nerves of the residents were a welcome mat, the crashers and crowds wore them out. Troubles began in the first month with "roving bands of drunks through the building. Rumour says that these guys are from a local frat....The police have been called in once already."[6] Crashers stole breakfasts and left messes. Often they were friends of the tenants in the ashrams, one resident complained, who were themselves irresponsible. Crashers wouldn't wash dishes, and they urinated in the halls. In one incident, six crashers were found at 4 a.m. sleeping in different storage closets with stolen dishes, cutlery, and food. "Some of them were very upset that anyone should 'dare' hassle them."[7] Dennis Lee and governing council member Paul Evitts issued a statement in search of a policy: "Some of these creeps who have no stake in Rochdale and use the building like their privy, we want pure and simply to dump. No principles involved."[8]

But, although the residents had become an Establishment by acquiring a building, the role didn't feel right. Who had the right to restrict entry? On what grounds? "None of us were screened when we arrived," said council member Jack Jones, "and it bothers our conscience to set up 'entrance requirements' for others."[9] The members of the Rochdale community in the first year, as chaotic and unformed as the community was, faced their first crisis of conscience. Crowd control needed cops, and no one knew quite how to take control while rejecting the principle of control.

Any time an effort was made to control entry, it met as much resistance from within as from without; "the cry of 'fascist' or 'paranoid' or 'square' is heard, and it paralyses all."[10] Door locks became the item that focussed the issue. In November '68, a 15th-floor meeting decided that one resident was "a bastard for stealing the lock from the kitchen door (so somebody would tell him why it was there in the first place, he says)."[11]

The front door drew the most fire. Late in 1968, the *Daily* recorded that "it was stupid of Rick to lock the front door on his own authority (if he did) and it was incredibly insane of Bernie civil servant Bomers to watch the door being locked a full week or two before non-resident MEMBERS get keys."[12] Then, according to a "Counterblast by Joel" in the *Daily*, a governing council member removed the front door lock early in 1969 and broke it. By a less contentious version, "the lobby door lock...failed repeatedly and was ultimately abandoned."[13] Yet another version said that the front door lock had been stolen three times by January '69. By all versions, the front door was wide open. Aside from the screening problems, it was impossible to buy tenant's insurance. The owner of a car that had been broken into twice appealed to the council for repayment of the $1,000 loss. His insurance company had refused to pay.

The building itself amplified the problems. The rooms in the east wing didn't have proper locks to begin with, so transients tended to discourage paying tenants. As well, the lack of living room space in the east wing led to crashers claiming space in bedrooms. The Ashrams, by design, invited public use with their lounges next to the elevators. In one case, twelve people in a 'responsibility unit,' intending to share a single Ashram, quickly became twenty-seven. Could a 'people's' area like an Ashram lounge be legitimately locked?

Recurring thievery eroded another ideal. Especially in the first few months, many Rochdalians felt that material possessions should be shared by all members of the community. Coach House Press, located in an alleyway behind Rochdale and closely associated with the new college, succeeded in this enlightened sharing, according to Sarah Spinks. "The Press, though it had expensive printing equipment, opened its doors to many people at Rochdale who wanted to come and learn to print. In a materialist society it is a revelation and a joy to watch a press-man walk out the door late at night, look over his shoulder at you gingerly squeezing ink onto a letterpress, saying: 'Make sure the rollers aren't down when you leave.'"[14]

In this case, the presses themselves and fast, tangible results created discipline. Karma is easily grasped when it is offset. But in too many other cases, thieves just grasped. The *Daily* printed a plea that appealed to reason: "An oval, black and white 'Dylan' poster and a colored 'Endless Summer' poster have been stolen from the 12th floor lounge—so if you happen to see them about your 'friend's' abode, help him realize that he's too old to be in this building."[15] Another *Daily* circulated a helpful motto: "Don't steal anything you can't use."[16]

Many times, things not stolen couldn't be used because they had been vandalized. The free phones were already gone, but Bell Telephone threatened removal of the payphones as well because of the number of long distance calls on phony credit card numbers. The *Daily* made the affair faintly subversive by publishing instructions on how to make those phony calls—using credit card numbers of large corporations.

As the discussion about locks continued its non-academic course, the residents started to realize that something so simple as an open door could be radically unlike the surrounding society, and could shift unpredictably into something the society would judge illegal. "There is a problem with runaways," said a November '68 *Daily*—"they have already been here and so have the police and although these kids need a place to sleep, if we take responsibility for them we could wind up in some legal shit creek."[17] The writer, however, still wanted to be helpful. "We could unofficially form a runaway underground and keep these kids elsewhere if we judge their case worthy of our risk."

Others were not so kind. A 4th-floor apartment displayed a sign: "WARNING! This apartment is protected by a 40-megaton nuclear device which will be triggered by the entry, or attempted entry, of any unauthorized person, chicks included. So watch it."[18] Crashers could see, written on a wall, that "Rochdale Doesn't Like Weekend Slobs. Are You a Slob?"[19] The *Daily* reported that "the Rochdale Clean-up-the-Crashers Committee...arranged volunteer labor to scrape from the terrace any crashers found on the higher floors."[20]

And along with the bluffs came more serious attempts. Early in 1969, an emergency meeting of the governing council banned crashers except as guests of residents, and an "Official Rent-Paying" petition assembled 250 signatures and declared that crashers were trespassers. But of course, no amount of banning and declaring managed to lock an unlocked door.

Most seriously, the college worried about increasingly obvious drug-dealing and taking. A room open to the public for film-showings and the 2nd-floor washroom already had a reputation as good locations to buy and sell drugs. On a weekend in January, two Rochdale members had pulled guns and had taken money from two people who were in the midst of a $750 hash deal.

What was going on? A changeling had been put into what was meant to be a cradle of education, and the changeling showed every sign of growing. Many members of Rochdale College, as well as their visitors, meant to learn about other kinds of consciousness—or other kinds of kicks. At the very least, the course taken in this college would be marijuana. Although not everyone smoked pot, everyone defended the right to do so. In October '69, even two members of the governing council were charged near London, Ontario, with possession of hashish and marijuana.

The worry about drugs was more accurately a worry that uncontrolled drug activity might—like the runaways who slipped in with the crashers—draw the attention of the police. In the first month of the College, the *Daily* passed on advice given by a lawyer to a Rochdale audience: "Grass itself is required for evidence. Ashes alone aren't too good. Watch for undercover boys who buy from you and use it as beautiful evidence. If you know about searches and come on straight, non-belligerent, cops will fuzz-off. If you get action, find out about suit. It's the only thing that really works."[21] A bail fund began, and more warnings appeared in the *Daily*.

Some of the people crossing the threshold—Rochdalian, visitor, crasher—weren't satisfied with marijuana and hashish alone. In 1968, for example, speed was a new craze and Toronto was being called the speed capital of North America. Those taking. speed became separated from the others inside by the strong effects of the drug, both the hyper-energy and the neuroses it promoted and the infections that resulted from the careless use of needles. With speed and other hard drugs came theft by users needing cash, and possible interference by motorcycle gangs who dealt in hard drugs.

A wide-open Rochdale College had two sides racing out of control at the same time. It somehow had to screen outsiders coming in, and throw unwanted insiders out. At all times, the college couldn't be sure what was now morally and philosophically In and what could be justified as Out.

In the early months of Rochdale, attempts at security were confused and ineffective. The first plan was to set up a night-watch with volunteers each taking a one-hour shift. The loose, co-operative approach had problems, however. When a motor-cycle gang took over an upper-floor lounge in December, ate all the food and refused to budge, a meeting of residents couldn't reach a consensus. Someone took his own initiative and phoned the police. At this point, the bikers didn't have their own security against police—and left.

In December, security had become part of a larger plan by solid, disciplined leaders like Dennis Lee and Judy Merril, an older woman, a writer and editor of science fiction who had come to Rochdale from the States. Their plan included a Communications Center at the front door. "A group of 'determined people' led by J.M. and D.L. (who cannot be named) are manning the desk by the entrance on a voluntary basis at first. 'We need to greet people with a "hello, what help do you need?"' said the Grandmother of the scheme."[22] The Communication Center would include a desk, files, telephone, and a volunteer member at all hours. The idea was introduced with an elaborate poll and balloting procedure, with all the twists and turns accounted for. The scheme was visualized in such detail that few Rochdalians faced the task of reading it. Like many of the campaigns by the serious leaders, it was 'prepared' to death.

That month, a general meeting elected "God" as night watchman and gave him authority to deal with crashers as he saw fit. The new night watchman patrolled the halls, but the position changed hands at least twice in the first two months of 1969 and sometimes no one knew exactly who was patrolling what. A nightwatch, however, was an easy concept to grasp and required only competent, trustworthy people to do it—unlike one Chief Nightwatch who "left Rochdale and Toronto abruptly, with a large sum of other people's money, reportedly collected as advance payments for undelivered drugs."[23] After four people attacked Turtle, a former crasher-turned-resident-and-nightwatch, and broke his jaw, pressure for a fulltime, uniformed doorman increased. A doorman? The doorman's uniform, the joke was, would consist of "green satin pants, red cape, and a sword."

Less easy to grasp was the concept of control for those who had become residents. In the struggle to sort out unwanted insiders, the college had only one, imperfect weapon. That weapon was eviction—an act of will by an organization that often couldn't tie its own shoelaces and wasn't sure it believed in shoelaces anyway. "What was taken more seriously than anything else," says former council member Jim Garrard, "was the idea that someone might be unjustly evicted. No matter what anybody did, they had somebody supporting them on some level, philosophical or personal or something."

An early attempt at evicting dealers was thwarted by a sense of fair play. At the end of January '69, four unidentified residents learned that an outsider—code-named 'Janus'—would join a patrol of the building. "The four of us talked to Bernie [General Manager Bernie Bomers] and he told us that this man was an investigator for a mining company downtown, and an acquaintance of Jack's; that he entered the building [and] had volunteered to go compile a list of dealers for Jack and Bernie, who intended to get the uncool dealers out of the building by asking them privately to leave."[24] The four insisted that no outside person do any such thing. "[We] went back to Rochdale, took the man's list (which made no human distinctions) away from him and set a deadline for his leaving. . . . At the same time we told [the people on the list] and others that we would very much like to see: no hard drugs in the building, no rip-offs or burns, and no chemicals being pushed without first being analyzed and published, and no big dealing to outsiders." Ironically, the dealers who were the intended targets of the message stayed—and the marksman was put out.

The night following, on January 31, 1969, Rochdale tried its most direct intervention. It was a Friday night and the masses were beginning to arrive. General Manager Bernie Bomers explained in the next day's *Daily* that a front door lock would take weeks to arrive. Also, residents afraid that the intercom system could be used to listen to activities in their rooms had sabotaged the units and thus, the intercom couldn't help screen friend from freeloader. Someone else would have to do it. At ten o'clock that night, Bomers pulled the Communication Center desk across the front door and began a Rochdalian form of sacrilege: he questioned the people who wanted to come in. He was joined by nine residents, five from the governing council, and they barricaded the door until 3 a.m. During that time, 400 people entered and an estimated 15 were turned away.

This, the Barrier Incident, was a "self-righteous vigilante escapade," according to resident Mike Donaghy.[25] Another resident, Ken Mason, watched the visitors being screened and decided that "the whole scene seemed a repeat of the trip to 'clean-up' Yorkville, or Montreal, of all those hippies, the trip we all condemned in the 'outside world'."[26] Mason sat on the desk and as quickly as people were turned away, he told them that the back door and the restaurant door were unlocked.

The Barrier was unauthorized and controversial, but its opponents need not have worried. Official steps had to be repeated and retracted repeatedly before it could be seen that nothing was being changed.

The next month, residents were still coming to the Rentals Department to complain about cleanliness and crashers, and Rentals' solution was both vigilante and democratic: "If your floor has cleanliness problems, do something about it! Too many crashers? Kick a few out! Appoint a head crasher, maybe, to regulate crasher traffic. But do something!!!"[27] By mid-month, Ian Griggs and his Cadet Corps began a 24-hour crasher patrol, and by March, security was being called The Watch. Crasher reactions became even more unrepentant. A group of crashers met "to plan (not to discuss) how crashers can seize their rightful share of power in Rochdale." A "Bonified Crasher Card"—and Proof of Chutzpah card—was proposed with the wording: "I declare on the one hand my intention to beat any system Rochdale sets up for us or over us which we crashers consider unfair. On the other hand I declare my intent to respect Rochdale's need for economic survival and agree not to exploit others in any way or to be servile."[28]

Some residents tried to integrate the crashers into the community by setting up a Crasher Co-op. Members of the Co-op would be given Rochdale membership, guest resident status, and meal tickets in return for cash or labor. Their privileges would be suspended "if found sleeping in a public area."[29] The Proof of Chutzpah card above had been inspired by the more benign "crasher card" proposed for the Co-op. It would carry the following inscription: "I will attempt to maintain good relations with the formal residents of Rochdale. I recognize and respect Rochdale's imminent need to reduce crasher cost to nothing. I further agree not to make a mess for others to clean up, not to con people, and not to exploit people in any way."[30]

Resident Bruce Maxwell drew up a list of tips for cool crashers: "If you jimmy the locked door with a spoon, don't. Find a resident with a key and be his guest when you are in the kitchen...Don't sleep in public areas. Residents will know that you did even if they don't wake you up, which most of us won't....Residents mostly are crashers with money. Don't treat us like cops."[31]

The "upper classes of the crashers became integrated" in the Crasher Co-op, but the turnover was too high for it to be more than a noble idea.[32]

Meanwhile, the issue of eviction continued to excite breast- and brow-beating. In February, according to Alex MacDonald, "a General Meeting passed a law outsiding speed freaks and then adjourned to go to the thirteenth floor hash room and beat up speed freaks." In the same month, Govcon voted 27-3 in favor of 24-hour eviction notices instead of five-day ones. Again, in the first weeks of May '69, council conducted a "sweeping vigilante-style eviction" of forty speedfreaks and dealers.[33]

A three-member Evictions Board was set up to report to council and a Secret Security Group began to carry out evictions and bouncing, "breaking up gatherings in public places. There were 'actions' in the lobby every Friday night.... The [2nd floor] Lounge was locked. The seminar rooms were locked. The movies were stopped.... Gary Segal was authorized to rent a safety deposit box to implement the arms control measure (How many guns are in the box, I wonder?)"[34]

All of the threats to security came together in one package when Rochdale faced the motorcycle gangs. In one small incident among many, in March '69, the Detroit Renegades had been hanging out for several days in The Same, a 24-hour restaurant in Rochdale, and the Coffee House. On a Sunday, four of their members found themselves separated by a locked door from three baggies filled with white powder and some pills that they had stashed on the roof terrace. Several Rochdale officials not only refused to give them the key, but called the police. The bikers "hit out" with their fists, but that wasn't the only scuffle going on. At the elevators below, two residents were trying to stop the police from going up. The motorcycle gang disappeared, one resident was charged with assault, and both residents were taken by the police to 52 Division. Later, a Rochdale man "went out on the 17th floor terrace to walk his dog and found another bag of drugs, which was flushed with great ceremony down the toilet in full view of a number of respectable witnesses. We pause here for all you crankers to take a good deep breath."[35]

By May '69, a "chicken-wire fence no-mans land" on the south side of the elevator lobby separated the public restaurant from the building—a futile but visible sign of Rochdale's skirmishes to find a border. Despite definite statements that 'so and so' was accomplished, the definite actions disappeared in the indefinite movements of hundreds of young people following their own notions of what was in and out, who belonged and what belonged to whom. Like the crashers, the visitors, and the drugs, the bikers would return again and again.

But the bikers too would change—and be changed by—Rochdale, itself a changeling constantly changing. When Dennis Lee outlined a territory he called 'liberal,' he didn't reckon on the wider ranges of 'free' and its wider powers. "Use that word 'free'," Lee said in December '68, looking at the buzzword that was cutting his ideal down, "and it triggers off an extraordinary number of reactions in people's heads.... I find people who don't live here wandering down the halls, banging on people's doors, wanting to know where the action is."[36] Where the action is—and freedom. "This cat who lived in a communal house in Buffalo said where he lived before freedom was a little kit who came up and licked you on the cheek and then ran away. In Rochdale, freedom was a tiger that jumped out at you and would maul you to death if you didn't learn how to grapple with it."[37]

NOTES

1. D, 20 Nov 69

2. AO

3. D, 3 Mar 69

4. D, FRB

5. D, 14 Aug 72

6. D, 24 Sep 68, CHA

7. "Counterblast by Joel—Listen!," D, 5 Feb 69

8. D, 25 Nov 68

9. D, 2 Feb 69

10. NOTE 7

11. D, Nov 68, CHA

12. D, Dec 68, CHA

13. MCP

14. SS

15. D, 19 Nov 68, CHA

16. LB

17. D, Nov 68, CHA

18. AE

19. BZ

20. D, 4 Feb 69

21. D, 6 Oct 68, CHA

22. D, 30 Dec 68, CHA

23. IR 5, 19 Mar 69

24. D, 4 Feb 69

25. D, 7 Feb 69

26. D, 2 Feb 69

27. IR 2, 16 Feb 69

28. D, 8 Feb 69

29. leaflet, Feb 69, FRB

30. D, 3 Feb 69

31. D, 14 Feb 69

32. RE

33. MS 6, 12 May 69

34. IR 5, 19 Mar 69

35. leaflet, FRB

36. MV

37. KG

AE   Alan Edmonds, "The new learning: Today it's chaos/Tomorrow...
      FREEDOM?," *Maclean's*, May 69

AO   Anthony O'Donohue, letter to Robert Andras, Minister of Housing,
      21 Oct 70, MRL

BZ   Barry Zwicker, "Rochdale: The Ultimate Freedom," *Change*, Nov/
      Dec 69, FRB

D   Daily, all versions including the Daily Planet

IR   InfraRochdale, several issues, FRB

KG   Kent Gooderman, "Come Live With Us" in P. Turner *There Can Be No
      Light Without Shadow*, 1971, MRL

LB   Linda Bohnen, "Rochdale Is Alive But Ailing," *Miss Chatelaine*, late 70

MCP   "Rochdale College: A Managerial and Corporate Paradox with
      Educational Overtones," Fall 69, pamphlet, FRB

MS   MaySay, several issues, FRB

MV   Michael Valpy, "Rochdale's reality is something else," *Globe,* 16 Dec 68

NOTE refers to note above, in same chapter

RE   Robert W. Ewart, "Rochdale," paper for Anthropology 420 (U of T?),
       23 Apr 70, FRB

SS   Sarah Spinks, "The Rochdale Experience," pamphlet, CHA

THE
THIRD DECADE

—

1987-1997

1 ERÍN MOURE

Excerpts from the poetry collection *Furious* (1988)

Ordinary Cranium

The grey heart touched by the lips turns red.
My red sweater, the colour of that touch.
Trees bowed trees bowed trees
Thinking of the poem <u>Snow Door</u>.
Bronwen writes me of her back yard in Kingston
& I am thinking of the grass growing there by the fence &
Bron inside the house at 11am, sleeping, blankets tossed over her.

A small photograph of the inside of the head shows
an ordinary cranium.
An empty vessel makes the most noise
the student tells me,
explaining his silence & my virtual
noise.

The connections between poetic syllables
have finally broken down.
We pushed on them so long our arms were hurting.

A glass carring.
Bron's boyfriend in the driveway, looking at a white canoe.

None of us has solved sexual longing.
At a café table, a woman sings the rock hero of New Jersey
more slowly than the record.
Already she is days behind.
We are only recognized from our passports
for five minutes at any border.

I'm on fire, she sings

Pure Writing is a Notion Beyond the Pen

All of this an avoidance of the script:
the small turquoise shirt rolled up over the shoulders, the narrow
angle of sun in the yard, the body, the body,
oh, the body
with its view of the cold dew on the grass this morning, silver,
like a ring
Dreaming over & over of
women's madness, my mother's madness, the madness of
the neighbour woman shut up in High River,
where I was caught in a blizzard once, drifts choking the road & cars

until there is no anger any longer.
Until none of us is angry
until our women's faces are the blindness of snow & refract light
until our house is so lit it has the sound of steel
until light becomes the absence of weight
& does not resemble us any longer

My brother out in his long yard stooped beside the hay-bin,
the thin swath of clover & timothy
drying in the sun, & the narrow muscle in his back, his head
completely vanished

into a place where there is no more childhood, just
the heat of August risen off New Holland equipment,
the connection   between   things & things,
the air hose & the tractor

air hose

tractor

In spite of us, the connection
between words, are words things, are they names of things,
the speed of light notwithstanding,
why do we go mad & forget everything, & be unable to speak of it,
as if: pure writing is a notion beyond the pen
she said, & held her head to keep the wind in,
& named it this

2 DAPHNE MARLATT

An excerpt from the novel *Ana Historic* (1988)

'Such rain here!—It rains day in and day out, a veritable curtain falling all around my Cabin. The trees weep, paths slip into small bogs, the chickens look as bedraggled as I feel my muddy skirts to be. I am orphaned here at the end of the world—Yet I feel no grief, for I am made new here, Father, solitary as I am—nor am I entirely so: daily a garrulous blue-black bird keeps me company, the young Cedar spared by my front door dips to greet me. Nor do these tell me what I must be.'

she writes as if she were living alone in the woods, her vision trued to trees and birds. she filters out the hive of human activity in which her 'cabin' sits, a tiny cell of light, late, after the others have been extinguished. in the dark (i imagine her writing at night, on the other side of a day in England she already knew) she can overlook the stumps, the scarred face of the clearing that surrounds her, and see herself ab-original in the new world (it is the old one she is at the end of). but why she had to erase so much is never given, it is part of what is missing, like her first name, like her past that has dropped away. we cannot see her and so she is free to look out at the world with her own eyes, free to create her vision of it. this is not history.

and this is why, perhaps, they think her journal suspect at the archives. 'inauthentic,' fictional possibly, contrived later by a daughter who imagined (how ahistoric) her way into the unspoken world of her mother's girlhood. girl? even then, teaching at Hastings Mill, she was said to be a widow, though young. but she married again, didn't she? she married Ben Springer and moved across the inlet to Moodyville, Moody's mill, the rival one. and her daughter? we know nothing of her, this possible interpreter of her mother's place in that world. it's hardly a record of that world, is it? no, it's Mrs. Richards' private world, at least that's what they call it. that's why it's not historical—a document, yes, but not history. you mean it's not factual.

what is fact? (f) act. the f stop of act. a still photo in the ongoing cinerama.

Mrs. Patterson, say, with her crocheted mitts and bonnet, the very picture of a 'Dame Hospitaller.' there is no image of Mrs. Richards. but if there were, she would be caught with a tiny frown between her eyes, lower lip dented by an apprehensive finger, pen idle before her, thinking:

'My keenest pleasure is to walk the woods, despite their scolding me most roundly as to its dangers. I do not hold stock in their stories of Bears!—The Siwash do not seem to fear them but wander as they will. If need be, I will lie face down as if dead, as they have told me.'

'More I fear their talk about me, their Suppositions. Perhaps because they understand me to be a Widow, the men think me most eager for their company. Capt. Soule yesterday insisted on escorting me, pointing out this and that—D'ye see those two peaks beyond the Inlet? he says, Sheba's Paps they call 'em. I did not know whether to shew myself insulted, for surely a School Mistress should be above reproach. Yet it was laughable—what did he imagine Sheba to be? I merely remarked that Burrard's Inlet must look very different from the Nile, which gave him the occasion to boast, Indeed ye'd get no timbers the size of ours from that desert. And so it passed. Should I have shown displeasure at a remark a gentleman would not utter in the company of a lady? And he a member of the School Board! Or does he speak freely because he sees me wandering of my own free will? I cannot keep only to drawing rooms and the School! I am. not a Proper Lady perhaps.'

Proper, she says, Lady capitalized, and it is barely sounded, the relationship between proper and property. the other Ladies at the mill would be wives or daughters-about-to-be-wives: Mrs. Alexander, Mrs. Patterson, Miss Sweney. she alone is without 'protection,' as they would say. subject, then, to sly advances under the guise of moral detection, subject to agonizing (your word, Ina), subject to self-doubt in a situation without clearly defined territory (because she is no one's property, she is 'free' without being sexually free), she feels her difference from the other women, hopes the Captain recognizes it as freedom of intellect (suspects he doesn't), is at home only with things without language (birds, trees) in a place she struggles to account for in her own words. words, that shifting territory. never one's own. full of deadfalls and hidden claims to a reality others have made.

lady, for instance, a word that has claimed so much from women trying to maintain it. the well-ironed linen, clean (lace at the cuffs, at the collar), well-tailored dresses and wraps, the antimacassars, lace tablecloths, the christening bonnets. beyond that, a certain way of walking, of talking. and always that deference, that pleased attention to the men who gave them value, a station in life, a reason for existing. lady, *hlaefdige*, kneader of bread, mistress of a household, lady of the manor, woman of good family, woman of refinement and gentle manners, a woman whose conduct conforms to a certain standard of propriety ('lady airs'— singing true again).

i imagine the ladies of Hastings Mill spent hours when they got together discussing the merits of various haberdashers in Victoria, New Westminster, centres of culture by comparison with Granville and the mill store with its red flannel. so hard to get anything 'decent,' they complained, for a decent lady kept herself well-covered, her sexuality hidden. no flag to taunt 'vigorous' men with. for if men couldn't control their desires, women could. women knew the standard of what was socially acceptable in conduct and apparel. just as you spent hours, ma, shopping for bargains, shopping department store basements or poring over Sears catalogues, dismissing things that looked 'cheap,' vainly trying to clothe us with the class you had in the tropics where your clothes were handsewn by Chinese tailors and our intricately smocked dresses came from the School for the Blind. now there was very little money and Harald wore good suits that 'lasted' ('slightly out of date, poor dear'), you tried bargain dresses ('dreadful—people here have no idea of fashion'), and struggled with our running around in jeans—'so unladylike.' exactly. skirts meant keeping your legs together as you so often told me (i didn't realize *why*), skirts meant girdles and garter belts and stockings...

— and i suppose it wasn't *your* crinolines i had to starch?

— i remember. crinolines and white bucks.

— and i suppose it wasn't you who pestered me for high heels?

— but it wasn't that i wanted to be a 'lady,' i wanted to be like the other girls, sexy but not too much, just enough to be liked, just enough to be cute.

— and what about 'nice'?

yes, nice girls don't...i didn't realize the only alternative to lady you knew, was tramp, though that was a line i heard often enough on one of your records. tramps were girls who smoked in the bushes behind the corner store (doo-wop, doo-wop). tramps loved Chuck Berry and *Little Darlin'*, wore pencil-line skirts with kick pleats, wobbled their hips, inked initials on their arms. tramps cut school or left it because they had to. i was fascinated with their flouting all the rules, but i didn't want to be one. tramp was a word nice girls used to brand those outside their group—tramp, slut, bitch.

i came home to *Red Roses for a Blue Lady*, the last pop song you bought. i came home to the peculiar silence of your growing naps, your obsessive washing the kitchen floor, your chronic exhaustion (sleep, the one great unsatisfied desire). 'that damn dog, they deliberately leave it out all night to torture me.' 'hell's bells, will no one give me any peace?' peace. a lady's respect for tranquility.

> *Oh, Jemima, look at your Uncle Jim,*
> *He's in the duck pond, learning how to swim;*
> *First he does the breast stroke, then he does the side,*
> *And now he's under the water, swimming against the tide.*

i didn't hear then what kind of stroking was meant. bathing was what you called swimming, as if to sanitize it. what did you do with all that pent-up energy? (besides paint walls). you taught us your fear, you taught us what you knew about a world where even uncles were not to be trusted. you grew more afraid as our sexuality came budding to the fore—foreground, fore-body, carrying these forward parts of our bodies. ladies do not draw attention to themselves. (is that you speaking or your mother or all the mothers?) ladies keep to the background. ladies *are* the soothing background their men come home to.

'The man suggests that he would like chicken for dinner. It is not a command, yet such is the harmony between them that his wishes are hers,' says one of your how-to-heal / how-to-fix yourself books (caught in a fix, castrated—what is the female word for it? i mean for the psychological condition?) Soul has 'positively no wishes of its own, no preferences. It stands forever as the servant of Spirit' and in this it is 'similar to a happy home.' the standard. Soul: generic feminine, it is the man who is Spirit, has spirit. what does Soul, what does a woman do with her unexpressed preferences, her own desires? (damned up, a torrent to let loose.) and this is what you were trying to live up to. the neuter.

3 NOAM CHOMSKY

An excerpt from the CBC Massey Lectures
Necessary Illusions (1989)

4. Adjuncts of Government

"It is very interesting," Senator William Fulbright observed in
Senate hearings on government and the media in 1966, "that so
many of our prominent newspapers have become almost agents
or adjuncts of the government; that they do not contest or even
raise questions about government policy."[1] These remarks are
not precisely accurate: the media do contest and raise questions
about government policy, but they do so almost exclusively
within the framework determined by the essentially shared interests of state-corporate power. Divisions among elites are reflected
in media debate,[2] but departure from their narrow consensus is
rare. It is true that the incumbent state managers commonly set
the media agenda. But if policy fails, or is perceived to be harmful
to powerful interests, the media will often "contest government
policy" and urge different means to achieve goals that remain
beyond challenge or, quite often, even awareness.

To illustrate, I have reviewed a few samples of the media's
contributions to the government project of "demonizing the
Sandinistas" while praising the violent terror states backed or
directly installed by the United States in the region. With all the
skepticism I have personally developed through studying media
performance over many years, I had not expected that they

would rise to this challenge. When writing in 1985 about the Reaganite disinformation programs concerning Central America, I did not compare Nicaragua to El Salvador and Guatemala to demonstrate the hypocrisy of the charges (where they were not outright lies); that seemed an insult to the reader's intelligence. Instead, I compared the allegations concerning Nicaragua with the behavior of the "model democracy" of Israel during the same period and that of the United States itself in wartime conditions, showing that the Sandinista record was respectable by these—admittedly, not very impressive—standards.[3] But my assessment of the media was naive. Within a year they had succeeded in portraying the murderous U.S. clients as progressive if flawed democracies, while the Sandinistas, guilty of no crime that even begins to approach those of Washington's favorites, had become the very embodiment of evil.

The review in the last chapter of two periods of intense debate over U.S. policy towards Nicaragua kept to the spectrum of expressible opinion. News reporting conforms to the same implicit premises. The dichotomous treatment of the elections in El Salvador and Nicaragua provides one example, studied in detail elsewhere. The periods reviewed in the last chapter provide another. Political scientist Jack Spence studied 181 *New York Times* articles on Nicaragua during the first six months of 1986; the conclusions are similar to those drawn from the editorial and opinion columns.[4]

Spence observes that Central America was virtually ignored until U.S. control faced a challenge in 1978. From 1969 through 1977, the TV networks devoted a total of one hour to Nicaragua, all on the 1972 earthquake. They ignored the 1972 election in El Salvador, when the apparent victory of the Duarte-Ungo reformist ticket was overturned by blatant fraud and intervention by the U.S. clients in Nicaragua and Guatemala, guaranteeing the military rule that continues until the present. There being no challenge to U.S. domination, the problem of establishing "democracy" did not arise, just as it did not arise in 1984 in Panama when the notorious drug dealer General Noriega, then still a U.S. favorite, ran a fraudulent election legitimized by the attendance of George Shultz at the inauguration, where he "praised the vote as a triumph for democracy, taunting Nicaragua to do the same," after having been briefed by the CIA and the U.S. ambassador "that Noriega had stolen upwards of 50,000 ballots in order to ensure the election" of his candidates.[5]

Through the 1970s, the media ignored the growing crisis of access to land in Central America that lies at the roots of the current turmoil.[6] In the first six months of 1986, Spence observes, the "crucial issue" of "access to land and land ownership patterns" in Nicaragua received one sentence in the 181 articles, and agrarian policy was also virtually ignored in coverage of El Salvador, except for occasional mention of El Salvador's "progressive" reforms without serious analysis. Similarly, "Nicaraguan issues such as the effects of the war on Nicaragua, Sandinista programs, popularity, and support were not part of the news agenda." Most of the stories "emanated from Washington" and presented Reagan administration doctrine without challenge or analysis, including the laments about freedom fighters forced to fight with only "boots and bandages" against advanced Soviet armaments and Cuban-piloted helicopters, brutal repression in this "cancer, right here on our land mass" (George Shultz), guns to Colombian terrorists and subversion from Chile to Guatemala, Cuban troops "swarming the streets of Managua by the scores" in this terrorism sanctuary two days' drive from Texas, a second Libya, and so on through the familiar litany. In its news columns, Spence observes, "the Times tacitly accepted [the Reaganite] views, seeking out no others, thus contributing to a drastic narrowing for public debate." "Regarding the charges leveled against the Sandinistas, almost no contrary view could be found in the Times [and]...supporting evidence was never present." "Four times the Nicaraguan Embassy was given a buried line or two," and in a few stories "the reporter added a background balance line": "it was as if the *Times* had a software program that, at rare and odd intervals, automatically kicked in a boilerplate 'balancing' graf beyond that story's halfway point." Critics of Reaganite *tactics* were cited, but virtually nothing beyond these limits.

As is well known, choice of sources can shield extreme bias behind a façade of objectivity. A study organized by media specialist Lance Bennett of the University of Washington investigated the distribution of attributed news sources for the month of September 1985 in the *New York Times* and the Seattle press. In *Times* coverage of El Salvador, over 80 percent of the sources were supportive of the government of El Salvador; 10 percent were drawn from the opposition. In *Times* coverage of Nicaragua, the pattern was reversed: more than two-thirds of sources selected were hostile to the government of Nicaragua, under 20 percent were from that government. The local media were similar. In fact, despite the apparent difference, the two patterns reflect the same criterion of source selection: in both cases, the primary sources were the U.S. government and its allies and clients (the government of El Salvador, the Nicaraguan political opposition and the contras). The study observes that in both countries, "the vast majority of Central Americans, the ordinary peasants, urban dwellers, workers and merchants, are virtually mute in U.S. news coverage of their lives." They account for 9 percent of attributed news sources, of which one-third are "U.S. individuals."

The study suggests that the reasons for these discrepancies may lie in the tendency to rely on "easily available 'official' sources" and other such "institutional factors." That is plausible, but one should not be misled. Opposition sources are, of course, easy to find in Nicaragua, where they operate freely and openly despite government harassment, while in El Salvador and Guatemala, most were murdered by the U.S.-backed security forces or fled; a nontrivial distinction that the media manage to suppress, indeed to reverse. In coverage of Afghanistan, the Kremlin is a more "easily available" source than guerrillas in the hills, but coverage is radically biased in the other direction (as it should be). Similarly, great efforts have been made to report the war in Nicaragua from the point of view of the contras. Reporting from the point of view of the Salvadoran or Guatemalan guerrillas, or the Viet Cong, has been next to nonexistent, and important sources that exist are often simply suppressed.[7] The same is true of publication of refugee studies, which typically reflects political priorities, not ease of access.[8] The "institutional factors" are doubtless real, but throughout there are conscious choices that flow from doctrinal needs.[9]

Spence found the same tendencies in his study of news reporting on Nicaragua in early 1986. Top priority was given to the U.S. government. Ranking second were the U.S. proxy forces. The contras received 727 column inches as compared to 417 for the Nicaraguan government, a discrepancy that was increased by 109 inches devoted to the U.S.-backed internal opposition in Nicaragua, overwhelmingly those who had refused to participate in the 1984 elections as the U.S. government had demanded. There were extensive reports of the concerns of the businessmen's association COSEP, harassment of the U.S.-funded journal *La Prensa*, one of whose owners was issuing thinly veiled calls for contra aid in Washington at the time, and other abuses. Coverage of the U.S. clients was largely favorable; only one of thirty-three stories on the contras focused on human rights abuses, and there were a few other references to atrocities that were by then reaching a remarkable scale. Like the State Department and Congress, the media preferred what human rights investigators described as "intentional ignorance."[10]

Turning to El Salvador, we find that the pattern is sharply reversed. Here, the guerrillas were castigated as Marxist terrorists, and the official line, as laid forth in *New York Times* editorials, was that things were improving under the democratic government of "the honorable Mr. Duarte," "the honest, reform-minded Christian Democrat," who is desperately trying to lead his people to a better life while "beset by implacable extremes," though he may have been "less than rigorous in bringing death squad operatives to judicial account" (in translation: he has done nothing to curb the security forces he praises for their "valiant service alongside the people against subversion" while conceding quietly that "the masses were with the guerrillas" when he assumed the role of front man for the war against the population). News reporting was similar in style. Duarte was portrayed in the major media as a victim, not as the willing agent whose role was to ensure adequate congressional funding for the state terrorists whom he protected. Analyzing over 800 articles in the major dailies from March 1984 through October 1985, journalist Marc Cooper found a consistent pattern of suppressing massive atrocities and "singing the praise of Administration policy." There were hundreds of column inches lauding Duarte's *promises* to end the rampant state terror conducted under his aegis, but virtually nothing on his actual record of apologetics for state terror and service to it, and not a single article "analyzing the nature of Duarte's alliance with the military establishment," the effective rulers.[11]

In the editorials reviewed over six and a half years, the *Times* never mentioned such matters as the assassination of Archbishop Romero or the raid by the security forces on the legal aid office of the archbishopric to destroy evidence implicating them in the assassination; the destruction and closure of the university by the army, with many killed; the physical destruction of the independent media and the murder and expulsion of their editors and publishers; or the Salvadoran state of siege from March 1980 when Duarte joined the junta, under which the atrocities were conducted with his backing and constant apologetics. In contrast, when Nicaragua declared a state of siege on October 15, 1985, the

Times bitterly condemned this demonstration of Nicaragua's lack of "respect for democracy and human rights," dismissing with contempt "President Ortega's claim that the crackdown is the fault of 'the brutal aggression by North America and its internal allies'"; the *renewal* of El Salvador's far more draconian state of siege two days later received no mention. The events ignored in the editorials were also largely suppressed or falsified in the news columns.

There was no hint or concern in the editorials, and little (if any) reporting, about the fact that "since 1981 the Salvadoran press has either supported the government or criticized it from a right-wing perspective," avoiding "stories critical of government forces from a human rights standpoint," as observed in an Americas Watch review of freedom of the press. The political opposition had been murdered by Duarte's security forces or had fled the country, so there was no need to report or comment on their problems.[12] Similarly, no second thoughts were aroused by the fact that one of the leading murderers was selected to be Duarte's Minister of Defense, having completed his service as director of the National Guard. Earlier, he had coolly explained that "the armed forces are prepared to kill 200,000-300,000, if that's what it takes to stop a Communist takeover," and he had acted accordingly as the Guard under his command administered its "pedagogy of terror." When he was named Defense Minister, this mass murderer and torturer was described by the *New York Times* as "a soft-spoken, amiable man who has a reputation as an excellent administrator." Conceding that the Guard under his command had been responsible for horrible atrocities, including the rape and murder of four American churchwomen and the assassination of two U.S. labor advisors, the *Times* adds that "in his defense, others contend that under his command the National Guard's reputation has improved to the point where it is no longer considered the most abusive of Salvador's three security forces"—an impressive achievement, doubtless.[13]

NOTES

1. Hearings of the Senate Committee on Foreign Relations, August 31, 1966; cited by Aronson, *The Press and the Cold War*, 226.

2. There are exceptions when interfering factors distort the operation of the system. Even powerful segments of the corporate world may be barred from ready access to the public forum; for one case, see the next chapter.

3. *Turning the Tide*, 72f., and my article in Walker, *Reagan versus the Sandinistas*. See also Michael Parenti, "Afterword," in Morley and Petras, *The Reagan Administration in Nicaragua*, and Michael Linfield, *Human Rights in Times of War*, ms., 1988.

4. Spence, "The U.S. Media: Covering (Over) Nicaragua," in Walker, *Reagan versus the Sandinistas*. On the election coverage, see appendix I, section 1, and sources cited.

5. Council on Hemispheric Affairs (COHA), "News and Analysis," Feb. 29, 1988.

6. More generally, it would be very difficult to find in the media any discussion of the impact of the Alliance for Progress in intensifying the crisis, with its emphasis on developmental programs that increased the GNP and human suffering (for example, by shifting production from subsistence crops to beef for export), led to serious ecological damage, and in general were a human catastrophe even where they were a statistical success.

7. For example, Katsuichi Honda published in the Japanese press extensive studies of life in villages controlled by the South Vietnamese resistance forces and under U.S. attack, but the English translation found no takers. Cambodia specialist Serge Thion reported his visit to Cambodian guerrillas in 1972 in *Le Monde*, but the *Washington Post* turned it down. *Le Monde* southeast Asia specialist Jacques Decornoy published his firsthand reports of the devastating bombing of Laos in 1968, but despite repeated efforts, no U.S. journal was willing to reprint his articles or even to mention the facts. Reports on the atrocities of U.S.-backed Salvadoran forces by foreign journalists and even direct testimony by House members were ignored. See *For Reasons of State, Towards a New Cold War, Manufacturing Consent*, on these and other examples.

8. Cambodian refugees on the Thai border in the late 1970s were not more accessible than Cambodian refugees in Phnom Penh a few years earlier, but the former had a useful tale to tell and the latter did not, and were therefore ignored. The Thai border camps were also not more accessible than Lisbon or Australia despite some remarkable claims by journalists who surely know better, but what the Timorese refugees had to say conflicted with the requirements of U.S. power, as distinct from those who fled Pol Pot atrocities. See *Political Economy of Human Rights* and *Manufacturing Consent* for discussion and details, in these and other cases.

9. Seattle Central America Media Project, *Out of Balance*, n.d. See also appendix v, section 6, on Times choice of sources within Nicaragua.

10. Donald Fox and Michael J. Glennon, "Report to the International Human Rights Law Group and the Washington Office on Latin America," Washington D.C., April 1985, 21, referring to the State Department reaction to their revelation of contra atrocities. Most studies were, like this one, ignored or dismissed.

11. For a review of *New York Times* editorials on El Salvador and Nicaragua from 1980 through mid-1986, see my article in Walker, *Reagan vs. the Sandinistas*. For comparison of the image of Duarte here and in Latin America, including El Salvador, see *Culture of Terrorism*, 101f. On Duarte's record and media appreciation for it, see *Turning the Tide*, chapter 3, sec. 5.2; Cooper, "Whitewashing Duarte," U.S. Reporting on El Salvador, NACLA *Report on the Americas*, Jan./March 1986.

12. See sources cited above for explicit references and further detail, here and below; appendix V, section 6, on the Central American media.

13. Lydia Chavez, NYT, April 24, 1983. Defense Minister Gen. Vides Casanova cited by Ray Bonner, *Weakness and Deceit* (Times Books, 1984, 106).

4 CHARLES TAYLOR

An excerpt from the CBC Massey Lectures
The Malaise of Modernity (1991)

X: Against Fragmentation

I argued in the preceding section that the institutions of a technological society don't ineluctably impose on us an ever-deepening
hegemony of instrumental reason. But it is clear that left to
themselves they have a tendency to push us in that direction.
That is why the project has often been put forward of leaping out
of these institutions altogether. One such dream was put forward by classical Marxism and enacted up to a point by Leninism.
The goal was to do away with the market and bring the whole
operation of the economy under the conscious control of the
"associated producers," in Marx's phrase.[1] Others cherish the hope
that we might be able to do without the bureaucratic state.

It is now evident that these hopes are illusory. The collapse
of Communist societies has finally made undeniable what many
have felt all along: market mechanisms in some form are indispensable to an industrial society, certainly for its economic
efficiency and probably also for its freedom. Some people in the
West rejoice that this lesson has finally been learned and make
the end of the Cold War a pretext for the celebration of their
own utopia, a free society ordered through and through by
impersonal market relations, with the state pushed into a limited residual role. But this is equally unrealistic. Stability, and

hence efficiency couldn't survive this massive withdrawal of government from the economy, and it is doubtful if freedom either could long survive the competitive jungle that a really wild capitalism would breed, with its uncompensated inequalities and exploitation.

What should have died along with communism is the belief that modern societies can be run on a single principle, whether that of planning under the general will or that of free-market allocations. Our challenge is actually to combine in some non-self-stultifying fashion a number of ways of operating, which are jointly necessary to a free and prosperous society but which also tend to impede each other: market allocations, state planning, collective provision for need, the defence of individual rights, and effective democratic initiative and control. In the short run, maximum market "efficiency" may be restricted by each of the other four modes; in the long run, even perhaps economic performance, but certainly justice and freedom, would suffer from their marginalization.

We can't abolish the market, but nor can we organize ourselves exclusively through markets. To restrict them may be costly; not to restrict them at all would be fatal. Governing a contemporary society is continually recreating a balance between requirements that tend to undercut each other, constantly finding creative new solutions as the old equilibria become stultifying. There can never be in the nature of the case a definitive solution. In this regard our political situation resembles the cultural predicament I described earlier. The continuing cultural struggle between different outlooks, different enframings of the key ideals of modernity, parallels on the institutional level the conflicting demands of the different but complementary ways we organize our common life: market efficiency may be dampened by collective provision through the welfare state; effective state planning may endanger individual rights; the joint operations of state and market may threaten democratic control.

But there is more than a parallel here. There is a connection, as I have indicated. The operation of market and bureaucratic state tends to strengthen the enframings that favour an atomist and instrumentalist stance to the world and others. That these institutions can never be simply abolished, that we have to live with them forever, has a lot to do with the unending, unresolvable nature of our cultural struggle.

Although there is no definitive victory, there is winning or losing ground. What this involves emerges from the example I mentioned in the previous section. There I noted that the battle of isolated communities or groups against ecological desolation was bound to be a losing one until such time as some common understanding and a common sense of purpose forms in society as a whole about the preservation of the environment. In other words, the force that can roll back the galloping hegemony of instrumental reason is (the right kind of) democratic initiative.

But this poses a problem, because the joint operation of market and bureaucratic state has a tendency to weaken democratic initiative. Here we return to the third area of malaise: the fear articulated by Tocqueville that certain conditions of modern society undermine the will to democratic control, the fear that people will come to accept too easily being governed by an "immense tutelary power."

Perhaps Tocqueville's portrait of a soft despotism, much as he means to distinguish it from traditional tyranny, still sounds too despotic in the traditional sense. Modern democratic societies seem far from this, because they are full of protest, free initiatives, and irreverent challenges to authority, and governments do in fact tremble before the anger and contempt of the governed, as these are revealed in the polls that rulers never cease taking.

But if we conceive Tocqueville's fear a little differently, then it does seem real enough. The danger is not actual despotic control but fragmentation—that is, a people increasingly less capable of forming a common purpose and carrying it out. Fragmentation

arises when people come to see themselves more and more ato-
mistically; otherwise put, as less and less bound to their fellow
citizens in common projects and allegiances. They may indeed
feel linked in common projects with some others, but these
come more to be partial groupings rather than the whole society: for instance, a local community, an ethnic minority, the
adherents of some religion or ideology, the promoters of some
special interest.

This fragmentation comes about partly through a weakening
of the bonds of sympathy, partly in a self-feeding way, through
the failure of democratic initiative itself. Because the more fragmented a democratic electorate is in this sense, the more they
transfer their political energies to promoting their partial groupings, in the way I want to describe below, and the less possible it
is to mobilize democratic majorities around commonly understood programs and policies. A sense grows that the electorate
as a whole is defenceless against the leviathan state; a well-
organized and integrated partial grouping may, indeed, be able
to make a dent, but the idea that the majority of the people
might frame and carry through a common project comes to
seem utopian and naive. And so people give up. Already failing
sympathy with others is further weakened by the lack of a common experience of action, and a sense of hopelessness makes it
seem a waste of time to try. But that, of course, *makes* it hopeless,
and a vicious circle is joined.

Now a society that goes this route can still be in one sense
highly democratic, that is egalitarian, and full of activity and
challenge to authority, as is evident if we look to the great republic to our south. Politics begins to take on a different mould, in
the way I indicated above. One common purpose that remains
strongly shared, even as the others atrophy, is that society is
organized in the defence of rights. The rule of law and the uphold-
ing of rights are seen as very much the "American way," that is, as
the objects of a strong common allegiance. The extraordinary

reaction to the Watergate scandals, which ended up unseating a president, are a testimony to this.

In keeping with this, two facets of political life take on greater and greater saliency. First, more and more turns on judicial battles. The Americans were the first to have an entrenched bill of rights, augmented since by provisions against discrimination, and important changes have been made in American society through court challenges to legislation or private arrangements allegedly in breach of these entrenched provisions. A good example is the famous case of *Brown vs the Board of Education*, which desegregated the schools in 1954. In recent decades, more and more energy in the American political process is turning towards this process of judicial review. Matters that in other societies are determined by legislation, after debate and sometimes compromise between different opinions, are seen as proper subjects for judicial decision in the light of the constitution. Abortion is a case in point. Since *Roe vs Wade* in 1973 greatly liberalized the abortion law in the country, the effort of conservatives, now gradually coming to fruition, has been to stack the court in order to get a reversal. The result has been an astonishing intellectual effort, channelled into politics-as-judicial-review, that has made law schools the dynamic centres of social and political thought on American campuses; and also a series of titanic battles over what used to be the relatively routine—or at least non-partisan—matter of senatorial confirmation of presidential appointments to the Supreme Court.

Alongside judicial review, and woven into it, American energy is channelled into interest or advocacy politics. People throw themselves into single-issue campaigns and work fiercely for their favoured cause. Both sides in the abortion debate are good examples. This facet overlaps the previous one, because part of the battle is judicial, but it also involves lobbying, mobilizing mass opinion, and selective intervention in election campaigns for or against targeted candidates.

All this makes for a lot of activity. A society in which this goes on is hardly a despotism. But the growth of these two facets is connected, part effect and part cause, with the atrophy of a third, which is the formation of democratic majorities around meaningful programs that can then be carried to completion. In this regard, the American political scene is abysmal. The debate between the major candidates becomes ever more disjointed, their statements ever more blatantly self-serving, their communication consisting more and more of the now famous "sound bytes," their promises risibly unbelievable ("read my lips") and cynically unkept, while their attacks on their opponents sink to ever more dishonourable levels, seemingly with impunity. At the same time, in a complementary movement, voter participation in national elections declines, and has recently hit 50 per cent of the eligible population, far below that of other democratic societies.

Something can be said for, and perhaps a lot can be said against, this lopsided system. One might worry about its long-term stability, worry, that is, whether the citizen alienation caused by its less and less functional representative system can be compensated for by the greater energy of its special-interest politics. The point has also been made that this style of politics makes issues harder to resolve. Judicial decisions are usually winner-take-all; either you win or you lose. In particular, judicial decisions about rights tend to be conceived as all-or-nothing matters. The very concept of a right seems to call for integral satisfaction, if it's a right at all; and if not, then nothing. Abortion once more can serve as an example. Once you see it as the right of the fetus versus the right of the mother, there are few stopping places between the unlimited immunity of the one and the untrammelled freedom of the other. The penchant to settle things judicially, further polarized by rival special-interest campaigns, effectively cuts down the possibilities of compromise.[2] We might also argue that it makes certain issues harder to address, those that require a wide democratic consensus around measures that will also involve some sacrifice and difficulty. Perhaps this is part of the continuing American problem of coming to terms with their declining economic situation through some form of intelligent industrial policy. But it also brings me to my point, which is that certain kinds of common projects become more difficult to enact where this kind of politics is dominant.

An unbalanced system such as this both reflects and entrenches fragmentation. Its spirit is an adversarial one in which citizen efficacy consists in being able to get your rights, whatever the consequences for the whole. Both judicial retrieval and single-issue politics operate from this stance and further strengthen it. Now what emerged above from the example of the recent fate of the ecological movement is that the only way to countervail the drift built into market and bureaucracy is through the formation of a common democratic purpose. But this is exactly what is difficult in a democratic system that is fragmented.

A fragmented society is one whose members find it harder and harder to identify with their political society as a community. This lack of identification may reflect an atomistic outlook, in which people come to see society purely instrumentally. But it also helps to entrench atomism, because the absence of effective common action throws people back on themselves. This is perhaps why one of the most widely held social philosophies in the contemporary United States is the procedural liberalism of neutrality that I mentioned earlier (in section II), and which combines quite smoothly with an atomist outlook.

But now we can also see that fragmentation abets atomism in another way. Because the only effective counter to the drift towards atomism and instrumentalism built into market and bureaucratic state is the formation of an effective common purpose through democratic action, fragmentation in fact disables us from resisting this drift. To lose the capacity to build politically effective majorities is to lose your paddle in mid-river. You are carried ineluctably downstream, which here means further and further into a culture enframed by atomism and instrumentalism.

The politics of resistance is the politics of democratic will-formation. As against those adversaries of technological civilization who have felt drawn to an elitist stance, we must see that a serious attempt to engage in the cultural struggle of our time requires the promotion of a politics of democratic empowerment. The political attempt to re-enframe technology crucially involves resisting and reversing fragmentation.

NOTES

1.   "Freedom in this field can only consist in socialized man, the associated poroducers, rationally regulating their interchange with Nature, bringing it under their common control, instead of being ruled by it as by the blind forces of Nature." *Capital*, vol. III (New York: International Publishers, 1967), p. 820.

2.   Mary Ann Glendon, *Abortion and Divorce in Western Law* (Cambridge: Harvard University Press, 1987) has shown how this has made a difference to American decisions on the issue, as compared with those in comparable Western societies.

5 NORTHROP FRYE

An excerpt from the CBC Massey Lectures
The Educated Imagination (1993)

III. Giants in Time

... There's a great deal of allegory in literature, much more than we usually realize, but straightforward allegory is out of fashion now: most modern writers dislike having their images pinned down in this specific way, and so modern critics think of allegory as a bit simple-minded. The reason is that allegory, where literature is illustrating moral or political or religious truths, means that both the writer and his public have to be pretty firmly convinced of the reality and importance of those truths, and modern writers and publics, on the whole, aren't.

A more common way of indicating that an image is literary is by allusion to something else in literature. Literature tends to be very allusive, and the central things in literature, the Greek and Roman classics, the Bible, Shakespeare and Milton, are echoed over and over again. To take a simple example: many of you will know G. K. Chesterton's poem on the donkey, which describes how ungainly and ridiculous a beast he is, but that he doesn't care because, as the poem concludes:

> I also had my hour,
> One far fierce hour and sweet:

> There was a shout about my ears,
> And palms before my feet.

The reference to Palm Sunday is not incidental to the poem but the whole point of the poem, and we can't read the poem at all until we've placed the reference. In other poems we get references to Classical myths. There's an early poem of Yeats, called "The Sorrow of Love," where the second stanza went like this:

> And then you came with those red mournful lips,
> And with you came the whole of the world's tears,
> And all the trouble of her labouring ships,
> And all the trouble of her myriad years.

But Yeats was constantly tinkering with his poems, especially the early ones, and in the final edition of his collected poetry we get this instead:

> A girl arose that had red mournful lips
> And seemed the greatness of the world in tears,
> Doomed like Odysseus and the labouring ships
> And proud as Priam murdered with his peers.

The early version is a vague, and the later one a precise, reference to something else in the literary tradition, and Yeats thought that the precise reference was an improvement.

This allusiveness in literature is significant, because it shows what we've been saying all along, that in literature you don't just read one poem or novel after another, but enter into a complete world of which every work of literature forms part. This affects the writer as much as it does the reader. Many people think that the original writer is always directly inspired by life, and that only commonplace or derivative writers get inspired by books. That's nonsense: the only inspiration worth having is an inspiration that clarifies the form of what's being written, and that's more likely to come from something that already has a literary form. We don't often find that a poem depends completely on an allusion, as Chesterton's poem does, but allusiveness runs all through our literary experience. If we don't know the Bible and the central stories of Greek and Roman literature, we can still read books and see plays, but our knowledge of literature can't grow, just as our knowledge of mathematics can't grow if we don't learn the multiplication table. Here we touch on an educational problem, of what should be read when, that we'll have to come back to later.

I said earlier that there's nothing new in literature that isn't the old reshaped. The latest thing in drama is the theatre of the absurd, a completely wacky form of writing where anything goes and there are no rational rules. In one of these plays, Ionesco's *La Chauve Cantatrice* ("The Bald Soprano" in English), a Mr. and Mrs. Martin are talking. They think they must have seen each other before, and discover that they travelled in the same train that morning, that they have the same name and address, sleep in the same bedroom, and both have a two-year-old daughter named Alice. Eventually Mr. Martin decides that he must be talking to his long lost wife Elizabeth. This scene is built on two of the solidest conventions in literature. One is the ironic situation in which two people are intimately related and yet know nothing about each other; the other is the ancient and often very corny device that critics call the "recognition scene," where the long lost son and heir turns up from Australia in the last act. What makes the Ionesco scene funny is the fact that it's a parody or take-off of these familiar conventions. The allusiveness of literature is part of its symbolic quality, its capacity to absorb everything from natural or human life into its own imaginative body.

Another well-known poem, Wordsworth's "I wandered lonely as a cloud," tells how Wordsworth sees a field of daffodils, and then finds later that:

They flash upon that inward eye
Which is the bliss of solitude;
And then my heart with pleasure fills,
And dances with the daffodils.

The flowers become poetic flowers as soon as they're identified with a human mind. Here we have an image from the natural world, a field of daffodils: it's enclosed inside the human mind, which puts it into the world of the imagination, and the sense of human vision and emotion radiating from the daffodils, so to speak, is what gives them their poetic magic. The human mind is Wordsworth's individual mind at first, but as soon as he writes a poem it becomes our minds too. There is no self-expression in Wordsworth's poem, because once the poem is there the individual Wordsworth has disappeared. The general principle involved is that there is really no such thing as self-expression in literature.

In other words, it isn't just the historical figure who gets taken over by literature: the poet gets taken over too. As we said in our first talk, the poet as a person is no wiser or better a man than anyone else. He's a man with a special craft of putting words together, but he may have no claim on our attention beyond that. Most of the well-known poets have well-known lives, and some of them, like Byron, have had some highly publicized love affairs. But it's only for incidental interest that we relate what a poet writes to his own life. Byron wrote a poem to a maid of Athens, and there really was a maid of Athens, a twelve-year-old girl whose price, set by her mother, was 30,000 piastres, which Byron refused to pay. Wordsworth wrote some lovely poems about a girl named Lucy, but he made Lucy up. But Lucy is just as real as the maid of Athens. With some poets, with Milton for example, we feel that here is a great man who happened to be a poet, but would still have been great whatever he did. With other equally great poets, including Homer and Shakespeare, we feel only that they were great poets. We know nothing about Homer: some people think there were two Homers or a committee of Homers. We think of a blind old man, but we get that notion from one of Homer's characters. We know nothing about Shakespeare except a signature or two, a few addresses, a will, a baptismal register, and the picture of a man who is clearly an idiot. We relate the poems and plays and novels we read and see, not to the men who wrote them, nor even directly to ourselves; we relate them to each other. Literature is a world that we try to build up and enter at the same time.

Wordsworth's poem is useful because it's one of those poems that tell you what the poet thinks he's trying to do. Here's another poem that tells you nothing, but just gives you the image— Blake's "The Sick Rose":

O Rose, thou art sick!
The invisible worm
That flies in the night,
In the howling storm,

Has found out thy bed
Of crimson joy,
And his dark secret love
Does thy life destroy.

The author of a recent book on Blake, Hazard Adams, says he gave this poem to a class of sixty students and asked them to explain what it meant. Fifty-nine of them turned the poem into an allegory; the sixtieth was a student of horticulture who thought Blake was talking about plant disease. Now whenever you try to explain what any poem means you're bound to turn it into an allegory to some extent: there's no way out of that. Blake *isn't* talking about plant disease, but about something human, and as soon as you "explain" his rose and worm you have to translate them into some aspect of human life and feeling. Here it's the sexual relation that seems to be closest to the poem. But the poem is not really an allegory, and so you can't feel that any explanation is adequate: its eloquence and power and magic get away from all explanations. And if it's not allegorical it's not allusive either. You can think of Eve in the Garden of Eden, standing naked among the flowers—herself a fairer flower, as Milton says—and being taught by the serpent that her naked-ness, and the love that went with it, ought to be something dark and secret. This allusion, perhaps, does help you to understand the poem better, because it leads you toward the centre of Western literary imagination, and introduces you to the family of things Blake is dealing with. But the poem doesn't depend on the Bible, even though it would never have been written with-out the Bible. The student of horticulture got one thing right: he saw that Blake meant what he said when he talked about roses and worms, and not something else. To understand Blake's poem, then, you simply have to accept a world which is totally symbolic: a world in which roses and worms are so completely surrounded and possessed by the human mind that whatever goes on between them is identical with something going on in human life.

You remember that Theseus, in Shakespeare's *A Midsummer Night's Dream*, remarked that:

> The lunatic, the lover, and the poet
> Are of imagination all compact.

Theseus is not a literary critic; he's an amiable stuffed shirt, but just the same his remark has an important truth in it. The lunatic and the lover are trying to identify themselves with something, the lover with his mistress, the lunatic with whatever he's obsessed with. Primitive people also try to identify themselves with totems or animals or spirits. I spoke of the magic in Blake's poem: that's usually a very vague word in criticism, but magic is really a belief in identity of the same kind: the magician makes a wax image of somebody he doesn't like, sticks a pin in it, and the person it's identified with gets a pain. The poet, too, is an identifier: everything he sees in nature he identifies with human life. That's why literature, and more particularly poetry, shows the analogy to primitive minds that I mentioned in my first talk.

The difference is more important. Magic and primitive religion are forms of belief: lunacy and love are forms of experience or action. Belief and action are closely related, because what a man really believes is what his actions show that he believes. In belief you're continually concerned with questions of truth or reality: you can't believe anything unless you can say "this is so." But literature, we remember, never makes any statements of that kind: what the poet and novelist say is more like "let's assume this situation." So there can never be any religion of poetry or any set of beliefs founded on literature. When we stop believing in a religion, as the Roman world stopped believing in Jupiter and Venus, its gods become literary characters, and go back to the world of imagination. But a belief itself can only be replaced by another belief. Writers of course have their own beliefs, and it's natural to feel a special affection for the ones who seem to see things the same way we do. But we all know, or soon realize, that a writer's real greatness lies elsewhere. The world of the imagination is a world of unborn or embryonic beliefs: if you believe what you read in literature, you can, quite literally, believe anything.

6 STEVEN HEIGHTON
Excerpts from the poetry collection
The Ecstasy of Skeptics (1994)

The Thief

We brought him down from the hill with the sun
hot on our shoulders, filed like apostles
past the woodlot's edge, into flourishing shade
where limbs of Lebanon cedar touched him

and left him there among deadfall, folding
the quick, dead hands, knowing his last escape
would go unwitnessed in the isolate
eye of the orchard, after the hawkers' cries,

the clamour and swearing, the brute barter
a cloak of noise that covered him. Fallen
here among olives, the soft inviolate shade
must have troubled him, surely, or would have, if...?

It was bad enough to be ignored at the end,
buckling, splayed like a plummeting angel
in the hot wind, his stammerings swallowed
by the mob's roar; after a lifetime of furtive silence

he must have had something to say to them.
But the congregation hadn't come to hear
and the guards went on to the day's main draw
while their cold carpentry did the trick.

And yet, though nobody listened
he must have found the word—we saw him shudder
and cough, groan, struggle to gesture
but there were nails through his crooked hands

and feet, the barest motion was a trial, the sun
a mass of molten gold. Late afternoon. Long after
the other thief had flagged, and the slender man
on the middle cross, crowned with thistles

grew too weak to amuse the crowd, storm clouds
clustered on the skyline, there was talk of rain
and the crowd thinned before a last fugitive
breath escaped him. As early darkness curtained in

and the dying prophet pleaded with the air
we freed the fallen thief from his cross
and brought him down from the hill.
        We left him lying in the fragrant deadfall

of an orchard, turned, filed away
in the fallen dark along aisles of olive trees
ripe with rain, yet felt on our shoulders
a warmth, like sun: the word on his tongue, still flickering.

The Machine Gunner

I saw them. They came like ghosts out of ground-
mist, moving
over ruined earth in waves, running

no, walking, shoulder to shoulder
like a belt of bullets or like
men: tinned meat lined on a conveyor belt as the sun

exploded in thin shafts on metal
buckles, bayonets, the nodding
spires of helmets. I heard faint battle cries

and whistles, piercing through the shriek
of fire and iron falling, the slurred
cadence of big guns. As they funnelled

like a file of mourners into gaps
in the barbed wire I made quick
calculations and slipped the safety catch.

But held my fire. Alongside me
the boys in the trenches worried them with
rifles, pistols, hand grenades

but they came on, larger now, their faces
almost resolving out of hazed hot
distance, their ranks at close quarters amazing

with dumb courage, numb step, a sound of drugged
choking in gas and green mud, steaming—
Who were these men. I saw them penitent

sagging to knees. I saw their dishevelled
dying. And when finally they broke
into a run it came to me

what they had always been, how I'd always,
really, seen them: boys
rushing toward us with arms

outstretched, hands clenched as if in urgent prayer,
sudden welcome or a reunion
quite unexpected. Yes. And more than this

like children, chased by something behind the lines
and hurrying to us
for rescue—
I spat and swung the gun around. Fired,
felt the metal pulse
and laid them three deep in the wire.

Were You to Die

Were you to die I'd be free to go off
and see the world, and sleep in every elsewhere
I might never arrive
—yet I might choose to travel alone
from window to window looking out
on the streets of your city
where your friends still expect to see you sometimes
or mistake you for someone, out of custom—love—

Without your thrashing, manic dreams, my body
would sleep better
but wake more tired, I'd let the garden go to seed
the way I always meant to
and when I looked out the window into the yard
I'd never miss the snowpeas, beets and roses
but your sunhat I might miss—you hunkered down
in a summer dress, your fingers
grouped like roots in the raised beds,
your stooped, stubborn nape, your cinnamon-
freckled shoulders—

Were you to die, my heart
would be free to pack a bag
and book passage for the riot of islands
I might have been, and shared
with the one and numberless "beloved" we fumble
our whole lives glimpsing
a moment too late
when Eden was always the one who stayed
rooted in her changes, and gave you
the island in her arms, and when you slept
somehow she travelled, and when you woke
she was changed—

Were you to die, my mind
would be free to twist inward
the way fingers fist, and fasten pat
on its own taut notions, theorems, palm shut fast
to the snow that pooled there and seemed to flow through
when the skin still flowered in fullest winter
and I loved you, and thoughts, like books,

were doors that opened outward
not coffins, closed,
not cells—

Were you to die and free me
my body would follow you down into the cold
prison of your passing, and warm you when all the others
had turned away, and try
bribing the keeper with a poem, or fool him
with keychains of chiming words—an elegy
so pure he'd be pressed to cry, eyes
thawing and the earth warmed, April
of carillons and sepals, your opened arms
that bore the sun down with you, warm.

7 JOHN RALSTON SAUL
An excerpt from the CBC Massey Lectures
The Unconscious Civilization (1995)

I. The Great Leap Backwards

... But why do we have this desperate need to believe that the solving of a single problem will solve all our problems? Or that a particular and absolute form of social organization will "bring history to an end"? "The need to fabulate," the French novelist Romain Gary said, "is just a child who refuses to grow up." *"Le besoin d'affabulation, c'est toujours un enfant qui refuse de grandir."*[1]

Yet there is no innocent childish charm hidden within our need to fabulate; none, for example, in Professor Fukuyama's declaration that his side had won and therefore we had come to *The End of History.* Rather there was an unpleasant air of self-serving propaganda. Fabulation in all of us suggests a fear of reality. A weakness for ideology. A need to believe in single-stroke, cure-all solutions. A taste for the intolerance of conformity when we come to public policy. All of which translates into a debilitating passivity when faced by crises.

This suggests that we have difficulty perceiving our own weaknesses. Let me put this another way. If we are unable to identify reality and therefore unable to act upon what we see, then we are not simply childish but have reduced ourselves to figures of fun—ridiculous victims of our unconscious. The conscious human holds happily onto a sense of his own ridiculousness.

Unfortunately, our sense of the ridiculous in ourselves seems to ebb and flow, but to remain dangerously weak when it comes to public affairs. And the weaker it is, the more we tend to slip into an unhealthy, unconscious form of self-contempt. Worse still, we cultivate this loathing in our elites. We encourage them to think of us—the citizenry—with contempt, and so to think of themselves in the same way.

If we cannot see ourselves, then we cannot act as humans. It is hardly surprising that the result is a loss of self-respect.

This self-loathing is key to our weakness for ideology. Those who have the "truth" are by definition a small minority. They are the elect. Their desire is not to convince the rest of us of their truth. It isn't a matter of democratic debate with all the compromise that involves. They have the truth. The aim of the ideologue is therefore to manipulate, trick or force the majority into acceptance. People whom you intend to manipulate, trick or force are people for whom you have contempt. And if they, the majority, allow themselves to be taken in, well then, they do have contempt for themselves.

The modern version of this process first appeared during the Reformation—on both sides of the debate. The Protestants who accepted predestination accepted a profoundly passive existence for themselves. It is true that spreading the word was important but good works would get them nowhere. God had already chosen who would be saved. Everyone had but to wait for death to find out their ultimate destination. If, however, a small group could somehow convince itself that it knew the mind of God and that its members *were* the chosen few—the elect—well, then, they could throw off their passivity and drive the condemned majority before them. All and any methods were justified because the elect alone held the truth.

This was also the mentality of Ignatius Loyola and his Jesuits, who picked up the Protestant methods, thus adding a firm rational structure to Catholicism. Their intent was to give shape and weaponry to the Counter Reformation. Here was the beginning of modern ideology and absolutism.

The Jacobins of the French Revolution, the Bolsheviks, the Fascists, and now the free marketeers, are all the direct descendants of predestination and the Jesuits. They are the chosen few—the minority who have the truth and therefore have the right to impose it by whatever means.

Am I really being fair, throwing in among such a violent, bloody crew the market disciples, with their Chicago School of Economics *bona fides*, and their endless Nobel prizes, to say nothing of the neo-conservatives who are in general wonderfully educated?

Listen to Michael Oakeshott, the English philosopher, now dead, who is one of the father figures of the neo-conservatives. Politics, he said, is "vulgar," "bogus," "callous," because of the sort of people it attracts and "because of the false simplification of human life implied in even the best of its purposes."[2] Politics, he believes, should be left in the hands of men from the traditional political families, not some democratic, ambitious person.[3]

This same loathing for the majority can be found in the political philosopher Leo Strauss, who gave birth, in a sense, to Allan Bloom, who in turn, with great intelligence and style, demonstrated to the American public via his book *The Closing of the American Mind* that most of them were of an inferior nature. Intellectuals here and there followed suit. Botho Strauss, the well-known German playwright, wrote a trend-setting article in 1993 for *Der Spiegel* along somewhat the same lines.[4] He wrote it in a high literary German, incomprehensible to the majority of readers. Yet this elitism somehow inspired the rising groups of violent skinheads in Germany. Here is a vibrant example of self-hatred. The skinheads were inspired by an argument which, in its very form, denigrated them.

A little bevy of youngish Americans, mainly the sons of either rich or well-established families, has constituted itself as the North American branch of this movement. These are the eager courtiers of neo-conservatism. The atmosphere which reigns in their language is one of an embattled minority elite seeking ways to manoeuvre, manipulate and fool the majority into passive acceptance. In a recent public conversation they could be heard saying such things as:

"We can't really go to poor black people and throw them off welfare if we haven't first gone to rich white farmers and thrown them off welfare."

and

"The big programs, like welfare, Medicaid and Medicare, will take a little time to get rid of. But there are a lot of little ones that we can get rid of right away."

and

"...it's dangerous for the Party to seem callous." (Note the word "seem.")

On the other hand:

"In the current environment being accused of callousness might even be to our advantage."[5]

Their air of cynical bitterness, in spite of their own comfortable situations, also suggests an unconsciousness of their own profound self-loathing. The tone throughout is one of religious sadomasochism. 'We have done wrong. We have had it easy. We indebted ourselves. Now we must pay. We must don hair shirts. We must impose suffering upon ourselves.' Of course, the suffering will fall on others, but that is beside the point.

The Italians have a wonderful word to describe a mummy's boy—*un mammone*. When I hear or read these people I can't help thinking of a daddy's boy. *Un pappone*. Someone who tries to be as tough as or tougher than his father.

In any case, their approach is pure Reformation politico-religious rhetoric. And like those church leaders 400 years ago, the new variety must, as the Canadian writer, M. T. Kelly, puts it, "create the other—the devil." This demonization is also essential to deny any "goodness or moral value to the other side."[6]

In fairness to the courtier tradition, it is important to add that by no means all of them have been, like the neo-conservatives, bitter and cynical. History has been full of men and women who had to sing one tune or another for their supper. Often they had no choice if they wanted to play a public role. They were victims of the reigning social structure. Our society today is very much like that. The highly educated, technocratic, specialized elites who make up more than a third of our population are caught in structures which require of them courtier-like behaviour.

Today, as in history, their ranks are filled with people who try their best. They put up with the indignity of their role in order to eat—yes, we all must eat—but also in order to serve a good cause.

On the other hand, history also records a group of courtiers who have taken pleasure in the humiliation which their status demands. Often they were successful precisely because their self-loathing and cynicism allowed them to make the most of a situation that rewarded crude ambition and manipulation.

Shakespeare was particularly good at portraying the two types of courtiers, side by side. Inner strength versus weakness. An ethical centre versus vain ambition. A sense of the public good versus a wounded sense of having been personally wronged. Kent versus Edmund in *King Lear*. Rodrigo versus Iago in *Othello*.

The Iagos and Edmunds of our day are by no means limited to the ranks of neo-conservatism. As we gaze around at ministers' offices, at departmental administrations, at corporate executive suites, we can see courtiers of all sorts making their way.

But the neo-conservative courtiers do appear to fall almost as a group into this category. Given that they are of age and legally responsible for their actions, this must be treated by society as a matter of their own choice.

NOTES

1. Emile Ajar (Romain Gary), *Pseudo*, Mercure de France.

2. Robert Grant, *Thinkers of Our Time: Oakeshott* (London: The Claridge Press, 1990), 15. The construct of these quotes is taken directly from Grant, an admirer of Oakeshott.

3. Grant, 62. Again the formulation is taken from Grant.

4. *Le Monde*, 24 February 1995.

5. *Harper's*, March 1995, 43-53.

6. Conversation with M.T. Kelly, June 1995.

8 MARIE-CLAIRE BLAIS

An excerpt from the novel *These Festive Nights* (1997)

The long silent street that ran down to the ocean in the moonlight appeared to Luc, who was chatting with his friends from
the open window of a bar where he sat swinging his legs, someone asked why he didn't go out every night as he used to, and
what had happened to that friend of his, a cultivated man, a little
self-conscious, sometimes arrogant, they didn't see him around
any more, smoking his hashish all alone at the bar, Jacques, yes,
where was he now, caustic, droll too, amusing and seductive,
people still remembered his birthday last Easter, the town was
still talking about it, surrounded by this din of voices, of deafening music, draped in a solicitude he preferred not to respond to
that night, Luc felt a need to leave, and in a leap he spun around
on his skates, catching his breath and then travelling almost
soundlessly down Bahama Street, over the sparkling asphalt,
climbing onto cracked sidewalks where, as he glided along at a
nearly fluid speed, he felt dry, thorny flowers raining down on
his head; light-headed from the perfume of the bougainvillea, of
the magnolias and acacia that were all in bloom at this time of
year, he grabbed hold of a branch of crimson flowers, bit it off
with an agitated rustling that brought a woman in a nightgown
onto her balcony, who is that, she asked, another one of those
drug-crazed Negroes, the dogs, call the dogs, Luc raced away on
his skates, spitting flowers as he went, at last he saw the ocean
glittering in the moonlight and he let himself be carried along

to the wharf, in the phosphorescent green wake that emanated from his skates, from their laces, their straps, he listened to the waves rolling under the boards of the pier where the boats had tied up till the next day, and suddenly he came to a halt, scowling, for he hoped to travel far away, as far as Australia, where with Paul he would learn to be a cattle trader, a horse breeder, a farmer brimming with health, the head of a family perhaps, all of it, so he could forget the precariousness of existence, from now on he would have to hide from Jacques the sight of those stains on the sheets, that brownish liquid discharge whose odour soiled everything, but the elegant cruise ships Luc had seen berthing in the harbour that morning were already sailing towards other islands, the fishing boats, like the small sailboats lined up along the pier, inviting the tourist on safaris that would strip the bloom off the lacy underwater fauna adhering to the coral, borrowing its colours, each of those boats, thought Luc, each of those sailboats, with the shadow of its masts wavering in the moonlight on the water, would soon be a house being driven out to sea, a house, a dwelling, perhaps his own one day, where behind the curtain in his cabin he would live among his books, with a dog at his feet, in the company of a faithful love, fishing for shark and dolphin every day with Paul, he would escape the line of fire they heard rumbling in the sky, was it the sound of lightning as it struck the trees near the house, or a bomb exploding in the depths of the ocean, the approaching flames would be their warning, it would keep them awake, coming closer and closer both in the churning water and in the silent bedroom where the sick man was confined, stretching his feeble arms out to the sun at the window, the weather had been beautiful the day they got the news, they were at the home of a writer who was celebrating his belated but magnificent success by having a swimming pool put in, even though he didn't have a house yet, and it was there, around a marble pool, leaning over water not yet cleared of the leaves and debris left by a storm, that they had been sipping their martinis, laughing, when they saw him, heard him, and though the day was glorious, Luc had seen the lightning rend the sky, what was Jacques saying in veiled terms, in a low voice, as he stood next to them, what was he saying with his quiet but feigned assurance, while his blue eyes peered at them with bitter resignation, a dirty business, my friends, it has to end quickly, very quickly, they had seen the nervous tension in his smile when Jacques suddenly left his hosts and went home, the air and the sky were blazing that day, and with a brutal gesture that seemed suddenly to separate him from the rest of the world, Jacques had thrown his still-lit cigarette into the pool, and shortly afterwards Luc had seen him disappear around the corner near the Cemetery of the Roses, Jacques was wearing a short-sleeved blue shirt, light blue like his eyes, buttons open on his powerful chest; determined, hostile, and alone, he would not turn around as he walked, that day Luc had heard the rumble of a storm brewing in the sky, the funereal music seemed to well up by itself, he could hear it in the sound of the waves beneath his feet, in the sky where a cloud veiled the moon, it was the evening breeze that was stirring his soul, he thought, Luc and Paul would live for a long time, one day they'd be seen greeting their friends from those elegant ships that set out every day for distant seas, he was late, borne along by his skates, the iridescent light of their straps and their laces, Luc travelled down the street again, he opened the garden gate that Jacques never closed against thieves, in his celestial flight along the streets and sidewalks, swept up in the nighttime intoxication, stretching out his arms on either side of him, Luc had the impression that he was running towards Jacques, that he was unfurling wings around him, and as he pushed the wooden gate before him he could sense in the roots of his hair the tinkling of small oriental bells, the bells purchased after a visit to a temple, when Jacques had walked barefoot through Bangkok because someone had stolen his sandals, for a long time, Luc thought, the tinkling of those bells at the garden gate, the sound of those bells among the flowers, had announced the return of the carefree pilgrim, you could still hear the engaging timbre of his voice when he called to his friends, hop over the wall and come have a drink, and suddenly that voice was barely audible, or was merely a sigh, soon the voice rising from the big hospital bed that had been transported to the bedroom would be heard no longer; as he was taking off his skates on the path that led to Jacques's room, Luc could see the sick man dozing by the window, he seemed more rested, his sleep was calm, the bedside lamp that illuminated his face shone as brightly as the moon, all the way to the back of the room, onto the books scattered over a table, its harsh light setting fire to Jacques's unclothed body amid the sheets that he pulled out all around him every night, as if he was afraid they would smother him, it was true, thought Luc, that he could suddenly hear heavenly arpeggios, because *Amadeus*, the film Jacques had wanted to watch, was still running, and sitting at the foot of the bed with its fetid odours, Luc compared the lovemaking of the young Mozart with his own desires, his passion for amorous adventure, even tonight on a beach he had once again yielded, quickly, he would be more cautious tomorrow, it was as if they'd been at sea on a raft some windless night, Luc and Jacques were sailing far away from the bedroom where they were both prisoners, thought Luc, surrounded by the heavenly music they could hear, one of them asleep, the other awake, his spirits brightened by alcohol, where were they sailing like this if God didn't want them in His mansion, let them drift and sing as they used to when they went sailing with Paul, devoting themselves to underwater fishing, let the sun spread its warmth over them, let them laugh and sing and never know pain, rancour, anger, or humiliation, let them stream through the waves on their sailboards, run along the beaches, the sandy shores of the ocean, until dawn, or let them travel so far into the peace of the waters that they lost their way, with the stigmata on their bodies that were once so beautiful, let them disappear into the waves, fade away without voice or cry, while above them flickered those luminous green signals that guide ships in the night, in his sensual breathlessness Luc had often been touched by the sense of radiant intimacy with another, he experienced it now while listening to Mozart, those few brief seconds of pure, palpable love in the arms of men, those shoulders, those backs sealing a hidden authority, arching with delight under the caresses of his lips, the smell of those rough, voluptuous skins whose fears he untangled amid cries of deliverance, had he known anything more enduring on this earth, the brevity of those seconds, those moments, had overwhelmed his simple soul which asked for nothing more, and soon, perhaps, he would be alone, for he had seen the lights of the final hour flare up on the sea, each of those boats, those sailboats, would leave without him, in the glittering night, with opalescent globes at the summit of their masts, the young captain who had approached him on the beach an hour ago called his dog back to the gangway with a whistle, he had shut the door to his studious cabin, tonight he would open Conrad's book, which he had not had time to read when he was cut off by a storm in the Bahamas, he would listen to Vivaldi while he sailed towards the Indian Ocean, heading for Madagascar, which would be his destination this time, the captain had first gone to sea at seventeen, he had seen Panama, Tahiti, he'd been imprisoned in Australia, in Costa Rica, he'd been wounded in one knee, his dog came running towards him along the gangway, they would all set off again without Luc, without Paul, each of these sailboats, each of these craft in the night, and those fetid odours rose from the bed where Jacques lay moaning, I'm coming, here I am, said Luc, approaching him with all the firmness, the assurance of the movements he had learned with men, Luc freed Jacques of his soiled sheets, he washed him, cleaned him, smiling and chatting all the while, used a towel soaked in cologne to wipe away the traces of brownish discharge from Jacques's thighs, his belly, it's time, said Jacques, yes, the time has come to call the doctor for the shots, I've had enough of this filth, when will it be over? And taking the sick man in his arms Luc said, you should get some sleep now, I won't leave you, Paul will be back soon, it's time to close your eyes and sleep, said Luc, and he began to laugh nervously because it seemed to him that this cascade of warm laughter that suddenly shook him would save them both, would rekindle the green signal lights a navigator followed when he was in peril at sea, and those iridescent globes at the summit of the main masts, and Jacques, who in the past had so enjoyed laughing and having fun with his friends, Jacques in turn laughed a huge laugh, as if he'd been surprised once again by those little pleasures life could bring him, an orgasm—hesitant but serene—a burst of laughter in the night, while a vigorous boy tried to soothe him by rubbing his back and his skeletal shoulders, freshening his soiled flesh with an oily cologne, Jacques thought, when all was lost, all was lost, as he got up to put on the tape of *Amadeus* again he had felt that sudden pain in his guts, the release of the revolting brownish stream that spread around him, so all was lost, and yet celestial music was still coming from the TV set at the back of the room, was it the song of the bassoon, of the oboe he could suddenly hear in the depths, in the obscurity of his suffering, for he knew now that all was lost, tomorrow Luc would call the nurse for the injections, they would summon his sister, they'd let Tanjou know, and meanwhile—how ironic, he thought—Mozart was asking Salieri for a little break; laying down his pen, he was asking for a little break before he finished writing his Requiem, no doubt the traitor Salieri represented the banality of fate, the executioner of mediocrity was hounding the child beloved of God, as he listened to these words, the little break, with the song of the oboe, the bassoon, he thought Mozart had felt their notes falling around him like lightning flashes, as he turned his head Jacques thought he could hear the prelude to that eternity he was unsure what to make of, while Mozart's eternity, like his life, seemed to have been laid out in advance; for hadn't God thought of everything in his child's chaotic path, the surfeit of solemn notes like the sarcasm of archbishops and princes, even the yawning of an emperor who had destroyed masterpieces, the entire assemblage had been conceived by God alone and, who knows, for His own glory, the man who was known as Herr Mozart had never had to look for his birth certificate, any more than for the common grave in which he would be buried, the spectre of the sovereign father would follow him everywhere, and not until it was time for the little break that was suddenly so long would Heaven's divine buffoon rest at last, not to sleep but to hear the indescribable song that had been born in him, upon this earth; Luc and Jacques had laughed together, for demented though that laughter might be, it had the spontaneity of misfortune and good fortune combined, as Luc was still there and Paul would be home in an hour, and one must bow to divine will when, like Salieri, one embodies a banal destiny that goes astray, a light that travels by itself, with no harbour, no attachments, no shore, when all is lost, all is lost.

Translation by Sheila Fischman

9 ESTA SPALDING

Excerpts from the poetry collection *Anchoress* (1997)

What she sees

Because what she believed was
big enough for this world—or it was

too small, something anyone
could pack in an overnight bag, strap on
a back, carry at the end of a stick (not even
drooping under the weight), because

it was dangerous, incendiary,
uninspected. Because those who could strike

the match were miles away, boarding
helicopters, hugging wives, sons, daughters,
waving to the crowd (with closed fingers),
were in choppers lifting off from aircraft carriers
(stirring up the brine—the names of the dead
lifting off the waves towards them
in a speech they cannot interpret),

because what she believed crawled
in her belly, rumbling through
the tunnels in her body, shaking her skin

(I put my hand on her wrist
and felt it),
it was not satisfied by rhetoric.

Because it was beautiful
and she fed it.

.   .   .

A painted ibex
in the headlights,
a whale in an ice
sheet, frozen

by her love. Nothing
like her had ever touched me before,
I was in a cavern whose markings I did not recognize.
No recipes.
Colours from a different spectrum.
It was blood inventing channels into new life,
it stung. The way life stings.
The way it hurts to eat when you've been
hungry.

When a despot wants to starve the people
he does not burn their rice, he breaks
their cooking pots.

I came to her without a vessel.

.   .   .

Students thick in the quadrangles,
the sun lecherous

on the white stone buildings, that grey city,
mound of bones, she squats below
the flagpole, dog chain around her neck
and hung from it the sign, *Peace*,
she means this, lifting the heavy metal
canister and bending her neck forward,
as a woman washing her hair will bend
her neck forward, her hair falling over her face

she soaks in gasoline, pours it down her neck,
heavy canister, sloshing gas on her back,
ribbons of gasoline
splash on her jeans, her feet, the snow
on the ground catches it
in pools that rainbow around her, furious
birds overhead, and squirrels, feeding,
oblivious

Helen's poem

My feet are for burning,
are for burning, to send up an SOS.

My back is for burning,
is for burning, a signal flare, a promise.

My face is for sweet burning,
is for sweet burning, my only gift.

And I am for burning, a black candle lit for you.

. . .

On fire, dancing. Everyone could see
her eyes, their screaming, someone ran to her
released the rope from the pole
wrapped her electric body
in the flag.

. . .

Helen's song

Come into my ship, Love, light the lantern's wick, for I have
trailed too long elsewhere, come Love, I was so near melting
into something, bird, beast, butterfly, threatening to be only
human, Love, I twisted for your taste, waited for you, to feel
you uncurl, flag in me, candle
    I want all atoms to open, dust, the silent stretches
between them, unfurl long rows of cables strung, post to
post, the rich fuel of oxygens to burst, mercury flung
    Breathe to inhale one another, breathe to eat other lives,
how they build, rumble, stretch, lift the stiff filaments of
their wings, roil into compounds, attached, unattached to
the throng of this body,
    The world is too dispersed already, Love, too cyanide,
too bereft, *love is nearer death*
    Spooling, nursing on its elements—nitrates, phosphates,
benzene, each ring, my ring—*I live without living myself, and
in such a way I hope, I die because I do not die*
    My bones, match sticks, knots of mineral, each envelope,
cell, turned inside out, *arriving in magic, flying, and finally,*

insane for the light, I am Oroboros: searing, raining majestic
ruin, honeying, the velocity of my love for this world.

. . .

Did she reach Baghdad?
Did she, did she, reach it? Give her body?
Did she meet them on the bridge
over the slow river
from New Chicago to the other world,
say, *here I am with you,*
I know how burning is?

Helen's dialogue

If you burn I will burn too.
I never really believed in life.
I believed only in life, I loved all of you,
I never loved you, I loved only
myself, let me take you into my arms, my house,
my life, *none of these is mine to give, good-bye,*
the earth is home, *death is home,* the earth
is all we have, *no, no, death is what we're working for,*
yes, *no,* I love you, I am you, *I can love*
no one, can never understand you, I am,
I die, I die because your life is worth everything,
your life is worth nothing for I am willing
to give up mine.

10 JEAN VANIER

An excerpt from the nonfiction book *Becoming Human* (1998)

II. Belonging
The Difficult Place of Those Who Are Weaker

...Those who are weak have great difficulty finding their place in our society. The image of the ideal human as powerful and capable disenfranchises the old, the sick, the less-abled. For me, society must, by definition, be inclusive of the needs and gifts of all its members; how can we lay claim to making an open and friendly society where human rights are respected and fostered when, by the values we teach and foster, we systematically exclude segments of our population?

I also believe that those we most often exclude from the normal life of society, people with disabilities, have profound lessons to teach us. When we do include them, they add richly to our lives and add immensely to our world.

Our society is geared to growth, development, progress. Life, for most of us, is a race to be won. Families are about evolution: at a certain stage, children are encouraged to leave home, get married, have children of their own, move on in their lives. But people with disabilities have no such future. Once they have reached a certain level of development, they are no longer expected or encouraged to progress. There is no "promotion" for the disabled and what forward movement there is seems frequently to be either erratic or cruelly sped up: many move quite quickly from childhood to adulthood without passing through a period of adolescence; others age quickly. Our society is not set up to cope very well with people who are weaker or slower. More important, we are not skilled at listening to the wisdom of those whose life patterns are outside of the social norm.

There is a lack of synchronicity between our society and people with disabilities. A society that honours only the powerful, the clever, and the winners necessarily belittles the weak. It is as if to say: to be human is to be powerful.

Those who see the heart only as a place of weakness will be fearful of their own hearts. For them, the heart is a place of pain and anguish, of chaos and of transitory emotions. So they reject those who live essentially by their hearts, who cannot develop the same intellectual and rational capacities as others. People with intellectual disabilities are excluded; it was never intended that they be included as equal partners with the powerful, with you and me.

Our notions of society and our belief systems flow from our own fundamental experiences of life, of death, of joy, and of anguish. If we have never experienced a love that is liberating, how can we talk of love as valuable? If our journey through life has been one of conflict and power, then our image of the ideal person will be of one who prevails in conflict and wields power with assurance.

The history of our world is the history of conflicts, of one group demonstrating its strength over another. Weakness is at the heart of the need to belong; weakness that we may fear, because we have been hurt. So we band together in groups in order to share our common strength. So easily from this does conflict arise. Each group is secure in certitudes and ideology. From there it is a small step to indifference, to despisal, and to suspicion: the fear and hatred of others.

In all conflicts between groups, there are three elements. One: the certitude that our group is morally superior, possibly even chosen by God. All others should follow our example or be at our service. In order to bring peace to the world, we have to impose our set of beliefs upon others, through manipulation, force, and fear, if necessary. Two: a refusal or incapacity to see or admit to any possible errors or faults in our group. The undeniable nature of our own goodness makes us think we are infallible; there can be no wrong in us. Three: a refusal to believe that any other group possesses truth or can contribute anything of value. At best, others may be regarded as ignorant, unenlightened, and possessing only half-truths; at worst, they are seen as destructive, dangerous, and possessed by evil spirits: they need to be overpowered for the good of humanity. Society and cultures are, then, divided into the "good" and the "bad"; the good attributing to themselves the mission to save, to heal, to bring peace to a wicked world, according to their own terms and under their controlling power.

Such is the story of all civilizations through the ages as they spread over the earth by invading and colonizing. Differences must be suppressed; "savages" must be civilized. We must prove by all possible means that our culture, our power, our knowledge, and our technology are the best, that our gods are the only gods!

This is not just the story of civilizations but also of all wars of religion, inquisitions, censorships, dictatorships; all things, in short, that are ideologies. An ideology is a set of ideas translated into a set of values. Because they are held to be absolutely true, these ideas and values need to be imposed on others if they are not readily accepted. A political system, a school of psychology, and a philosophy of economics can all be ideologies. Even a place of work can be an ideology. Religious sub-groups, sects, are based upon ideological principles. Religions themselves can become ideologies. And ideologues, by their nature, are not open to new ideas or even to debate; they refuse to accept or listen to anyone else's reality. They refuse to admit any possibility of error or even criticism of their system; they are closed up in their set of ideas, theories, and values.

We human beings have a great facility for living illusions, for protecting our self-image with power, for justifying it all by thinking we are the favoured ones of God.

And this is not only something from past history; it is our world today. The civil wars in Algeria, the genocide in Rwanda, the conflict in the former Yugoslavia, the tension between Israelis and Palestinians, the way men and women are treated in the most abominable way for their beliefs, and the way the weak, those with disabilities, are written out of the equation of life, are all signs of this need to dictate that one group is right and the other wrong.

How difficult it is for human beings to move from the recognition of the ultimate value of their own particular culture and way of life to the acceptance of the value of other cultures and ways of living. This movement implies a weakening in our own certitudes and identity, a shifting of consciousness and a lowering of protective walls. The discovery of our common humanity, beneath our differences, seems for many to be dangerous. It not only means that we have to lose some of our power, privilege, and self-image, but also that we have to look at the shadow side in ourselves, the brokenness, and even the evil in our own hearts and culture; it implies moving into a certain insecurity.

THE

FOURTH DECADE

—

1997–2007

1 A SAMPLING OF THE POETRY

LYNN CROSBIE
Excerpts from the poetry collection *Queen Rat* (1998)

Nine Hammer Blows
(FOR KENNETH HALLIWELL)

John, we used the language as if we made it
    — Robert Lowell

People don't like to be told
that you're sick
and then be forced
to watch
you
come
down
with the hammer.
    — Anne Sexton

A deliberate form of frenzy—John, who sleeps so easily, and I, setting out barbiturates, grapefruit juice: *If you read his diary all will be explained. Especially the latter part*, I wrote,

and crushed his skull with nine hammer blows. He is still warm when
     I lie down.
My eyes closing, I see blood on the Magdalene, the mandolin, my design—

it has come to this. The latter part—eight pages—has disappeared,
     the diary ends
and what, what became of us in early August. It was painfully bright;
     I do not care
what others think, and pause at the black-spiked entrance gate,

drawing its points across my throat. You're sick, he says and leaves,
     more often these days, or
presses a napkin to the telephone. I hear murmured devotions, *soon, patience
my love*—

he loved me once, that I was sick, the things I saw. Spider monkeys in
roses, a ladder of cats' heads.

               sometimes I love poverty, a friend wrote; I miss everything.
               I was the first

to explain tragedy to him (*not wisely but too well*), to lubricate
     my fingers
and open him, tenderly easing the petals of the rosette, my tongue in his
     urethra, a taste of honey

much sweeter than wine, music, slipping between our single beds to kiss
     and the slow sedative
caress. The poppy is the first bloom I place on the walls, radiant, it
     pollinates the field

I attend with my paste and scissors. I do not have his facility with
     words, the orderly entries, dated,

detailed. The scent of cherry, urinal stones, the cup of a stranger's hand
      on his balls,

my orchids. I iron his briefs and pillowslips, trying to smooth the
      disorder, sheer terror is all I feel,
and the walls become heavy with paradise, marble gods recast, the
      choir invisible, angels striking

Moroccan princes. We were so still in the sand I thought we may
      never rise, the funereal
smoke of *kif* burning in censers, yellow-shirts embalming us with their
      religious lips.

I was his shadow, paling behind him a little cloud. The hammerclaws
      leave two impressions
on my palm. That he cannot leave me, so much is lost already (slivers
      of paper, haloes, shields),

how necessary shadows are. The fastened grey shape that retreats in
      pursuit, that may precede you.
Revealing your presence, gesturing to the distance of the sun,

I had to remove my clothing as I fell to my knees. Dying, you were still able
      to produce antiphony,
red flares of blood shining in the eclipse, the yellow fire in me.

Close to you I try to touch you, I see eight sheets fall like linens, like spirits.
As immaterial as purity, as sacred as the shadows

that seek me and falter, erased in the flames, a disclosure—

      We went to bed early. Kenneth was looking wan.

      Monday 31 July 1967.

The Snake Pit
(FOR TONY)

I know the purity of pure despair
— Theodore Roethke

He is often tired this fall, his eyes—purple shadows,
narcotic flowers. Glassine bags, black envelopes, ill-concealed secrets
I discover, sunflower dust, faint streaks of powder.

His horror of water, its purity and the sweetness he desires;
his mouth is burnt sugar, a honeycomb
where gorgeous insects recline.

I am afraid of anger, exhaustion: I'm just tired, my mother would say,
        as she
retreated to her bed; she would not speak for days. James sleeps
        and wakes
in strange furies: *you've never loved me, you wish I could take you places—*

into the water, his body washing to the shore wreathed in seaweed
        and fire-coral.
Beyond recognition, he lies, and I believe him. Because I have my
        own secrets,

the same sweet tooth, the blue dissolution, a desire for serenity. When
the world is too much with me, and I revile myself,

forget to breathe. The first time I met him, shooting stars, once, twice,
my veins recoiled from the needle: *Is this what you want?*

I wanted to retreat, to see beautiful things—the scars on his wrists,
our dishevelled hair, the cracks in the tiles—transformed;

he once lived by the water, collecting dead flowers and fish bones. He
        came to me with nothing,
and never left. We began to assemble these things together.

Broken elemental objects, as mysterious in origin as he, as the
        painting he made,
where he levitates above me, dormant and formless,

I'm just tired, he said, and disappeared. Later, there is a call; he has
        been institutionalized,
a breakdown. I visit him often, finding him in the long antiseptic corridors,
in the ice of his prim white bed.

We listen to someone play the piano—*some say love, it is a river,*
        I kiss him,
and ask him to get better. At night, he combs the winter streets for
        heroin, and sinks deeper
into the glacial corners of his sheets.

When he finds his way through the bleak cold he sees something
        growing—a fast seedling,
unattended, irreducible. It is as trite and as ravishing as the tentative music
that played for us,

the seed, *that with the sun's love*, in the spring,

becomes the rose.

Vive Karaoke (Kensington and Baldwin, 1993)

Tên Bán Nhac: "You Light Up My Life"

So many days: spent at the old Quoc Té. Formerly Peter's punks-
drugs-music clubhouse, now a karaoke bar—rumours of back
alley garrotting, gunshots. One night a Vietnamese gang gets
close, is deflected by our bracelets: sandalwood beads & glass
Buddha. They sing for us instead **Now mothers tell your children, not to do what I have done.**

I'd sit by my window, waiting for someone to sing me his song:
Afternoons are for Marjorie, we are alone in orange hooker wigs,
letting discs ride, clapping for each other. Our loneliness and pale
desires—her voice too much like air, and my one gig at the
Paddock, singing "I Fall to Pieces," falling to pieces I am so afraid.

                    [later at the bar by the Grand Ole Opry I
will sing the hell out of this song where Hank Williams rests,
drinking and writing, knowing that he is pulling up dead]

Nights with Chris or Richard or Andrew (dressed as John
Shaft), other serenades:

I'm just a jealous guy.

So many dreams, kept deep inside me: of blue smoke, the brilliant
facets of the mirrored ball, cocktails coursing through me, ice
and tonic: wanting to kiss everyone, to kill them (in one prism
my green sleeves a praying mantis). They ride Spadina north
home, waving white

handkerchiefs I keep folded in my pocket
                              made up, my tears are black.

Alone in my heart, but now you've come along: He isn't drinking
anymore but he follows me down Kensington, slipping away.
Pretending I need protection and I ask him to duck downstairs
for a quick song. Dangerous, what William calls **scaraoke**, we
order double scotch, drain them, two songs and no one has
missed us. Feeling as though I have met my match

gunslinger liar inscrutable thrillseeker, it has always sounded like
this—

It can't be wrong when it feels so right: Because the Night Belongs
to Lovers seeps into the backseat we have ignored—all night
our only chance to meet him, because the night covers us, long
before Love is an Angel

it is cruel and left-handed,

singing the words in another language, summoning the day.

                    When we walk through the Market the sun is bright
                    Pain and pleasure unite us, walking past VIVE

He tells me the only thing a gambler needs is a suitcase and a
trunk.

Packs his clothes so neatly, they are like crescent rolls. And pops
them in the drawer I have marked M:

a Peter Lorre film about compulsion, that it cannot be helped.

MICHAEL REDHILL
Excerpts from *Light-crossing* (2001)

Cependant

In the traces of creosote from the neighbour's walls, a memory, not mine
of the settlers' smoky outbuildings, the black tar seeping into the green
where later the vested conquerors played golf. One had massed his troops
too far east, guarding the mouth of the river, the other climbed the cliffs
with the future in his teeth. This morning, the song of finch and grackle
weave the air, two language, and the neighbour's new basement yields
pottery fragments where he crushes his cigarette (wondering
what grainy soups were once spooned up from it). The book in front of me forces
caincailleries and cependant up through the yellow air but I forget words
as soon as I learn them, stumble back onto standbys, communicate
without expressing. In the old city, foreign brides are defrocked en masse, later
they stand under the statues squinting in the river-reflected light. Walking
through the plains later, I see groundhog whelps nested in a cup of
red fabric, their blind heads searching through the gold thread for milk.

Sudden

I

Black and yellow, a sepiaed X ray, the edge and centre of a bruise. Shallow
water at the lake-rim is yellow, looking down from a canoe (the distant
chirring of a chipping sparrow, cicada in birch, the whonk of beavertail)
the water is black, bracken and mud closed to the sky's wingfilled blue. Sharp
Halloween colours, bringing memory of Toronto fall, yellow leaves, wirey
air. But here, anaphylaxis, honey-gold venom and my mother dead at fifty-six.

II

Or rescued, the luck of a smalltown ambulance trundling past, the attendants
eating popcorn in the front seat out of their oil-grimed hands, the radio
alive with bad news. She's alabaster pale, her own death tribute, coldsweat
and hivey red on the table, her stomach war-mapped with red dots showing
the enemy positions. Ministrations: cuff and cold disk, a sting for blood, the old
nurse's lessons coming back as she diminishes, every cell shrunk in stark refusal
and back at the lake, the ice cubes are melting slowly in her drink.

III

A few weeks later, Benjamin discovers birds. Lying flat on my chest he follows
the pale grey-and-white shapes crossing the sky. Sham unity comes apart:
everything moves independent, is separate, things can disappear. Near us,
    nectar-drunk
bumblebees lumber from one flower to the next, airborn bison, a mistake
that works. Somehow, they get home and deep in those nests the sugar cures
to thickness and is never suspect although it can kill a child. There is a
    trace of poison
in pleasure. With those new teeth, he bites when he kisses.

IV

Hysteria parts the traffic, manic lights flashing the siren raw as a voice saying
it's you, it's you, it's you, it's her, gas-masked and resurfacing. My father
follows behind, rational as math, papering hornetlike round and round

the claw-filled panic. But she lives, she lives, and her birthday will come again
and there will be cake and the childhood wax-scent of candles, and later,
the morbid puns: venom I ever going to hear the end of this I-almost-died
    story?
But not thoughts of nearly nor the extra minute somehow not wasted nor
all of us in the city, happily ignorant, nor her, black-humoured saying
today you would have buried me.

V

From a maze of others, out of the cramped dark, you came looking for quiet
and solace in the dozey heat. lack and yellow like a bruise, a memory of
    the fall,
or the striped corduroy turtlenecks she once dressed me in: she didn't know
better, neither did you, settling in the cool dark of a pantleg. But this is
not an elegy, tiny power, not for you, although after this, everything is
    forgiven,
you are forgiven, you with your accidental death clenched in you like a shout.
Spent and empty you became weightless and sudden in a hand and we
    read your name
in the field guide, yellowjacket, and this was the last thing said of you.
    Bade home,
you weren't missed, although you died for your mother, who made you, and
    now goes on.

July 1999

JOHN BARTON
Excerpt from *Hypothesis* (2001)

Case History

there is a need, sometimes, for clarity, otherwise the heart
which they say is neither male nor female, too freely associates

the body preoccupied with such a vortex of near particulars
it dreams its own country where exiles trade in the fitful

custom of desire—meanwhile the hand held out in love is delicate
but the sad unlacquered nails are bitten to the quick, the boy told

almost since birth he was altogether otherwise so soon beginning
despite what they had taken from him, to remember himself

remembering even today shoulders he caught once in the mirror
squared under a dress whose torn hem his mother lovingly repinned

what was taken from him they said is what made her and would
make her so, without clarification—not necessarily one who

would grow to be desirable or beautiful but one who might
love and adopt, when the time comes, should she, despite all

else she might have longed for, conceive of wanting a child of her
own—a life of certain particulars only clarity could ever make

for her; it would be, they said, otherwise too late for him, every
thing too quickly answered before she could have questions

.

for him there was never any question, for him clarity, so-called,
was not absent but taken before he could remember; if only

by accident—the current, he now knows, coursing too harshly
through some instrument used to untighten his constricted

7-month-old foreskin, 'clarity' in its entirety burned to near 'ablation'
before it 'necrosed' and they 'sloughed' it off but like his 'monozygotic

XY twin' down at the gene level the variables of X and Y still plotted
the same ardent trajectory otherwise rising exponentially between

the spread legs of the graph, the particular line he would come
to trace, the nerve to do so opening through him centrally

at puberty despite whatever they plotted to subtract, despite any
'contingencies' they would have, in all certainty, attempted to add

.

what they have taken from him he knew early on in his heart
is not some thing otherwise consequent—what makes him

sexy is the brain, its ecstatic rush finally reassigned to him
hypodermically, helping him to grow a light beard and chase

after girls he took to with such confidence, taking out the very
ones who before never once thought he was ever in any way

one of them, in whom at last they found no ambiguity
liking the particular cut of his jeans and how he was remade

to fill them in ways he had so long ago began longing for, liking
his open-necked shirts, the muscled body he still trains and does

not conceal despite the soft line of his jaw and the scarring
and all else leftover it is now too late to ever take away

.

for him it is not that the body clarifies, though he knows it
sometimes reveals more than it hides, it is just his sons make

him a father purely by what he does for them, the hockey games
he watches them play at the local arena all through the cold winters

of childhood no one else could understand perfectly like him—
what they have he cannot take from them, even if he tried to

the Y of the men their mother coupled with, her X he cannot hope
to shelter them from, the otherwise surprising interior weather

of whatever in particular has been left them—instead all he wants is
for each boy to stand in the eventual eye of his own storm, enter

the country no one can claim for him as completely each one
gives himself to the private transformative legacies of lightning

DENNIS LEE
Excerpt from *Un* (2003)

Scribblescript portents unfurl, world-
to, worldfro.
And to comb the signs, to
stammer the uterine painscape
in pidgin apocalypse—how now not
gag on the unward, the once-upon, us-
proud planet?
Scarlight, scar-
blight in the chronifrag of no-man's:
sublingual agon.
Rolled scarlight up the hill, got
crushed, rolled
scarlight up the hill.

Of palaeopresence. The extra
space around what is.

ADAM SOL
Excerpts from *Crowd of Sounds* (2003)

The Calculus of a Man Striking Water in Relation To a Boat Striking Wood, and the Pieces Shattering

Here is where the boat broke through barriers as a hand goes through a screen. How the timbers trembled. And a boy on the bridge whistled like an old man, waveringly. We have seen how the captain used his throat to imitate the ocean. Three girls on the shore were throwing stones at the water, and we wondered whether someone had lost his way watching them. But the boy on the bridge was without guile, and when the boat came through he could only gape, like a window.

The sound of wood breaking is familiar to all of us, even the unborn, but the girls stopped throwing as if their ears had only just opened. And the captain, launched from the deck, made us all think of our drowned fathers, our drowned brothers, our drowned sons. These are things even the boy on the bridge would know by now. In this town there are those who love the drowned, and there are the drowned.

Not even air pushed through the boy's pursed lips could change the shape of the captain's hand as it grasped for the clouds above the water and found only the shreds of the dock.

So we see the boat, the captain, the dock, the boy, the girls, the stones, and the tremblings of the frustrated water, all in relation to each other. And we can use these fixed points to calculate how the boy will return to his mother's home, how he will omit the story of the crash and of the captain thrown from the deck, but how he will repeat the whistled song in reference to the girls throwing stones at the water and the sound of the spray against the falling hand, and the floating wood.

Solve.

On Jays

Songs are poor, mostly raucous.
— Birds of North America

There's a story of a dozen jays dive-bombing a cat
to keep it from a fallen chick. And the one about a cat
who hunted down a dozen jays. Scraps of blue
strewn about the lawn like a broken balloon.
I heard that one at a party while trying to eat roasted garlic cloves
with someone who resembled the Grinch. I miss those parties.
There is always plasticware left over.

There are countless tales of jays chasing sparrows and chickadees,
even squirrels, from feeders. There should be a study
of the various creatures who thrive near humans. Enough
of these *National Geographic* specials on the snow leopard,
the California condor, the humpback whale. I'd like to see
a one-hour program on pigeons, or mosquitoes.

Mammals of the New York Sewer System!
Birds of Suburbia: wrens, grackles, and jays. Turns out swans
don't always mate for life. We could learn
something from these programs about what it takes
to live with people. For instance, all these animals are cruel.

Crows, chipmunks, gulls. And of course the roach,
Crown Prince of the Urban Habitat. Roaches would be much less
repulsive if we couldn't hear them walking.
I once said that roaches only want to live together peacefully,
but I'm not so sure now that I've spent more time in New York.
I think roaches are waiting, like you wait at the house
of a sick uncle whose piano you'd like.

Jays eat roaches. When it has one, it looks like the jay
might just be transferring it to a roomier apartment, it holds
the creature so carefully in its beak, and the roach moves its legs
with what could be wonder.
Tickles the tongue, all that horror in the mouth.
Then a quick flick of the head, like swallowing a pill,
and it's just the jay lifting its feet, crooning a raucous jazz.

A.F. MORITZ

Excerpts from *Night Street Repairs* (2004)

North American Song

I have a mild case of everything.

I starve a little but not like they do in Ethiopia.
Life is empty for me but not like it is in Stockholm.

I'm lyrical and obsessive though not as much so
as a bird: one might better compare me to the bands,
the poet bands of New York and California:
everything repeated, everything lost, every day.

If there's one thing I know, or one thing I know better
than anything else, it's that the difference between mild
and wild is just the inversion of a letter.
By this means the revolution is accomplished.

I'm a little bit homeless and a wanderer
but not like the people sleeping in the doorway,
and am gently rich—yet not for me
are ornate palaces endlessly deep:
no, just a front door, a room or two, and out the back.

I am in opposition but would never want
to seem invisibly strange, so let it be said
that I worship intensity, but not as the living or the dead.

The Helmet

The greatest twentieth-century work of art is not a poem or
    a painting

but the steel helmet: so said some Nazi curator. And indeed the
    German helmet

from World War II that I own does satisfy our obsession with
    elegant design.

Its lines and volumes, simple yet intricate, and the way light
    passes over it

as if it were a planet while the skull-hole is filled with
    darkness: these

fulfil design's one great promise or perception, that a thought,
    even a life,

can express itself with beautiful inexplicitness, and there truly is
    paradise:

the heaven of dynamic patterns and self-cancelled phrases where
    all are equal.

Here is the example, unique for each who confronts it, of a mass-
produced,

ineffable and unsayable impression. Democracy, art for all. Who
has not seen

these helmets? Millions owned them. Tens of thousands took
them from the dead.

This one, for instance, I have from a relative, who received it from
a friend,

a Berber, one of the Free French, assigned with the Americans,
who taught him

the tools and techniques of modern war. But this man also loved
traditional means.

At night he used to take a serrated bayonet and pass through the
lines. In the darkness

nothing could be seen, so he felt for helmets: rough ones meant
the American army,

and he went farther. Smooth ones: he was among Germans and
started cutting throats.

This additional work he did for the pleasure of danger and skill,
hatred of the enemy,

and love of his foreign friends. A stoical man, with outbursts of
frantic exalted delight,

he went home after the war to a strict life in the desert south of
   Marrakesh.

Now I've turned his helmet over on its back like a small-boy-
   tortured turtle,

and I use it to plant flowers in: those shade-lovers I always call
   "patience"

when I know impatiens is their name.

SUZANNE BUFFAM
Excerpts from *Past Imperfect* (2005)

Sir Gromore Somyr Joure

That was a happy station, full of sunshine and cabbage.
You could sit among the thinkers for hours,
thinking anything you wanted. You could think
about your kingdom and feel a small stab of remorse,
or you could cultivate an interest in the funnel-shaped
webs leading down through the grasswort
towards what toothed and cruel centre lay waiting.
Knees were for kneeling. Lashes were for looking
at the sun. The river was slow and it hurried.
Trains slowed down but did not stop.
Wherefore was the question on everyone's lips
though none spoke it, nor plucked it away
but let it hang there like an overripe pear
left out for the gleaners to dispute in the fall.
Every horse had three different names, each one
more purple than the last. Sir Gromore Somyr Joure
took the day every day until the very day
he retired. Did I love that dark horse?
I did not. His breath stank of cabbage.
He bit the hands that fed him. He would stand
in bad weather and refuse the boxwood gate.
But I was there in the fray and the fanfare,

I was there in the dooryard, and I was there
when they laid him down cold to the earth.

Shapes at Midnight

Across the street the artists are still working in their studios.
Through my curtains I can see them, moving now towards,
now away from the assorted shapes and colours
on the walls, each private artist vibrant in her cell.

On the second floor, a woman reaches out
as though to grasp a wedge of blue and reposition it,
    a careful
movement, full of a new love of ideas and distrust
of the heart. At the last second, before her hand connects

up with the colour and commits, she draws it back
and stands there, in the centre of her life, lit starkly
by the swinging bulb above her. Hoisted in the branches
of the maple is the moon

that dropped behind the poplars last November, when you
first introduced me to this version of despair: halfway
we cannot bear yet here
we long to stay: the artists in their studios, the sentimental

rectangles of blue, the moon, the ramifying
branches of the maple through the window,
halfway between the woman I am watching
and myself, beginning at this hour to lose green.

KEVIN CONNOLLY
Excerpts from *Drift* (2005)

Domestic Lyric

Out west, it's so dry, the rain vanishes before it hits the ground.
That's heavy, dude, write a poem about it.

And that kitten, it glides over the hardwood like, I dunno, mittens.
That's heavy, babe, write a poem about it.

You know, Frida Kahlo, she did some fucked-up pictures of herself.
That's sweet, man, write a poem sequence *about it.*

And Hemingway blew his brains out when his dick wouldn't work.
Harsh! But are you thinking what I'm thinking?—Poem!

And Lewis Carroll, paddling around with all that underage tuna.
That's fucked-up, hombre, but a big opening for a poem.

Not to mention my ex-wife, sticking it to that grad student.
Miserable liar, what say we drop a poem on her?

And the November trees, they're like sad fingers, you know?
And that's such a freaking poem I totally can't believe it!

Drift

> *There is so much Everything*
> *that Nothing is hidden quite nicely.*
> —Wislawa Szymborska

The Killim Haus, Delia's Esthetics,
Shawarma Hut, all of them duck before
the same sullen pleasures—
the village of tomorrow undone
almost by accident, a loose coalition
of strip malls and strip malls and strip
malls: Quik-E Convenience,
Cheers Fine Foods, Fish and Cheeps—
a pet store. In the absence of real stars,
repetition has its consolations—
random lights conscripted into the opera,
reimagined as sheet-metal thunder,
Sea of Rains Dry-Kleen,
two-for-one Szechwan lobster.

What endures, a piece of it, is weather,
the snap and cuddle of clouds,
on-and-off pressure of traffic,
treasured debris of childhood
cohabiting the same shrunken rooms,
the same lint-frosted airducts,
same breezeway assignations after
bridge or curling or cribbage:
Where's Dad? Did Beth leave?
Who signed what in who's yearbook,
who conjured the calamity—the deep

tension-emptying sigh before
the garage door dumped its
gust of impossible light?

It's all good because it's all decided.
The dream mall closed for business,
its flummoxed architect returned
to Europe with his tale between his teeth.
But who'll hike out the salvage?
The anchor-stores crumbling, time-
shares stuttering, the buckling credit
of the jury truants: *No flyers, please;*
No one home; Not at this address—
all of it a tough-love lesson in
the pitfalls of earnest simulation.
Desperation among toothpicks,
unlit gatehouses, vacated parking
booths—hard edge trembling in
a wilderness of signs.

Swallows

It would almost be worth it, he thinks—basting a chicken
on a gas grill with a beer can up its ass, swallows diving
in the evening light—to have four years instead of forty, eight
instead of eighty (no longevity stats on swallows forthcoming),

to *move* like that, hit a rogue current, throw up your flag and
hang with it, hollow-boned acrobat that you are. To be
tossed over the gloom and lightning, properly terrified
of your speed, your height, for as tall and thirsting as your fame

no ground can claim you, no stone so fast and hard and fleeting
though the air flirts hard and the tan light gives it legs.
Swallow enough anything and it's euphoria. Strangled or
drowned, we all die drunk—no vexed loves, no stowed

slights, just a hole at the top of a column that thunders and
beckons and brightens, then, tightening, flees the scene.

SHARON THESEN
Excerpts from *The Good Bacteria* (2006)

How to Stay Sane

Despite all that's wrong
     I'd like to go for a walk someday
          among the pearls and carriages
merriment and weather

untoward anything

you talk about volition and overcoming
     I, margarine
          in the aisles of hope
in butter-coloured tubs and pots

geraniums
     mystical, alone and latent
          in the sheds of winter, winter's
shelter, they are

a shade of pink nail polish
     from this season's Greek Collection
          (last year's British Collection
was darker, verging on plaid)

I for one am glad of these mood-lifting changes!

from another yummy shop
        many tasteful items
                carefully tableau'd

luggage and overcoats, mug sets
        at the Great Canadian Superstore
                at Costco

she exclaimed, "I'm here all the time!"
        and had just finished writing the real estate exam.
                Wow, I think, yet aver

too much paperwork.
        Help yourself is my motto
                when it comes to stuff sitting around

like the bags purple in the freezer with last summer's berries.

Not to mention miracles in maroon leather
        to be found at Zambesi's
                a world away in Wellington

maroon and pumpkin, a different and distant place
        from office hours with monitor, minotaur

squatted centre stage
        concealing Zambesi cookies.
                A three-ring binder on my lap.

Going over a story.
        The student is large in the room.
                The banners of May yell.

Going to Skidegate

I take my homunculus and my purse
        Across the busy parking lot on a hot day
                To the Pharmasave where it is also busy.

People waiting for the blood pressure monitor.
        People picking and choosing their Scratch-and-Wins.
            People with Mars bars and aspirins—

That was the lady behind me. I had a glossy uplifting
        Magazine and a jar of night cream
            And a pair of warm soft socks

So my homunculus would be comforted while the ferry heaved
        And bucked across the Hecate Strait
            And we'd have Mars bars to eat

And magazines to trade
        Once we got to Skidegate.

KEN BABSTOCK
Excerpts from *Airstream Land Yacht* (2006)

The World's Hub
after Pier Paolo Pasolini

Not poor, but adjacent to that, I lived
in an outer suburb, undistinguished but
for the mauve-blue mirrored panels of glass

alongside the feeder lanes. Not country
and no sort of city. Everyone drove, to all points
within the limits of nowhere; the rest

incarcerated on public transit: packed
in the high-wattage strip light
sat the poor, the mad, the adolescent

and license-suspended, the daylight
drunk, and Malton's newly arrived.
Hours-long treks through air-quality

alerts, fingering vials of hash oil and
transfers back. Or earlier, at the thin edge
of long dusks, the Bookmobile

dripping grease on clean tarmac
nudging the lower leaves of young maples,
I kissed a Jamaican boy with three

names, his loose jheri curls
looked wet and right, black helices
in the bay windows' blue glow.

And something inside me took root;
a thing mine that I didn't own, but cared
for, as I had for a pink-eyed rabbit,

loved without reason and was returned
nothing in kind, and so what? The flurry
of rose-brick façades being raised

on cul de sacs without sidewalks, outlets
and outlets, the sameness, and grimmer storeys
of the projects beyond the ballpark

were a weird history I was casting love
upon even as I wanted to leave it. I worked
retail, weekends, from within an awareness

of myself as Self; the brown carpeted tiers
of the library, ravine parties, parading
my young body through malls. The world's

hub, improbably, here, under untranslatable
verses of powerlines, kestrels
frozen above vast grassland of what used

to be farm. November like a tin sheet
blown up from the lake over Mimico, with
garbage and refuse I'd build

a hilltop to the moon over Mississauga—
chip bags, flattened foil wrappers, shopping
carts growing a fur of frost, the shocking

volume and echo of squat women's voices,
here from blasted South Balkan huts
via Budapest; Filipinos, Croatians

with income come to make good
and did, dressed us in suede pantsuits
at ten, or terry summer halters, confident

with adults, curious, clean. Damp
electrical storms, bloated purgings
of rain turning the avenues to linked lakes.

The low slung buses veering, Albion-bound
but stalled in a monoxide cloud
somewhere on the usual grid...

it was the world's hub.
If you feel otherwise, that it constituted negative
space, I can only say it's a postulate

without need of proof but for the love
I had for it. I knew before I could speak
of it—that great, horrible sprawl

folded under airport turbulence, advancing inland
each year, breeding signposts, arteries, housing—
it was life as it was lived. Raspberries. The smell of gas.

Compatibilist

Awareness was intermittent. It sputtered.
            And some of the time you were seen
                asleep. So trying to appear whole

               you asked of the morning: Is he free
          who is not free from pain? It started to rain
a particulate alloy of flecked grey; the dogs

wanted out into their atlas of smells; to pee
           where before they had peed, and might
              well pee again—though it isn't

               a certainty. What is? In the set,
           called Phi, of all possible physical worlds
resembling this one, in which, at time *t*,

was written 'Is he free who is not free—'
           and comes the cramp. Do you want
              to be singular, onstage, praised,

               or blamed? I watched a field of sun-
           flowers dial their ruddy faces toward
        what they needed and was good. At noon

they were chalices upturned, gilt-edged,
        and I lived in that same light but felt
            alone. I chose to phone my brother,

          over whom I worried, and say so.
      He whispered, lacked affect. He'd lost
my record collection to looming debt. I

forgave him—through weak connections,
        through buzz and oceanic crackle—
           immediately, without choosing to,

          because it was him I hadn't lost; and
      later cried myself to sleep. In that village
near Dijon, called Valley of Peace,

a pond reflected its dragonflies
        over a black surface at night, and
           the nuclear reactor's far-off halo

          of green light changed the night sky
      to the west. A pony brayed, stamping
a hoof on inlaid stone. The river's reeds

lovely, but unswimmable. World death
        on the event horizon; vigils with candles
           in cups. I've mostly replaced my records,

          and acted in ways I can't account for.
      Cannot account for what you're about
to do. We should be held and forgiven.

2 GAÉTAN SOUCY

An excerpt from the novel *The Little Girl*
Who Was Too Fond of Matches (2000)

I followed them, and I tried to be a pitiful sight with my mouth
and my eyes and all my airs and graces so they'd treat me nicely,
so they would help my heart in all this suffering, so they'd think
I was a handsome youth. The priest didn't look nasty. Because
his soutane was all dungy and covered with chalk dust I felt
safe, he looked more like a neighbour than the others, papa had
been a priest too when he was a fine-looking lad. The other
individual had a revolver in his belt, which startled me, because
from the pictures I'd seen I had always thought firearms were
very small, whereas in reality, my goodness, this one was as big
as father's balls.

While I walked I rememoried in bits and pieces what our life
had consisted of to date, and what it would no longer be as everything passes here below, for instance the sound that papa made
upstairs while he was doing his exercises, or when we all ate
together and we tied a bib around our frog for a laugh and fed
her flies, and the care that papa lavished on the Fair Punishment
in the woodshed when he took it out of its box, which would
now be more berefted than ever, I thought about all that and it
helped me be a pitiful sight because it turned me every which
way in my sadness and I felt something like an urge to cry. It's a
pretty word, rememory, I don't know if it actually exists but it
means to recall things.

Now I'd like you to pay close attention because what comes next will be difficult.

First of all they showed me into the town hall, that's what it's called according to what I could read above the door, and it was a very pretty house, so clean that you felt like applauding and walking around inside dressed like Adam and dancing barefoot among the manikins of light. We walked down a corridor, which evoked for me the portrait gallery on our estate, I'll certainly have something to say about that later because of the sudden light these portraits would shed, a few hours from now, on my own origins here below, then we entered a small room equipped with tables, seats, and lamps that were attached to the wall by ropes and created light through the power of magic. The two men who accompanied me hadn't said a word to me along the way but between themselves they talked a great deal, energetically and anxiously it seemed to me, and the priest said officer to the man who was wearing the firearm with its breathtaking dimensions. The first thing I noticed in this little room was that there was someone else inside it, at first I could see only the feet crossed on a desk and the hands because a screen concealed the head, but right away I felt safe because the hands were opening a dictionary entitled the flowers of evil. They sat me down and then the officer's questions began.

"You live in the house on the other side of the pine grove, don't you? And your father is mister soissons? And it's his horse that was with you?"

I moved my torso from side to side as if I were humming a little song inside my bonnet, I stared vacantly into space, but I didn't reply. Incidentally, the strange thing about that word soissons is that sometimes I would nod off in the middle of my dictionaries and all at once, perfectly clearly, I would hear the word soissons whistle very quickly past my ear and flee like a trout that slips between our legs when we walk barefoot in the lake in summer, and I had the impression that the word had something to do with me, that it belonged to the most intimate part of me more than any other word, I'm saying it the way it seems to me, and that word soissons brought me out of my dozing all surprised.

The priest and the officer went on reviling me with questions, and it seemed that I annoyed them with the way I appeared not to hear the vulgate, but I meant no harm and they got lost in conjecture and other calculations of the sort and, let me tell you, even though I had the strongest sense of such things, never would I have believed that my father was such an important man. The officer even had a big grey moustache as if he wanted to imitate him! That moustache was so much like his, you'd have thought it had flown from papa's face like my friend the dragonfly, as it's said that our soul flies away when we die, and had settled above the lip of the officer, as true as I'm.

The gentleman in question, along with the soutane, soon opted for speaking to me as if they'd known me all my life, thinking that would sound better between my ears, and when they asked me if something had happened to my father I finally showed them that I understood the human tongue like everybody else, and I answered, he died this morning at dawn, which made an impression.

They asked me to repeat it, it was a piece of news that would travel far if proved correct, but repeating isn't my strong point. "We found him hanging this morning at the end of a rope that he was clinging to like one man without a by-your-leave," I said instead. The priest made the sign of the cross on his belly. The officer seemed calmer. Mind you, he didn't have a crucifix around his neck that he'd be constantly tempted to play with, the way kid brother does with you know what. He told me in a voice full of tact, as if I were something infinitely fragile that had to be treated sensitively:

"You said, 'We found him.' Who is we?"

"Papa has two sons," I said. "Me and my brother."

They drew back their necks in stupefaction the way pigeons do when they walk, they gazed at me as if I'd said something outrageous, just try to understand them, my contemporaries and friends. The officer moved his hand as if to say, we'll come back to that later, and he asked me:

"What about your mama? Isn't there a mother living with you?"

"There have never been any sluts in our house," I said.

From the look on their faces I realized clarifications were called for, so I added:

"All mothers are sluts but you can say blessed virgins too if you fancy, the nuance is infinitesimal."

I received two very quick whacks from the man in the soutane, one with the flat of the hand, the other with the back, both with the right hand and in less time than it takes to write it down. I'd have liked to put my fingers in my underwear and flick blood at him, but I didn't have any blood that day, it had healed over until next time.

Then the third man, of whom I'd so far seen only the hands and feet, got out of his chair and I immediately recognized my neighbour who'd come to my house to importune me, the prince that brother teased me about and said I was in love with, humph. He seemed interested in everything we were saying but he said nothing himself, in the manner of cats and wise men. He had crossed his arms and he rested his shoulder against the wall and he was looking at me with curiosity and gravity for some reason I'm unaware of, maybe he was in love too. Just seeing him gave me a kind of urge to run my tongue all over his face, to put his nose in my mouth, things sometimes happen in my head and in my body that are genuine riddles for me. He still had his diction-ary in his hand and he'd made a bookmark with one of his fingers and I liked that detail because it was something I very often did too when I broke off my reading to dream about the handsome knights the pages talked about, I'd make a bookmark with one of my fingers. As for the priest, he had withdrawn to a chair in the corner and he was staring at the floor with eyes like saucers. For a man who had promised not to harm me, it struck me that, despite the soutane he was wearing, his word had no more weight than a comet that emerges from our hole.

But getting back to sluts, I tried to explain to them that I did indeed have a very distant rememory of a blessed virgin who'd held me on her knees and smelled good, and even of a cherub on the sweet-smelling virgin's other knee who was as much like me as a bubble, as my brother tried to convince me. But was that a memory? And was she a slut?

The priest had come back and with a stunned look, like the one kid brother had the time he told me dog had just died, whereas I didn't give a hoot owl as my father would say, he repeated: "She's crazy. Or possessed." Soutanes don't know the genders of pronouns, if I'm any judge. What's more, I don't know what that priest did with his saliva but in the corners of his lips he had a sort of dry verdigris foam, mouth-kelp if you'll believe me, that I was seeing for the first time on a neighbour, I don't know if it's rare or what, in any case I have a horror of it, if you'll give credence to these words of mine. For want of blood I flicked contempt at him with my eyes, which were always filled with little thunderbolts according to my late father.

They started talking between themselves again, I mean the officer and the priest, with no concern for me aside from the glances they shot at me now and then, glances that froze them for a moment in a kind of horrified stupor, and I'm choosing my words carefully. But there was also the prince and he was observing me with touchingly friendly eyes and when I saw him smile at me I turned my face away, shrugging and putting on airs, because who did he think I was anyway?

The serious matter that seemed to overwhelm the other two, which they kept harping on like a refrain, was the fact that my late father was the owner of the mine and his death was going to cause changes, and they seemed to have a horror of change if you want my opinion. They finally told me that I was going to be obliged to take them to papa.

"Papa has disappeared."

"What's that? What do you mean? Have you lost his remains?"

"His body is there," I said, "but he himself has disappeared."

That shouldn't be hard to understand.

"Then you'll have to take us to his remains."

To show them that such a thing was completely out of the question I went into a stoppit. Don't worry, it wasn't a real one, it was just to impress them, which it did. The prince said gently, his gentleness even et cetera:

"Can't you see you're frightening her? She's trembling."

Another one who thought I was a slut, I suppose he was going by my inflations and I told him so with my eyes.

"Mister mine inspector, I would ask you not to get mixed up in this. Go back to your poems." It was the officer who said that to the prince.

"Precisely. As mine inspector it seems to me that it does concern me just a little, don't you think?"

Those two seemed not to like each other, to put it in black and white. I must also point out that the officer had in common with my brother the fact that he looked like someone who never sticks his nose in a dictionary, which fills such people with jealous contempt for those who make a bookmark with a finger, and I thought to myself that even though he'd called me a slut, in the event of out-and-out warfare I wouldn't make a big fuss, I would side with the mine inspector, all daggers drawn. What can you do with someone who never sticks his nose in a dictionary?

The priest and the mustachioed officer concluded that it was a case of force majeure and that it was their duty to advise the mare, who had been prevented from following the grocer's funeral by the flu, and I told myself that they definitely knew nothing about what words mean, but then I realized that no doubt they meant

mayor and not mare, because watch out!—the secretarious is a
reader. They told the mine inspector to keep an eye on me in the
meantime and then they were off like gushes of piss.

I'll tell you, had I been able to foresee that I'd be having a tête-
à-tête with the mine inspector before the day was over, I think,
all things considered, I'd rather have hanged myself with papa's
rope, because I was a little frightened by the urges of my heart,
to say the least, and according to the dictates of nature and religion it's obviously my brother I should fittingly be in love with,
not another man.

Translated by Sheila Fischman

3 SHEILA HETI
An excerpt from the story collection *The Middle Stories* (2001)

The Poet and the Novelist as Roommates

The poet went softly to the novelist's bedroom, while the novelist lay asleep, sleep coming out heavy like a stink through his nose. The poet stood in the doorway, watching, pressing down on the doorframe.

He loved his roommate. But not like that. It was four in the morning and why had he woken? Sleep was a burden for a man like him. And yet here was a man who slept through the night. "He must be in a state of guilt," the poet thought, before turning and going to bed. Padding through the hail he asked himself quietly, "What am I doing in this city? Even looking at the clouds I feel I have lost my imagination."

On the woman's first day at work the poet helped her with her boxes, but as he was helping he was looking away.

"Do you know this is my seventieth sick day since I started here?" he asked.

"But you're here," she said.

"Yes, I know." And he went to the bathroom and peed blood.

When he returned she was sitting upright, typing at her computer like a good girl. There was a calculated grace about her and it was this that caused him, eyes drooping and weary, to lean over the partition and say to her face, "Come with me after work. I will show you a good place to drink around here."

"I'll come, sure," she said, looking up, and there was no guile expressed, just a big round smile and those hateful eyes that only women understood.

When the workday ended he took her by the arm and led her to The Poodle, which was seedy and disreputable and no place for a woman from a cubicle to be. He looked around. She was wearing a bra on tight beneath her clothing.

"Sit down here at this booth," he said, pushing in her body with both his hands, "and I will get you a soda water."

"I take gin in my soda water," she said hopefully, and the poet walked away with a shudder. These modern women. They had no sense of their own indecency.

When he returned with the drinks he slipped into the booth and began to twitch in boredom as he listened to her story.

"I have a husband and three children," she began.

"But you look eighteen," he said mournfully, and swished his drink. A husband and three children. "You should not be dressed like that then," he concluded.

She furrowed her brow and sucked up her drink with pristine fury. "Thank you for this," she said, smacking down the glass and dropping the straw from her lips as she walked.

When he returned that night he found his roommate working on his novel. Looking up from the computer his roommate beckoned him over.

"I think there is a bug behind the glass," said the novelist, pointing to a place on the screen, then tracing it, following it.

"I don't see it," the poet replied, eyes crossed in intoxication.

"Go to bed," the novelist said, and the poet did.

When the poet woke he remembered the woman, the one with the husband and the three lovely kids. Probably right now she was frantically diapering them, or shoving sandwiches into their boxes, not thinking anything, just scurrying around with a phone in her chin, talking to her sister in Ottawa.

"It has been so in politics, it has been so in religion, and it has been so in every other department of human thought," he thought, and got up and undressed and went to the shower and rubbed himself hard, and went to his room where he dressed in brown and walked in the rain to work.

When he arrived the woman in the cubicle was already there. Her spine was haughty and tense and she was turned away. But as he sat and arranged his folders he knew that she was thinking of him. "She can't do any better than me," he determined. Yes, he would destroy her. This woman with the husband and the three lovely kids: she was looking for an affair, a real sweaty romance, he could smell it on her skin.

Indeed, by the coffeemaker at eleven a.m. she said, "I would like to go home with you tonight. I would like to see where you live."

"It is not a sight for a lady," he said, dangling this info in front of her. "It's a small place. A man's place. I'm a poet, you see, and I live there alone with my roommate of seven years who is cruel. Women fall in love with him but he cannot love them back. He is a novelist. He's very messy."

"I want to come home with you," the woman said, pressing her eyes into him and spilling the coffee.

That night they sat around the table: the poet, the novelist, and the woman from the cubicle. The woman from the cubicle, eyes all alight, looked back and forth from one to the other. One was so gruff and silent and thick, like a real man! and the other was disinterested and distracted and edgy, like a real man! She was falling in love with them both.

The novelist, feeling violated for reasons he could not understand, got up and left the table and went to his computer and peered in, and again saw the bug behind the screen. "Damn it!"

he cried, pounding his fist into his desk. The poet looked dreary and did not respond.

The woman said, "Please, tell me about your life. You must be fascinating. I have never known a poet before, except for one in high school. And I don't even know if he's still a poet."

The poet said darkly, "Don't tell me that." Then, "Come with me to the bedroom. It is my bedroom and I should like to show it to you."

The woman put down her fork and followed in behind. She was delighted. She felt so bohemian. She wanted to take off all her clothes.

"Good," he said, turning on a lamp. "You can see now on my wall two letters from Al Purdy, telling me I am good but not good enough."

He sat on the bed which was low to the floor and spread apart his legs and looked up at her as she walked around the narrow space, fingering all the things.

"That is a picture taken of me when I was in Poland. I was a professor."

"You look very Polish here."

"I know."

He lay his back on his bed and looked up at the ceiling, hands adjusted behind his head. "Do you smoke?" he asked.

"No."

"Please go into the next room and get a cigarette from my novelist roommate. He should have a pack beside him on the desk. Tell him it is for me; he will understand. If he refuses to give you one or throws a fit, leave the room at once. Sometimes it bothers him to be interrupted while writing."

The woman left the room and walked down the hall and saw the novelist hunched before his computer, deep in his chair, pressing his fingers to the screen. "Come," he said, when he heard her approach, and she moved towards his desk and placed her hands upon it and leaned archingly forward. He put one hand on her ass, felt it shifting beneath her dress.

"Do you see a bug?"

She held her breath, did not move. Then she looked evasively away and said, "I have come here to get a cigarette for the poet. He says you'll understand."

"Sure I understand." He sombrely pulled two cigarettes from the pack and she took them. She left the room and walked numbly through the hall towards the poet, and on the walk she remembered a dream. "I dreamed once I was in a room with other people."

When the poet saw her he sat upright on the bed. "Close the door," he said. "The novelist gets very jealous."

She closed the door and sat down beside him. She put the cigarettes in his hand. He looked down at them dumbly. She wanted him to throw his leg across her, push her down on the bed, slap her and rape her hard.

"Two," he said. "He must like you."

"Yes. He touched me on my bum."

"Let me see."

She lay down on her stomach and he examined her through her dress.

4 THOMAS KING
An excerpt from the CBC Massey Lectures
The Truth About Stories (2003)

V. What Is It About Us That You Don't Like?

. . . The truth about stories is that that's all we are.

"There are stories that take seven days to tell," says the Cherokee storyteller Diane Glancy. "There are other stories that take you all your life."[1]

I like Coyote stories. And one of my favourites is the one about Coyote and the Ducks. Not the one where the Ducks dance around with their eyes shut while Coyote grabs them one by one and tosses them in his hunting bag. And not the one where he tries to talk the Ducks into teaching him how to fly.

The other one.

The one about the feathers.

And it goes like this.

In the days when everything was beginning, and animals were still talking to humans, Coyote had a beautiful fur coat of which he was very vain. Every day Coyote would come down to the river and look at his reflection.

Goodness, but I have a lovely coat, Coyote would whisper to the water, and then he would give himself a hug.

One day while he was admiring his fur coat, he saw six Ducks singing and dancing and swimming around in circles. Back and forth they went, spinning and turning and diving and leaping in the sunshine. Now, in those days, Ducks had lovely long feathers that shimmered and flashed like the Northern Lights. And when the Ducks had finished singing and dancing and swimming around in circles, they carefully cleaned each feather and straightened it and fluffed it up, so that it glowed even more than before.

That is certainly a wonderful song, said Coyote, who was a little dizzy from watching the Ducks swim around in circles. And that is certainly a beautiful dance.

Yes, said the Ducks. We sing to keep everything in balance, and we dance for peace and generosity, and we swim around in circles to remind everyone of our relationship to the earth.

And those are certainly lovely feathers, said Coyote.

Yes, said those Ducks, they certainly are.

I would certainly like to have one of those lovely feathers, said Coyote. It would go so well with my excellent fur coat.

Now, in those days, Ducks were very agreeable. All right, they said. Just be careful with it, for we are quite fond of our feathers.

I will, said Coyote, and he stuck the feather behind his left ear and ran off to show it to all his friends.

What do you think of my feather? he asked everyone he saw.

It certainly is unusual, said Bear, who tended to be more critical than he needed to be. Too bad you only have one, for now you look a little lopsided.

Oh, dear, said Coyote, and he ran back to the river to find the Dancing Ducks.

Excuse me, Coyote shouted, would it be possible to get another feather?

Another feather? said the Ducks.

Yes, said Coyote, as you can see, having only one feather makes me appear lopsided.

Ah, said the Ducks. You're right. You do look a little lopsided. And the Ducks gave Coyote another feather. But this is the last one, they said. Don't ask for any more, for we need our feathers.

I won't, said Coyote. I promise.

And Coyote stuck the feather behind his right ear and ran off to show it to all his friends.

Aren't these the most beautiful feathers you've ever seen? said Coyote.

They certainly are, said Raven. And such an improvement on that ratty fur coat.

You don't like my wonderful fur coat? said Coyote.

Fur's okay, said Raven, but feathers are so much better.

They are? said Coyote.

Certainly, said Raven, stretching out one wing as far as she could. Anyone who is anyone has feathers.

Well, you can imagine poor Coyote's distress. If Raven was right, and she was seldom wrong, then fur had somehow fallen out of fashion. Oh dear, oh dear, said Coyote, I'm going to need more feathers. And back to the river he went.

When the Ducks saw Coyote waiting for them on the bank, they raffled their feathers and looked quite annoyed.

We hope you haven't come to ask us for more feathers, said the Ducks.

I wouldn't do that, said Coyote, and he smiled so all his teeth showed. I've come to protect you.

Protect us? said the Ducks. From what?

Human Beings, said Coyote, who on occasion can be clever. I heard them talking. They plan to steal all your feathers.

Steal our feathers! shouted the Ducks.

They might even try to eat you, said Coyote.

Eat us! said the Ducks. Human Beings eat Ducks?

Coyote pretended to shudder. You'd be amazed what they will eat, he said.

But then who will sing for them? said the Ducks. Who will dance for them? Who will remind them of their relationship with the earth?

Never mind that stuff, said Coyote, and he lowered his eyes and lowered his voice and looked around to make sure no one was watching. I have a plan that might save you. You give me half of your feathers and I'll pretend to be a Duck and I'll let the Human Beings chase me around until they get tired and give up.

Half our feathers? said the Ducks.

You'll get to keep the other half, said Coyote. And you'll be safe.

So the Ducks talked it over, and they agreed that half their feathers was better than no feathers, and certainly better than being eaten.

But what happens if they catch you? said the Ducks.

Oh, don't worry, said Coyote, they won't catch me. For I am exceptionally fast and very tricky.

Well, you can imagine just how good Coyote looked with his long shimmering Duck feathers. Even Bear was impressed.

They're okay, said Bear. If you like that sort of thing.

Look at me, Coyote cried, as he ran through the woods and over the mountains and down into the valleys, the feathers trailing behind him, flashing in the light. Look at me!

But Coyote was not very careful with the feathers. He didn't clean them or straighten them or fluff them up as the Ducks had done, and, after a few weeks, the feathers were bent and dirty and ragged, and they looked very, very sad, for they no longer shimmered and glowed.

We can't have this, said Coyote, and he threw the feathers away and went back to the river.

When the Ducks saw Coyote without the feathers they had given him, they were concerned.

What happened to all our feathers? said the Ducks.

The Human Beings took them, said Coyote. They caught me while I was sleeping.

How horrible, said the Ducks.

What's worse, said Coyote, is I need more feathers.

More feathers! shrieked the Ducks. Absolutely not! No, no, no, no!

Then, said Coyote, puffing out his chest as best he could, we'll fight them together.

Fight? Fight whom? said the Ducks, who were well versed in the rules of grammar.

Human Beings, of course, said Coyote. For they can be very fierce when they don't get what they want.

Well, the Ducks didn't know what to do. They talked about flying away but their long feathers made flying tiring, and they talked about swimming away but they didn't know where they would go, and they talked about running away but their legs were too short to do that. Besides, they were happy just where they were.

These Human Beings, said the Ducks, what is it about us that they don't like?

Oh, they like you well enough, said Coyote. They just like your feathers better.

Now, I could finish this story but you already know what's going to happen, don't you? The Ducks are going to keep giving up their beautiful long feathers. Coyote is going to make a mess of things. The world is going to change. And no one is going to be particularly happy.

Besides, this particular story is a long one that takes days to tell. A good storyteller can keep it going for a week. We don't really have the time. And there are other stories that are just as much fun and much shorter.

Such as the one we like to tell ourselves about injustices and atrocities and how most of them have happened in the past. We tell ourselves that, as we have progressed as a species, we have gotten smarter and more compassionate. We say of slavery, for example, yes, that was a horror. We know better now, and we won't make that mistake again. Of course, segregation was a problem, too, wasn't it.

And if we do make such a mistake in our lifetime, say, for instance, dumping raw sewage into the ocean or dropping bombs on people, we say that this was an aberration, a creature of the moment. We say that it was the times, that the fault was in our stars, that you had to have been there. As if what we did was set in motion by natural forces outside our control, something that caught us unawares or took us by surprise.

Indians, for example.

.　.　.

You might suppose that in the story about Coyote and the Ducks, eventually, Coyote winds up with all the Ducks' feathers, and, in fact, that is what happens.

Sort of.

While the Ducks do give up all their large feathers, the new feathers that grow in are much smaller, and they don't shimmer quite so much and they don't glow quite as brightly as before, and Coyote leaves the Ducks alone for the moment as he looks around for more valuable acquisitions.

With Native people, while our land base was drastically reduced in the early years of treaty making, that erosion has slowed. Even stopped in some areas. Mind you, we don't have much land left, but feathers are feathers. And even if all the large ones are gone, after a while, Coyote is going to come back, looking for the smaller ones. For he has an insatiable appetite.

NOTE

1.　Diane Glancy, *The West Pole* (Minneapolis: University of Minnesota Press, 1997), 70.

5 MICHAEL WINTER

An excerpt from the novel *The Big Why* (2004)

Because of the storm we decided to lie to in Harbour Grace.
Twenty-five thousand Newfoundlanders, Prowse said, migrate to
Labrador each spring. Some, the livyers, stay all year. They live
the winter in shacks on flour, tea, and molasses.

All hands aboard the *Industry*, he said, are Christian. Except
you and the sailmaker.

I go to church, I said.

Yes, and he smiled.

Is it that obvious I'm not religious.

Let's say an independent mind stands out.

The ninety crew aboard the *Industry* were permanent. They
caught green fish. The fish were laid in salt in the holds of the
boat. Sometimes a salt banker would come by and more salt purchased. If the fishing was good.

Belowdecks we checked out the quarters. Most of the hold was
salt. On top of the salt was bedding and luggage. We found Niner
Harris and his parents, Mag and Mose. They were stationers and
late in the season. They were to join Mag's brother in Turnavik.
They shared a bunk on top of the salt—their faces just inches from
the beams and planking of the deck above them. A piece of sail-
cloth divided them from the next bunk. They cooked and washed
on deck but slept and changed down here.

Mose Harris, joking, We came aboard to get away from you, Kent.

We passed a coper selling tobacco and alcohol to the fishermen. Illegal, Prowse said, but done openly and freely. The rum and gin then sold in shebeens onshore.

Aboard at night the dark was devoted to stars.

Prowse, looking up: Made in vain.

Me: I wonder about that—is it all in vain.

I'm speaking of the Milky Way, he said. They call it the maiden vein.

We slept at anchor along the Labrador coast. Anchorage was marked by a naked man on the shore. In the evenings the officers fished for salmon near the mouth of a river. We had salmon for lunch. The king of fish, Prowse said.

We stopped into Cartwright for the day, and he invited me to court. You might find these cases sad but interesting.

I took a seat in back so I could leave if I got bored. A man was brought before the judge and admitted he was a ship's captain. He was in charge of a vessel outside Lloyd's security. The claim by him was that his ship had foundered and was wrecked on the rocks off Blanc Sablon. Insurance was received, the ship sold. It was sold back to him.

This is all true, your Honour, and legal.

The charge, Prowse read, is that you intentionally wrecked the ship.

It had been a bad season with no fish, your Honour.

Yes, but your crew says you forced them to ram the ship onto a shoal.

I hardly rammed it, sir. A bit of misfortune. She was put up on a low-tide sunker.

You claimed the ship was beyond repair.

He shrugged.

You claimed she was played out, got your money to compensate for a poor season. You bought her back and salvaged her.

That's about how it's done, sir.

Prowse's head in his big hands. Crew claims you bought the vessel for a dollar.

I tendered the only bid, your Honour.

I bet you did. You had her careened, and then sailed home in her.

That is correct, your Honour.

Prowse fined the captain seventy dollars. He seized the ship and gave it to Lloyd's. Not for a moment did the captain think he had done something wrong.

The next case was against an entire southcoast community. There had been a true shipwreck the winter before. A salt banker had been trapped in a galloping surf and crushed on a reef. The crew in the frozen sea, hanging to the bowsprit. They wrapped themselves in canvas. They held on to chopped-down masts. And while they drowned and perished of hypothermia, a small gang from the town had rowed out in a chain of dories and stripped the banker of plates and silver and manila rope and tobacco. They had gathered spoons and money and a mantel clock while the salt dissolved around them. They had pushed survivors aside for the booty. This was the charge against fourteen residents of the town. There had been one survivor, and this was his testimony. The man was helped into the stand, for he had lost both his hands and one leg. He said they had been at sea for months. Had sailed from Cadiz and meant to land in St John's with a load of salt. There was smallpox on board, and beriberi. There was scurvy, he said, typhus, lice, nervous exhaustion, and venereal disease. There was blood poisoning and influenza. There was hypothermia, he said, and frostbite and gangrene. Then this storm. Our rudder, he said, holding up one handless wrist, was sheered off, and a makeshift one cut away. We didnt put up a stitch of canvas. We were pushed north, away from St

John's. We saw the birds of Funk and then the island, but we couldnt hold the island, so Captain told us to better crack on sail. We hove west like that for a day. Captain figured it was an emergency, so we lowered the colours and turned them upside down. That's what they saw.

Prowse: Did you see them?

We got in close to a rough shop.

Please explain.

We fell victim to a canal effect, your Honour. A change in pressure, it pushes your vessel towards the land. So we got sucked up onto these here rocks. That's when I saw them coming out in small boats. We was hoping yet to free ourselves. The masts were cut down, both to raise the level of the deck and to offer the crew something if we had to abandon ship. We tossed over the salt too, to lighten her. Hoping she'd come off the rocks. But her jawbones were broke, so we covered her with a sail to see if the water could be stopped from reaching the engines. I climbed into the shrouds and saw it all as they come out in their boats. We thought they come to help us.

The shrouds.

What gives the mast lateral support. The men, your Honour, were clinging to the chopped-down masts. Some were rolling under and losing their grip. All they had to do was throw a line made into a loop. A man in water will reach with his weakest hand and can often not hold on to a rope.

You saw the death of one mate.

Yes, before they were through with him they stripped him of his clothing. They appeared pleased with his death.

They knew the man.

He was from there. One often hates the mate.

You stayed above in the rigging.

I had bread and salt pork in a handkerchief. When I saw what they done to the mate, well, I stayed up there. The ship was doomed.

You've been after having three operations to amputate hands and one leg.

My genitalia just recently was removed. Your Honour, my hands rotted off during the seventeen weeks I spent here. The man in charge would not agree to ferry me to St John's. They was hoping I'd perish. I was put into a cold hut downwind from town.

After the people left the ship, what did you do.

I went down aboard her and made a raft of some planks. I put my feet in a box meant for ship's papers. I found a hen basket with four hens dead in it. I paddled to a fellow shipwreck, who was in a broken boat. We found a barrel of cider. We were to use a hoop off the cider barrel to repair the boat. But neither of us had the strength to turn the boat over. We had to paddle ashore up to the chest in water. He perished then. I kept on. Seventeen weeks, sir, without proper treatment.

A woman came up to testify. She was gaunt and open around the eyes. She looked insane and starved and determined and sorry but vexed with a dilemma. You could tell she knew starvation well, and she was intimidated by the formality of court. I thought she too must be a survivor, but she was one of the fourteen on trial.

Is the charge before you accurate, Judge Prowse asked.

She replied, bitterly: Why did they have to go up on the rocks. And tempt us like that?

The way she said it. There was nothing more to be said.

6 MARGARET ATWOOD
An excerpt from the essay collection *Moving Targets* (2004)

Dennis Revisited

When I was asked to write a small piece on Dennis Lee, I began by counting up the number of years I've known him. It came as a slight shock to discover that it was over twenty. I first met him, ludicrously enough, at a Freshman Mixer at Victoria College, University of Toronto, in the fall of 1957. I was somewhat in awe of him, since, like everyone else, I knew he'd won the Prince of Wales Scholarship for the highest grade thirteen marks in the province of Ontario; but nevertheless there I was, shuffling around the floor with him, while he explained that he was going to be a United Church minister. I, on the other hand, was already doggedly set on being a writer, though I had scant ideas about how this was to be accomplished. At that time I thought, in my intolerant undergraduate way, that poetry and religion—especially the religion of the United Church—did not mix, which brought us to the end of the dance.

Then there was a gap, as Dennis was in mainstream English and I had digressed into Philosophy and English, foolishly thinking that my mind would thereby be broadened. But logic and poetry did not mix either, and in second year I switched back, having missed Bibliography forever. Some time later, Dennis and I became friends and collaborators. I suppose it was inevitable. Art of any kind, in the late 1950s, in Toronto, at Victoria College, was not exactly a hot topic, and those of us who (bred to risk incurring the pejorative label "arty") practised herding and defensive dressing. We worked on *Acta Victoriana*, the literary magazine; we wrote on, and acted in, the yearly satirical revue. At one point. Dennis and I invented a pseudonym for literary parodies, which combined both our names and which lingered on after our respective departures: Shakesbeat Latweed. "Shakesbeat," because the first thing we wrote was a poem called "Sprattire," variations on the first four lines of "Jack Spratt," as if by various luminaries, from Shakespeare to a Beat poet. According to my mother, we laughed a lot while writing it. Dennis, then as now, had a faintly outrageous sense of humour concealed beneath his habitually worried look.

Dennis took fourth year off and went to Germany, thus enabling me to get a Woodrow Wilson fellowship (if he'd been there, *he'd* have got it). After that I was away from Toronto for the next ten years. So it must have been by letter, or during one of my infrequent visits back (I seem to remember Hart House theatre, at intermission; but intermission of what?) that he contacted me about the House of Anansi Press. Some people were starting a publishing house, he said, and they wanted to reprint my book of poems, *The Circle Game*, which had won the Governor General's Award that year but was out of print. He said they wanted to do two thousand copies. I thought they were crazy. I also thought the idea of a publishing house was a little crazy too; it was still only 1967. But by this time both Dennis and I were cultural nationalists of a sort, though we'd come to it separately. We were both aware that the established publishing houses had been timorous about new writing, particularly in prose fiction, though also to a certain extent in poetry. The dreaded "colonial mentality" was not yet a catchphrase but it was on its way. The first four Anansi authors got small grants from the Canada Council, most of which we bumped back into the company. It amazes me now to realize how little money it took to start Anansi. But it took a lot more blood and guts, much of both Dennis's.

During the late 1960s—the period of Anansi's rapid growth and the establishment of Dennis's reputation as an editor—I was in Boston, then Montreal, then Edmonton, so was in touch only by letter. I worked in various ways on three Anansi books with Dennis: George Bowering's *The Gangs of Kosmos*, bill bissett's *nobody owns th earth*, and, less intensively, Michael Ondaatje's *The Collected Works of Billy the Kid*. When my own book, *Power Politics*, was ready to be seen, I felt it was an Anansi book and took it to Dennis. I returned from England in 1971, joined Anansi's board, and worked with various writers (sometimes with Dennis, sometimes alone), including Paulette Jiles, Eli Mandel, Terrence Heath, P. K. Page, John Thompson, and Patrick Lane; and Dennis himself, with whom I edited the second edition of *Civil Elegies*. Our most engrossing collaboration at that time, however, was his editing of my critical work *Survival*. Dennis was indispensable for the book, and in top editorial form: fast, incisive, full of helpful suggestions, and, by the end, just as exhausted as I was.

Small publishing is an energy drainer, as anyone who has done it will testify. By 1973 Dennis was withdrawing more and more from Anansi, and shortly thereafter so was I.

I think it was in the summer of 1974 that Dennis read the first draft of *Lady Oracle* for me, with the usual helpful results. The editorial conference took place on the top of a rail fence, which was typical of Dennis as an editor. The process was never what you would call formal. Given the choice of a dining-room table or a kitchen full of dirty dishes and chicken carcasses and cat litter boxes, Dennis would go for the kitchen every time.

This is as good a place as any to throw in my two cents' worth about Dennis-as-editor. The reputation is entirely deserved. When he's "on," he can give another writer not only generous moral support but also an insightful, clear view of where a given book is trying to go. This is usually conveyed not in conversation alone but in pages and pages of single-spaced, detailed, and amended notes. I have never worked with an editor who delivers so much in such a condensed mode. His willingness to enter so fully into a book's sources of energy make him more than usually vulnerable to invasion by the author's psyche and to the demands of the author's clamorous ego. At one stage of his life he was acting not only as surrogate midwife but as surrogate shrink and confessor to far too many people. It's no wonder that he's fled from the editing process from time to time. It's no wonder too that he's sometimes become bored or impatient with the Super-editor uniform. He is also a writer, and both his own time and the attention and acclaim of others has often gone to the editing when it could or should have gone to the writing. It's his writing that's of primary importance for Dennis. It's also, I think, the hardest thing to talk to him about and the hardest thing for him to do.

When I try to picture Dennis to myself, it's the anxious wrinkles on his forehead that appear first, like the Cheshire Cat's grin. Next comes the pipe, eternally puffing, or sometimes a cigar. Then the rest of him appears, on the run, rumpled, harassed by invisible demons, replete with subterranean energy, slightly abstracted, sometimes perplexed, in spite of it all well-meaning, kindly in an embarrassed and hesitant way; and, when he's talking to you about something important, working very hard not only at but towards saying exactly what he wants to say, which is usually complex. Sometimes Dennis is less complex when he's had a few drinks and is playing the piano, for instance, or when he's making a terrible pun. This maniacal side of Dennis is most visible in *Alligator Pie* and its sequels, and probably keeps him sane; but friendly old Uncle Dennis is of course not the whole story.

I don't have the whole story, and it's clear to me after twenty-odd years that I'm not likely ever to have it. Dennis isn't what you'd call an easily accessible person. In any case, the whole story isn't finished yet. There's more to come.

7 A.L. KENNEDY
An excerpt from the novel *Paradise* (2004)

I can't do this.

No sleep, not practically any kind of rest, your night full of crawling, the presence of crawling, and dirty rags of something, the taste of rags, of death, and first the morning pouncing down alight and now leering through the windows of the car and coming in to get you, only a pinch of glass to keep it back, and so much of it in your surroundings because Simon is driving you, taking you out to the airport, no matter what you think.

I don't want to go.

And he's repeating about the money—the cost you didn't ask them all to pay—and the reasons why they can't afford it, the coming baby and its needs, the toll of the communal sacrifice. You didn't want it, didn't know about it, would have told them not to, but there it is, past recalling, such a monstrous sum spent and with nothing to show, because they have laid down a kind of bet on you, something unwieldy for you to carry with you on your trip to this clinic, this hospital, this spa, this holding tank you cannot visualise no matter what name it has. They think it might help you to go there and they have this love for you: this hard, immovable, weight of love they are levering down on to your breathing—Simon and Mrs Simon and your parents and the child unborn—the five of them sending you off to win their bet and recover yourself, grow respectable and better until everyone can pretend that's the way you were made.

So I won't go then. I can decide.

But the countryside is rushing ahead of the car, faster than the windscreen, reckless, and sucking you on until you feel very sick and all the while you're plunging downwards to the point where your family's wishes are going to make you disappear.

Please.

To the place with the aeroplane smell—jet fuel and vomit, diseases and sweat and travelling too fast to keep your soul. The scent of all those souls abandoned, tearing, you kick it up when you walk. Simon checks you in like your luggage—you can't think where your luggage came from—and there are men with guns here and surely that could lead to bad mistakes and you should go home now, it's time for that, but your brother tells the desk woman that you won't smoke and will sit near the aisle and that you are carrying no explosives and here is your ticket and boarding pass and here is your passport in order, although it contains the picture of someone who is not truly you and, judging yourself against your papers, it's terribly easy to spot the forgery. The cheap, dull fake.

But Robert knows me—he knows that I'm real and like this and correct.

No Robert with you here, though, only Simon who keeps you drinking coffees, drenches you with them so much that your small bones have started to trill and he's got you reined in where he can watch you, gauge you, until the last possible call when you have to be freed, allowed to go off and be somewhere you'll disappoint him, suspend all bets and disgrace yourself and drink.

He doesn't meet your eye as you spin and wave to him, because he can already see you failing. You are good money going after bad.

At the metal detectors you leave your keys in your pocket—so used to being locked in, you forgot that you had them—and the uniform people pat at you and search you and pass you through with frowns and you ask where the crowds are, the travellers, but no one says and you are very loud here, this corner being full of nods and whispers, which is strange. You are strange, but this is stranger and maybe, along with everything else, you are going deaf.

For their own reasons, individuals bump into you very often, even though they are so few and there is so much space. Not that it matters, because now you are walking, your path is fixed through the things you can buy: ways to tell time and smell not like a monster and ways to smoke and calm the hands and hide the eyes and ways to spend money to make yourself happy and ways to feel filthy because of it, as if you were thumbing through porn, as if people were fucking you here with your own cash.

No.

Fuck them. Fuck that.

That isn't happy. That's sad. And it isn't important, because you don't want anything: you're only looking for a friend. Robert would be one if he was here and you will phone him soon, but you can see your other friends now, your darlings, your sweet dreams.

Although there are so many you can't choose, and the shelves begin to loom, which is a cause of nervous tension.

Never mind, though, you find something, grab at something, and hold on to it like a lifebelt until you can pay.

£11.75.

Which is momentarily—you seem—it is mislaid—but about you, very close—you can assure.

£11.75.

They gave your clothes back, not your money. But you can assure. You look again. There must be something.

Simon, you prick.

The announcement announces your flight. Wallet. You have that. Card—no cash machine, no time—but you may have money on the card, in it, in the card, may have £11.75. You have to try, in any case. Time draining out as the girl at the cash desk, a child in fact, tinkers with your plastic, has to type its number out, and then the line is down, or broken, decomposing, and then another slow attempt and mechanical noises follow and, throughout this, she holds fast on to your bottle, as if it might not be completely yours, when she is absolutely much too young to drink and cannot understand a single part of anything about the depth of adult and liquid relationships.

£11.75.

You wait for the paper to curl up and out, the signable receipt that will confirm the possibility of purchase. You concentrate on making your signature seem like your own. You smile with your fullest integrity and charm.

£11.75.

YES.

So God is with you—and, in that case, who is not?

You suit each other, you and God, you're both alone.

In the concourse there's murmuring, faces not in focus, time-delayed, and newspapers in their hands and they're staring like cows, like standing flesh.

The toilet is more civilised and smaller, no one here, and that cool, true friend is yours now and you can see much more, hear much more, even before it's open and too soon and also, to be truthful, not fast enough, there's the beauty of swallowing, the loveliness, the sharp breath from the bottle's neck and the handsomeness of that first taste, it shouts out, shudders the walls.

Then you can ring him—Robert. You can try the card again, persuade it to bear a phone call. You're more than equal to doing that.

'Canada, going to Canada—' telling it to his machine, not to Robert, Robert isn't there—'Sorry. Canada—' his answering machine, which doesn't answer, just repeats the words he left it months ago. 'Canada, that's . . . Four weeks. I mean, I don't know. I can come back straight away.'

But you'll be better soon. If they've spent so much money to make themselves happy, to make you happy, then soon it must come true and you'll be cured.

You will give yourself up. You will be helped. You are a habit that you can't afford.

That makes sense, that's quite believable.

Although not as real as the press of that bet, the drag of expectations impeding you as you run towards the gate.

But you're weightless by take-off, no further burden to anyone— your limbs hollowed out with rushing and your heart thinned to pure motion, a soft knot of blood that evaporates, burns into joy. And more joy in the quiet, whiskey rattle at your feet, the living, stirring 40 per cent proof of perfection. Add it to yourself and make 100, without fail.

Man behind's kicking your seat. Multiple twitching and flickers from every tiny movie screen and up to the toilet with your proof in its nice bag and back and food you don't need and your eyelids dosing harsh against your eyes and swallowing slow and this child in the gangway and she's staring clear inside you and up to the toilet with your proof in its nice bag and back and over you climbs your neighbour who smells of moss and more proof from the attendant and man behind's kicking your seat and a kind of sleep and safety in the blank grind of engines and the half-light and up to the toilet with your proof in its nice bag, but leave it now because it's dead, it's empty, and this makes you sorry and then sit in your seat and watch the attendant take your nice bag from the toilet and look at it and laugh and man behind's kicking your seat and

'What?'

You want to know why he hates you, why he is doing this— sitting and reading the paper and doing this to you. But then the headline on his lap distracts you. You want to ask about it.

'What?'

There are military pictures, which you didn't expect.

'What...'

He's laughing, smirking, undistracted and wiping his hands on his sleeves—some sort of oozing there—and then there's a jolt through the airframe and...

You see the headlines again.

'Ah, because, when did this...'

Asking your neighbour now—man behind hates you and is no use—so you call towards your neighbour.

'We're at war?'

And you can't think how something so large could have occurred so unawares, a whole war without your knowledge, and your neighbour hands over her paper, looks at you as if you are dead and empty and you can't see the print or the pictures, because they move and make you colour-blind, stone-blind, and everything in the cabin has no proof now and smells of bombs and you are sliding into a restless dark where you float, where you are naked, stripped to your sin, and under you there is nothing but hot, wet earth, no sign of a human past remaining beyond this slaughterhouse stench that catches you, sinks you, drags you above it until you touch, until you are slithering over the thick, red ding of mud and, here and there, it jolts beneath you and this has a meaning you understand—that the dead are kicking up, that they remember you and hear you and can taste that you are there. They want you down. They want you buried down with them.

8 RONALD WRIGHT

An excerpt from the CBC Massey Lectures
A Short History of Progress (2004)

III. Fool's Paradise

... As I mentioned earlier, the wrecks of our failed experiments
lie in deserts and jungles like fallen airliners whose flight record-
ers can tell us what went wrong. Archaeology is perhaps the
best tool we have for looking ahead, because it provides a deep
reading of the direction and momentum of our course through
time: what we are, where we have come from, and therefore
where we are most likely to be going.

Unlike written history, which is often highly edited, archaeology can uncover the deeds we have forgotten, or have chosen to
forget. A realistic understanding of the past is quite a new thing,
a late fruit of the Enlightenment, although people of many times
have felt the tug of what the Elizabethan antiquarian William
Camden called the "back-looking curiousity." Antiquity, he wrote,
"hath a certaine resemblance with eternity. [It] is a sweet food of
the mind."[1]

Not everyone's mind was so open in his day. A Spanish vice-
roy of Peru who had just seen the Inca capital high in the Andes,
with its walls of giant stones fitted like gems, wrote back to his
king: "I have examined the fortress that [the Incas] built ... which
shows clearly the work of the Devil ... for it does not seem possible that the strength and skill of men could have made it."[2]

Even today, some opt for the comforts of mystification, preferring to believe that the wonders of the ancient world were built by Atlanteans, gods, or space travellers, instead of by thousands toiling in the sun. Such thinking robs our forerunners of their due, and us of their experience. Because then one can believe whatever one likes about the past—without having to confront the bones, potsherds, and inscriptions which tell us that people all over the world, time and again, have made similar advances and mistakes.

About two centuries after the Spanish invasion of Peru, a Dutch fleet in the South Seas, far to the west of Chile and below the Tropic of Capricorn, came upon a sight hardly less awesome, and even more inexplicable, than the megalithic buildings of the Andes. On Easter Day, 1722, the Dutchmen sighted an unknown island so treeless and eroded that they mistook its barren hills for dunes. They were amazed, as they drew near, to see hundreds of stone images, some as tall as an Amsterdam house. "We could not comprehend how it was possible that these people, who are devoid of heavy thick timber [or] strong ropes, nevertheless had been able to erect such images, which were fully thirty feet high."[3] Captain Cook later confirmed the island's desolation, finding "no wood for fuel; nor any fresh water worth taking on board." He described the islanders' tiny canoes, made from scraps of driftwood stitched together like shoe leather, as the worst in the Pacific. Nature, he concluded, had "been exceedingly sparing of her favours to this spot."[4]

The great mystery of Easter Island that struck all early visitors was not just that these colossal statues stood in such a tiny and remote corner of the world, but that the stones seemed to have been put there without tackle, as if set down from the sky. The Spaniards who had credited the Devil with the splendours of Inca architecture were merely unable to recognize another culture's achievements. But even scientific observers could not, at first, account for the megaliths of Easter Island. The figures stood there mockingly, defying common sense.

We now know the answer to the riddle, and it is a chilling one. *Pace* Captain Cook, Nature had not been unusually stingy with her favours.[5] Pollen studies of the island's crater lakes have shown that it was once well watered and green, with rich volcanic soil supporting thick woods of the Chilean wine palm,[6] a fine timber that can grow as big as an oak. No natural disaster had changed that: no eruption, drought, or disease. The catastrophe on Easter Island was man.

Rapa Nui, as Polynesians call the place, was settled during the fifth century A.D. by migrants from the Marquesas or the Gambiers who arrived in big catamarans stocked with their usual range of crops and animals: dogs, chickens, edible rats, sugar cane, bananas, sweet potatoes, and mulberry for making bark cloth.[7] (Thor Heyerdahl's theory that the island was peopled from South America has not been supported by recent work, though sporadic contact between Peru and Oceania probably did take place.[8]) Easter Island proved too cold for breadfruit and coconut palms, but it was rich in seafood: fish, seals, porpoises, turtles, and nesting seabirds. Within five or six centuries, the settlers had multiplied to about 10,000 people—a lot for sixty-four square miles.[9] They built villages with good houses on stone footings and cleared all the best land for fields. Socially they split into clans and ranks—nobles, priests, commoners—and there may have been a paramount chief, or "king." Like Polynesians on some other islands, each clan began to honour its ancestry with impressive stone images. These were hewn from the yielding volcanic tuff of a crater and set up on platforms by the shore. As time went on, the statue cult became increasingly rivalrous and extravagant, reaching its apogee during Europe's high Middle Ages, while the Plantagenet kings ruled England.

Each generation of images grew bigger than the last, demanding more timber, rope, and manpower for hauling to the *ahu*, or altars. Trees were cut faster than they could grow, a problem worsened by the settlers' rats, who ate the seeds and saplings. By A.D. 1400, no more tree pollen is found in the annual layers of the crater lakes: the woods had been utterly destroyed by both the largest and the smallest mammal on the island.

We might think that in such a limited place, where, from the height of Terevaka, islanders could survey their whole world at a glance, steps would have been taken to halt the cutting, to protect the saplings, to replant. We might think that as trees became scarce, the erection of statues would have been curtailed, and timber reserved for essential purposes such as boatbuilding and roofing. But that is not what happened. The people who felled the last tree could *see* it was the last, could know with complete certainty that there would never be another. And they felled it anyway.[10] All shade vanished from the land except the hard-edged shadows cast by the petrified ancestors, whom the people loved all the more because they made them feel less alone.

For a generation or so, there was enough old lumber to haul the great stones and still keep a few canoes seaworthy for deep water. But the day came when the last good boat was gone. The people then knew there would be little seafood and—worse—no way of escape. The word for wood, *rakau*, became the dearest in their language. Wars broke out over ancient planks and worm-eaten bits of jetsam. They ate all their dogs and nearly all the nesting birds, and the unbearable stillness of the place deepened with animal silences. There was nothing left now but the *moai*, the stone giants who had devoured the land. And still these promised the return of plenty, if only the people would keep faith and honour them with increase. But how will we take you to the altars? asked the carvers, and the *moai* answered that when the time came, they would walk there on their own. So the sound of hammering still rang from the quarries, and the crater walls came alive with hundreds of new giants, growing even bigger now they had no need of human transport. The tallest ever set on an altar is over thirty feet high[11] and weighs eighty tons; the tallest ever *carved* is sixty-five feet long[12] and more than *two hundred* tons, comparable to the greatest stones worked by the Incas or Egyptians. Except, of course, that it never budged an inch.

By the end there were more than a thousand *moai*, one for every ten islanders in their heyday. But the good days were gone—gone with the good earth, which had been carried away on the endless wind and washed by flash floods into the sea. The people had been seduced by a kind of progress that becomes a mania, an "ideological pathology," as some anthropologists call it. When Europeans arrived in the eighteenth century, the worst was over; they found only one or two living souls per statue, a sorry remnant, "small, lean, timid and miserable," in Cook's words.[13] Now without roof beams, many people were dwelling in caves; their only buildings were stone henhouses where they guarded this last non-human protein from one another day and night. The Europeans heard tales of how the warrior class had taken power, how the island had convulsed with burning villages, gory battles, and cannibal feasts. The one innovation of this end-period was to turn the use of obsidian (a razor-keen volcanic glass) from toolmaking to weapons.[14] Daggers and spearheads became the commonest artefacts on the island, hoarded in pits like the grenades and assault rifles kept by modern-day survivalists.

Even this was not quite the nadir. Between the Dutch visit of 1722 and Cook's fifty years later, the people again made war on each other and, for the first time, on the ancestors as well. Cook found *moai* toppled from their platforms, cracked and beheaded, the ruins littered with human bone. There is no reliable account of how or why this happened. Perhaps it started as the ultimate atrocity between enemy clans, like European nations bombing cathedrals in the Second World War.[15] Perhaps it began with the shattering of the island's solitude by strangers in floating castles of unimaginable wealth and menace. These possessors of wood were also bringers of death and disease. Scuffles with sailors often ended with natives gunned down on the beach.[16]

We do not know exactly what promises had been made by the demanding *moai* to the people, but it seems likely that the arrival of an outside world might have exposed certain illusions of the statue cult, replacing compulsive belief with equally compulsive disenchantment. Whatever its animus, the destruction on Rapa Nui raged for at least seventy years. Each foreign ship saw fewer upright statues, until not one giant was left standing on its altar.[17] The work of demolition must have been extremely arduous for the few descendants of the builders. Its thoroughness and deliberation speak of something deeper than clan warfare: of a people angry at their reckless fathers, of a revolt against the dead.

The lesson that Rapa Nui holds for our world has not gone unremarked. In the epilogue to their 1992 book, *Easter Island, Earth Island*, the archaeologists Paul Bahn and John Flenley are explicit. The islanders, they write:

> ... carried out for us the experiment of permitting unrestricted population growth, profligate use of resources, destruction of the environment and boundless confidence in their religion to take care of the future. The result was an ecological disaster leading to a population crash.... Do we have to repeat the experiment on [a] grand scale?... Is the human personality always the same as that of the person who felled the last tree?[18]

The last tree. The last mammoth. The last dodo. And soon perhaps the last fish and the last gorilla. On the basis of what police call "form," we are serial killers beyond reason. But has this always been, and must it always be, the case? Are all human systems doomed to stagger along under the mounting weight of their internal logic until it crushes them? As I have proposed, the answers—and, I think, the remedies—lie in the fates of past societies.

Easter Island was an isolated mini-civilization in a constrained environment. How typical is it of civilization in general? In the previous chapter, I offered a technical definition: that civilizations are large, complex societies based on the domestication of plants, animals, and human beings, with towns, cities, governments, social classes, and specialized professions. Both ancient and modern are covered by that. But Easter Island doesn't meet all the criteria. At 10,000 people, it was small; it lacked cities, and its political structure was at best that of a chiefdom, not a state. However, it did have classes and professions (the stone carvers, for one), and its achievements were in a league with those of far bigger cultures.[19] Its isolation also makes it uniquely important as a microcosm of more complex systems, including this big island on which we drift through space. Easter Island punched way above its weight; but it boxed alone, as if in a looking-glass, and we have been able to replay the moves by which it knocked itself out.

NOTES

1. Quoted in Daniel, *The Idea of Prehistory*, pp. 14-15.
2. Letter of Francisco de Toledo, March 25, 1571, quoted in Luis A. Pardo, ed., *Saqsaywaman* no. 1 (July 1970): 144.
3. From The Journal of Jacob Roggeveen, trans. and ed. Andrew Sharp (Oxford: Clarendon Press, 1970). Quoted in Paul Bahn and John Flenley, Easter Island, Earth Island (London: Thames and Hudson, 1992), p. 13, and more fully in Catherine and Michel Orliac, Easter Island, trans. Paul G. Bahn, (New York: Harry N. Abrams, 1995), pp. 98-99.
4. Orliac, *Easter Island*, p. 17.
5. Both land and sea were, however, less rich in species than large tropical archipelagoes such as Fiji and the Tahitian islands. Like the Marquesas, Easter Island lacks a surrounding coral reef.
6. On an extinct species closely related to the Chilean palm.
7. Most of these were ultimately of Southeast Asian origin. The sweet potato was indeed from South America and is known throughout Polynesia (*pace* Bahn and Flenley, *Easter Island*) by versions of its

Quechua name, *kumara*. For reasons unknown, the pig did not make the voyage.

8. In their otherwise excellent book on Easter Island, Bahn and Flenley (ibid., p. 46) are wrong in stating that the ancient Peruvians lacked ships with sails. There was a sophisticated sailing culture, using ocean-going *balsas*, along the South American coast since Tiwanaku times (the first millennium A.D.). In Inca times, such craft made regular trading voyages up the coast of the empire from Chincha, and other ports south of Lima, to Guayaquil and from there to Panama. The ships were similar to the *Kon-Tiki* design but larger and more sophisticated. Equipped with multiple centerboards, they could tack against the wind and were still making round trips to the Galapagos in the eighteenth century—600 miles (almost 1,000 kilometres) each way. Pizarro learnt of the Inca Empire in 1526 by intercepting a trading fleet heading for Panama from their home port of Tumbez. The craft he boarded had a twenty-man crew and was carrying thirty tons of freight. The Spaniards compared it, in its size and sailing gear, to their own caravels. It is also known that pre-Inca Peruvian seafarers reached the Galapagos on several occasions, leaving behind distinctive pottery. It is just possible that pre-Inca Peruvians reached the Marquesas, which may have been the migration "hub" for Easter Island, Hawaii, and other island groups. I think it equally possible that Polynesian canoes occasionally reached the South American coast and returned to their home islands. Spanish chroniclers recorded accounts of a fifteenth-century expedition by Tupa Inca Yupanqui (Atahuallpa's grandfather) to inhabited islands two months' sailing from Peru—see Thor Heyerdahl, *Sea Routes to Polynesia* (London: Allen and Unwin, 1968), chap. 4 and 5, for a review of this evidence and its influence on early Spanish explorations. It seems unlikely that an Inca ruler would personally sail away from his empire for a year, but he may have commissioned such an expedition.

9. 166 square kilometres.

10. Bahn and Flenley, *Easter Island*, p. 214.

11. Nine metres.

12. Twenty metres.

13. James Cook, quoted in ibid., p. 170.

14. Ibid., p. 165.

15. In general this was avoided, though not at Coventry and Dresden.

16. Roggeveen killed at least a dozen. Attacks by foreigners later became systematic, as "blackbirding," the enslavement of Polynesians, took hold throughout the Pacific. In 1805, the American ship *Nancy* killed many islanders while kidnapping others for forced labour. In 1822, the whaler *Pindos* seized young girls to "amuse" her crew, flinging them overboard when the sailors had had enough. But the worst came in 1862, when Peruvian slave raiders took away half or more of the population to the "islands of death," the infamous British-financed guano diggings off the Peruvian coast, where labourers were chained together and worked until they dropped. Only fifteen made it back alive to Easter Island (after humanitarian appeals by the bishop of Tahiti), and they brought small-pox with them. By 1872, when Pierre Loti saw it, the island was a mass grave, with scarcely more than a hundred people left alive (Bahn and Flenley, *Easter Island*, p. 179).

17. Those standing today have been restored.

18. Bahn and Flenley, *Easter Island*, pp. 213, 218.

19. The island even had a form of script, called *rongorongo*, though many experts believe it to be post-contact in origin.

9 LISA MOORE

An excerpt from the novel *Alligator* (2005)

Madeleine

What she really wants right now is to spend an afternoon with Marty. Some hotel restaurant somewhere with a threadbare Persian rug and waiters in pressed jackets and the tea comes in a stainless-steel pot with a leaky spout and they have all the time in the world to discuss her film, that's what she wants.

Lately, she's been thinking about hitting him up for a loan. There have been unforeseen expenses. She misses him fiercely. She finds herself arguing with him in her head. He's in the room and he's cantankerous. She asks him what he thinks about this or that shot: the girl in bed, her red hair spread over the white night-dress, how pale and possessed she looks, and the surf smashing against the cliffs and the four white horses galloping over the road at night.

Archbishop Fleming's cape, the scarlet lining in the moonlight, the cracking whip. Newfoundland has never looked so beautiful and dangerous, she wants to tell him.

They'd just got married and had figured out the cities in Europe that were nine hours apart so they could sleep on the train and save on hotels. A honeymoon in Europe, this is 1961 and she is what?

Twenty-one?

Chairs, four to a cabin, unfolded into cots and the train rocked them. They slept in their jean jackets and made love with their clothes half on and hoped no one would interrupt.

Sometimes they shared the cabin, once with a girl from Switzerland with fat red cheeks and thick blond braids whom Martin mistakenly called Heidi, though her name, she said, was Giselle.

Madeleine socked her bum into his hips, his cock pressing against his fly and the seam in the bum of her jeans and that was as close as they could get under the circumstances. Good night, Heidi, Martin said over his shoulder.

They were both twenty-one and couldn't make love enough. There was never enough sex. They hung on to each other in their sleep, his arm under her shirt between her breasts, her chin resting on his fist. He always slept in longer than she did.

In the early mornings she made her way down the rattling train for coffee and she would see the fields, luminous green with blue shadows under the clouds, and the Alps, smoky and cold.

Cows that watched the train with profound interest and started a quick walk with their heads hanging low between their shoulders having decided to keep the train company and in midstep forgot what they were trotting after and stood as still as stone.

She saw villages, forests, and windmills sweep past and returned to the cabin and he was still sleeping.

She read *The Magic Mountain* and went for another coffee, but he did not wake until the very last minute when the train jolted, and screeched and emptied out. They had to take their knapsacks down. She pulled on the collar of his jacket and his eyes flew open as if he had been administered electric shock. He stretched his face and had a little shake and sat blinking, his fists dug into the cot, staring at the floor. He had no idea where he was.

Come on, she said. She was taking down the knapsacks by herself, grunting under their weight, Come, on, come on. By then she had lived a full life, felt vast gushes of euphoria and boiling impatience. The day was half over by the time he opened his eyes.

They brushed their teeth in filthy bathrooms with warped mirrors and naked light bulbs in mountain villages. The porcelain sinks had flares of rust and the drains went down into the earth and bubbled up close by. She thought about the phrase, *My husband*. She said it to herself, This is my *husband*, Martin. Or, *This* is my husband, Martin. She hated the word *wife*. It was not a word she could bring herself to say.

Husband, too, was questionable. It sounded stout, bifocaled, and involving of a cardigan.

There were things she would not do: she would not iron his shirts, she would not mow lawns or ever, ever, ever fake an orgasm or put her children in tennis or sailing or allow Martin to buy a motorcycle because she was afraid his head would get smashed in, though he wanted a motorcycle more than anything in the world, nor would she ever get fat or sleep on the couch or let the sun set on a fight or have an abortion or make meatloaf, although a recipe with orange rind and brown sugar had caught her eye.

She would not outright deny the motorcycle—how could she—but she would connive against it.

She would never freeze seven meals because she was going on a trip and didn't want him to have to cook.

It frightened her, what she had got into. In her mother's deep freeze there was a crown of rosebuds that she had worn and a wedge of wedding cake wrapped in tinfoil. Her dress had been cream-coloured, full of understated flounce, and belonged to her godmother. She'd stood on a stool at a dressmaker's with her arms out from her sides and had the zipper moved so the dress would fit in such a way that she could draw breath.

She had fully expected, at the dinner in which they announced their wedding plans to his parents, to be told they were too young, that they had their lives ahead of them, that they'd known each other for only six months and if they were not pregnant what was the rush? She already knew she wanted to make films and she knew the marriage would make it hard to make films but she did not know how or why and so she didn't think about it.

She'd worn a black turtleneck, a rust-coloured skirt, and square shoes and she can still see the way his parents looked up from their plates, how startled they were. How their eyes met and how they decided in unison what they thought of the news. They both took another forkful of food before they spoke.

She had called his parents' house once, looking for him, and they hadn't hung up the phone properly and she heard their conversation about the groceries they were putting away. She heard them say about the price of peas going up and then heard a can of peas, she assumed, slide across the cupboard shelf. She heard his mother say about her back, his father say about his card game. She was riveted to the phone. They chuckled at some remark about a turn of fate; Father Hearn had been dealt the ace just when all was lost in a game of bridge. They both chuckled, a comfortable, private chuckle, and the phone disconnected, but it had been a glimpse into an intimacy so rich it left her light-headed.

Their forks and knives, which had stopped over their plates, began to move again and she saw they were happy with the decision and she could not believe it.

The toilets were clogged and the floors were sometimes packed earth and straw, sometimes covered in a sluice of shit and chickens ran in and out, and they could not believe their luck. They were in Europe.

They hitchhiked to Madrid and fell asleep in a transport truck and the driver pulled over on a hill and got out to smoke under the stars and came back with a flowering branch of an almond tree cold with dew. She woke because the rain from the almond branch dropped on her cheek. She was disoriented and the flowers filled the cab with a green, sugary tang and the smell of cigarettes reminded her of her father, dead for years then.

Groggy with sleep, the flowers and cold night wind made her potently frightened. She was way too much in love.

Smell the flower, the Spaniard said.

I am too much in love, she said.

Smell the flower, he demanded. And he shook the twig near her nose and raindrops fell on her face. She wanted to know what was in the back of the transport truck. What they were carrying.

The landscape had been slipping past them for weeks and it felt like having a tablecloth pulled from beneath an elaborately laid feast.

For the rest of her life she would judge every trip against this trip and every love again this love and none would measure up.

No love would ever measure up.

The truck driver said they had come through the mountains and it had snowed. She saw a rim of slush outside the arc of the wipers and was surprised because two days before they had been swimming in the ocean near Marseille. Marty had pulled a pink starfish out of the waves, handed it to her, and the arms curled around her wrist.

10 PETER BEHRENS

An excerpt from the novel *The Law of Dreams* (2006)

Workhouse

After a while Abner stopped the cart and unbound him, and he sat with his legs dangling from the back as they continued along the road. He could smell the lard that greased the wheel hubs.

The company of soldiers following on foot.

With every jolt from the road, his legs flew up, kicking. He considered jumping down, scrambling over the nearest wall, fleeing across the field. Finding his way back up the mountain. Perhaps the soldiers would shoot, but he doubted it. Perhaps they would chase him. But probably soldiers would not like leaving the dry road to muddy their boots. Which they must clean and rub constantly, he'd heard, or be constantly beaten.

What did soldiers care for a tenant on the loose? It wouldn't mean any more to them than a hare. Probably less. Not worth a scramble. Not worth a bullet. Abner had untied him, after all, and might stand to let him go. He had strength to get himself over the nearest wall, but probably not much farther. He knew that if he lay down in a field he'd stop breathing. And he didn't wish to die there, with magpies pecking at his eyes.

So he stayed on the cart.

Abner passed him his fuming pipe. Fergus held the warm clay bowl in his paws and puffed and watched the company of soldiers veering off at the crossroads.

A dab of wild scarlet moving into the glen, disappearing.

Sunlight beckoned, then rain swept in.

The pipe went out as they were crossing a bog that was split with precisely cut trenches where the turf had been excised, and Abner had nothing to light it with. The donkey trotted on, passing isolated cabins and potato plots where leaves and stalks lay smashed on the ground.

Mother and father, dead. Sisters, dead. You feel very light: floating. Not much attaching you to the world it seems.

Cramps, in the belly, stiff with gas.

Entering Scariff, the road became a street lined with ruined cabins. He had visited the town every year, come to the fair to sell the pig, and it had always seemed exciting—threatening, hurrying—but now it was dead.

Roofs burned out, one after another. Abandoned cabins stared at one another across the road.

Scariff stank of the moldy thatch that was left, too wet to burn.

Beggars standing outside the iron gate of the workhouse were cawing like crows as Abner drew up the cart.

"Now, Fergus, it's the Poor Law Union, you know. The workhouse."

Fergus unwilling to open his mouth.

You guard what you have when it's nothing.

Emptiness, silence.

"Very good establishment they say it is, and you must do as they tell you." Abner was pulling him off the back of the cart. "They'll feed you and take care of you, never fear."

The other son, Saul, had always had a jeering tendency, but Abner was usually kind, and good at working cattle. Cattle could not be worked by anyone who hated them or feared them or did not comprehend their sensitivity.

You could have been cattle, or a horse. Or a rabbit. Fox, badger. Anything that lived on the mountain. A stone, a piece of turf, white root of a mustard plant.

The beggars outside, some clutching children, were hoping to be admitted to the workhouse, but they cleared the way respectfully for the farmer's son to approach the iron gate.

There was a porter's lodge just inside. The workhouse itself was a handsome stone building with a courtyard. Fergus felt Abner's grip on his arm holding him down; otherwise he might flutter into the sky, like a moth.

Where was his mind? If he were a plant growing on the mountain, or a stone too large to be shifted—

"Keeper!" Abner shouted through the bars. "Keeper!"

A bonfire was crackling in the courtyard, inmates herding around it, attempting to warm their hands.

A uniformed keeper stuck his head out a window in the little gate lodge, and the beggars standing in the street began screaming "Soup! Soup!" while holding up howling children.

"Go away!" the keeper shouted.

"Open up, you!" Abner's voice was firm. "My father's a ratepayer, and this poor fellow is ours."

Abner thrust a scrap of paper between the bars. "Here is the ticket all made out. Now come, you, and let him in."

The keeper's head withdrew and the little window banged shut. A moment later the lodge door opened and the keeper came out, buttoning up his blue coat. "You don't expect me to greet every pauper in the country, do you?"

"I don't expect nothing but your duty. Now let us in."

"You must hold off these ragged pigs."

"Hold them off yourself, it's not my concern."

"Let me see your ticket." The keeper glanced at it, then shoved it in his pocket and started unlocking the gate. The beggars were wailing and pressing, trying to get inside. The keeper opened the gate just enough for Abner to push Fergus through, then banged it shut, catching the wrist of a beggar, who began screeching like a cat.

"Do as they tell you now, *an mhic*," Abner was saying between the iron bars. "Good luck to you. God bless you, dear."

He was on the point of opening his mouth and pleading with Abner to take him back, to take him home, but something stopped him, and he remembered his father's silence. He watched the farmer's son climb aboard the donkey cart, crack his whip lightly, and start driving away.

Go, you hasty fucker. I'll get you.

"Look smart, boy." The keeper gave him a shove, pushing him toward the bonfire. "Here is the warden coming— Mr. Conachree. Strip off your clothes now, they go in the fire."

A small official was beetling across the yard, followed by an orange youth lugging a pail in each hand. Ignoring them, Fergus turned to stare at the fire.

Everything red, warping, and changing.

Water cascaded over his head. While he was still gasping and sputtering the keeper and the orange boy seized and pinioned him, peeled off his rags, and threw them in the fire. Then they held him while the official began clipping his hair with sheep shears.

Looking down at the flagstones, Fergus watched snips of his hair twitching with lice.

"Hold still or Warden might slip and snip off your ear," the orange boy warned.

He could feel the tears but fought them back. Humiliated, trying to hold on to some string of himself, he attempted to withdraw inside himself.

Are you just that voice inside?

Frightened, cagey. A rabbit dashing for a hole. Heart beating fast and hard.

Shearing done, the warden dropped the clippers into the pail of strong-smelling fluid and left without a word, walking across the yard and disappearing inside the building.

Fergus stood naked, shorn, gasping and shivering. The orange boy was pulling on a pair of leather gloves. "Close your eyes, man. This goo stings very wicked." Dipping his gloved hands into the pail, he began vigorously rubbing Fergus's scalp. The acrid solvent stung at cuts and welts, made his eyes tear.

He felt like a badger, trapped, killed, peeled.

The orange boy gave one last violent knead then pulled off the gloves. "There, that'll do you I reckon."

He would remember his shearing as the end of everything, therefore a beginning as well. A kind of birth, in sheep dip. He knew himself then—skin and soul and nothing else. He would not forget.

Digging into a sack, the orange boy dropped some clothes at his feet. "Put on your jacket, fresh fish. We dress like gentlemen here."

SEVEN

FOR THE

FUTURE

1 RAWI HAGE
An excerpt from the novel *Cockroach* (spring 2008)

My welfare check is ten days away. I am almost out of dope. My kitchen has only rice and leftovers and crawling insects that will outlive me on doomsday. I am lucky to have that bag of basmati rice and those few vegetarian leftovers from Mary the Buddhist's party. I helped myself to some food at her party while everyone else sat on the floor with folded legs, eating. I could hear their chewing like an incantation as they floated on Indian pillows, the humming inside their throats synced to the sound of Mary's old fridge and the cycles of the world.

I despise how those pale-faced vegans hold their little spoons, humbling themselves. Who do they think they are fooling, those bleached Brahmans? We all know that their low sitting is just another passage in their short lives. In the end, they will all get bigger spoons and dig up the earth for their fathers' and mothers' inheritances. But it is I! I, and the likes of me, who will be eating nature's refuse under sick trees. I! I, and the likes of me, who will wait for the wind to beat the branches and drop us fruit. Filth, make-believers, comedians on a Greek stage! They will eventually all float down, take off their colourful, exotic costumes, and wear their fathers' three-piece suits. But I will find them; I will recognize them through the stripes of their graying hair. I will envy them when they are perched like monarchs on chairs, shamelessly having their black shoes shined, high above crouched men with black nails who are feathering and swinging camel-hair brushes across their corporate ankles. At the tap of the shoe-shiners, they will fold their newspapers, stand up and fix their ties, scoop their pockets for change, and toss a few coins in the air to the working men below. And they will step onto the ascending elevators, give firm handshakes, receive pats on their backs, fix their hair in the reflection of the tinted glass of high-rises. Their radiant shoes will shine like mirrors, and their light steps will echo in companies' corridors to the sounds of "See you at the barbeque, and give my regards to your lovely spouse." No, none of these imposters are chanting to escape incarnation; they all want to come back to the same packed kitchen, to the same large houses, the same high beds, the same covers to hide under again and again.

I am out of toilet paper, but who cares? I always wash after I defecate. Though I must admit, during the water shortages in the wartimes, in that place where I come from, there were periods when I did not wash for a long time. One could hardly brush one's teeth. Oh, how I once gave priority to that which was most apparent; I would wash my face, and deprive everything else, with the little water I had. Every drop of water that ran through the drain made me want to follow it, gather it, and use it again. As a kid, I was fascinated by drains. I'm not sure if it was the smell, those noises and echoes that are suddenly released after the water is gobbled, or if it was just the possibility of escape to a place where all the refuse of stained faces, infamous hands, dirty feet, and deep purple gums made a large pool for slum kids to swim, splash, and play in.

Somehow, I manage to roll the thin sheets of paper and stuff them with weed. The burning coal on top of the joint shines its silver lustre against the backdrop of Mount Royal, which is partially framed in my window. There is a large metal cross right on the top of the mountain. I hold the joint vertically, stretch my hand against the window, and align the burning fire on the tip of it to the middle of the cross. I watch its fume ascend like burning hair. The fumes remind me that it is time to escape this permanent whiteness, the eternal humming of the fluorescent light in the hallway, the ticking of the kitchen clock, and my breathing, yes, my own breathing that is fogging the glass and blurring the outside world in a coat of sighs and sadness as the vapour from my tears moistens the window. It is obstructing my view of the world! But I can escape anything. I am a master of escape (unlike those trapped and recurring pink Buddhists). As a kid, I escaped when my mother cried, when my father unbuckled his belt, when my teacher lifted the ruler above my little palm. I disappeared as the falling blows glowed over my hands like thunder in landscapes of lifelines, long journeys, and travellers' palms. I watched the teacher's ruler as if it wasn't me who received those lashes across fingers extended like the red noon-tide above beaches lit by many suns. I alternated my six cockroach hands and distributed the pain of those blows. And when my palms burned and ached, I fanned my cockroach wings. I let the air cool off my swollen hands as I stood in the corner, my face and belly to the wall.

But I escaped most when I stole sweets, pens, chewing gum, and later on, cameras and cars. Primitive and uneducated as I was, I instinctively felt trapped in those cruel and insane surroundings that were saturated with humans. I loathed those grown-ups who were always hovering above me and looking down on me. They, of course, ruled the heights; they could reach the chandelier, the top of the fridge, they could fondle my hair any time they pleased, but I was the master of the underground. I always crawled under beds, camped under tables; I was even the kid to crawl under the car and get the ball, rescue the stranded cat, find the coins under the fridge.

When I met my mentor Abou-Roro, the neighborhood thief, he realized I had the capacity to slip through everything. But to make me reach the heights he would fuse his fingers, and I would step on his locked and open palms, and he would lift me up to small windows that only vermin can go through. Once I was inside a house, a church, or a school, I would go straight for the valuables. I stole it all; you name it and I stole. I crawled and gathered: silver sets, crosses, change, watches. I even took my time to nibble leftovers and kitchen-counter crumbs.

The underground, my friend, is a world of its own. Other humans gaze at the sky, but I say unto you, the only way through the world is to pass through the underground.

2 PASHA MALLA

An excerpt from stories-in-progress (spring 2008)

The Ice-Cream Man Cometh

The ice-cream man cometh, said Little Sunshine, so all the children paused for a moment to listen. Sure enough, there it was, the tinny jingling of the ice-cream man's bell carried through the humid air over the hills and down into the Classy Park Gated Community that sat, distant and oak-treed and muggy, in a valley at the edge of a seaside town.

It was just after lunchtime and all the children in the neighborhood were gathered around a fire hydrant that one of the local men (the sad one who had moved in without the aid of a rented van or movers; the sad one who had arrived with nothing other than a cardboard box of possessions sitting on the backseat of his wood-panelled station wagon; the sad one with the lazy eye; the sad one who had now lived in CPGC for over two weeks and had seemingly yet to emerge from his house, but occasionally sat visible in his living room with the blinds half-open, gazing into the street; the sad one, the other residents had heard, with the recently dead wife and recently dead kids)—anyway, him. Well, the sad man had taken a wrench to that fire hydrant and now it spouted water in a silvery spray onto the street.

The sad man looked into all that water and thought of that day—almost a month ago, now—but couldn't quite picture that day as a *day*, with weather and atmosphere. Instead he imagined it as a drawing one of his kids might have done with crayons: a sky the color of that liquid in TV ads for diapers and maxi pads, and the sun, a golden, burning O, and a few white scrunches of clouds, and the m's of birds flapping across the page, etc. But the sad man *did* remember the lake. He remembered it vividly, that first glimpse as he pulled into the parking lot in the family station wagon with the wood paneling, how the lake stretched to the horizon like a sheet of black ice, fringed with scrub and rippling. It didn't quite reflect the sky—more, it swallowed the sky; it ate the sky up like a greedy mouth.

The sad man shook the image of the lake from his head. He looked up from the water shooting from the fire hydrant, around at the children. The fire hydrant water was lukewarm and oddly sulfuric, and the eggy smell deterred the children from splashing about as the sad man had hoped. And it seemed that even the children's parents, who found the sad man weird, had also hoped. After all, it was the parents who had sent their children out in bathing suits when they had seen what the sad man was up to. They had said, Oh, look, and ushered their children out into the sunshine. Then they had poured themselves drinks and taken their places on porch furniture on their porches to observe and whisper surreptitiously to their mates.

But despite it all, despite their parents looking on expectantly, despite the stickiness of the summer day that had descended into the valley, and despite encouragement from the sad man, who knelt nearby in a pair of jean shorts and flip-flops and kept saying, *Okay!* and *Get in there!* in a voice that had steadily dwindled from fun to desperate, the kids stood around in their swimsuits, sniffing the air. The sad man had looked up and around to the children's parents for support, but he received little more than vacant stares, before the parents returned to whispered conversations and sipped primly from fruity vodka-spiked drinks, or beers.

Even Little Sunshine had only toed the water. She looked apologetically to the sad man, who in turn, lazy eye lolling off in an indefinite direction, looked pleadingly to her. He knew she was the one who had been leaving things in his mailbox. That first day, trudging up the driveway with his cardboard box of belongings in his arms, he had seen her hiding in the bushes at the side of the house, spying. The next morning, there had been a pencil-crayon drawing of a pie, replete with wavy steam-lines of deliciousness, waiting for him within a sheaf of junkmail and forwarded sympathy cards in his mailbox. Underneath the pie was written: WELLCOME. The following day there had been a drawing of a can of baked beans. And the day after that, a drawing of a can opener.

With the fire hydrant pouring eggishly onto the street, the sad man and Little Sunshine exchanged looks and seemed about to exchange words—but then Little Sunshine had heard something, perked up, listened again, and made her announcement. As the children turned away from the hydrant toward the hills and the jingling bell of the ice cream man, the sad man withered. He had only wanted to make the children happy. And when the children turned away, the floundering boat that was the sad man's spirit capsized, finally, and sank. He squatted there on the lawn beside the fire hydrant, rocking on his heels, watching the water spray out onto the street. And then sat with a *whump* onto the grass.

On that day at the lake, the sad man's wife had been wearing a yellow dress, a yellow sunhat, and yellow sandals. His kids had been wearing mirrored sunglasses with neon rims that kept sliding down their noses. While the kids went down to the side of the lake to catch minnows, the sad man had taken off his t-shirt and hung it on the antenna of the car while he and his wife lugged stuff out of the trunk: a cooler, a blanket, the four life jackets that they would sit on, instead of wear. It's calm today, his kids had said. Do we have to wear them, Dad? The sad man's wife had nudged him and said, Yeah, Dad, do we have to? with a half-smile that suggested something conspiratorial, but also: love. At that moment, the sad man knew, he had been very, very happy.

3 ELISE PARTRIDGE

Excerpts from the poetry collection
Chameleon Hours (spring 2008)

First Death
for Renée Sicalides

Jean's father died one morning before school
—the first parent we knew to go: a stroke.
She came, red-faced, blank-eyed, to crew that day;
we lugged our racing eight to river's edge.
The honey-varnished hull was balsa-frail—
thrust a heel wrong, you'd splinter through to cold.
We teetered from the slip, clutched inch-wide gunwales,
balancing on one leg like storks; tied in;
brushed past the safety rope, slack as a clothesline,
unraveling by the eager waterfalls.
Jean, who stroked the boat, drove upriver;
all backs coiled with hers, our shoulders strained.
Putt-putting after in a stubby tin launch,
black anorak, black megaphone, our coach.

We shivered under the gloom of a railroad bridge
where kids lobbed chunks of coal at startled boats
and swaying snakes of boxcars, dried-blood red,
rattled away to their obscure horizons.
Two-mile warmup; we slid to rest by the isle,

riding uneasily on the shifting current.
A mallard family bobbed nearby, the male
off on his own, neck-sheen green changeable silk.
What could we say? "Jean—how're you doing?"
Amelia, seven-seat, leaned to pat her arm.
When Karen started a story about her dad,
Irene poked her, brightly changed the subject.
In silence we sat half-listening to the coach—
"Let's try some moves to help you stay together"—
kept glancing at Jean, trying to steady the boat.

One bridge to go; past its black arch, the river
fast that day, funneled into a froth;
if we weren't careful, we'd ricochet
off squeezing rocks. "Hold water, port!" The cox
yanked the card-size rudder till it nicked the hull.
We were veering, light as a pencil. "Starboard,
pull! Come on," Jean cried. "Trying!" yelled Marie.
The boat, a minute-hand, swung stiffly; stuck,
dragging. Dig in, dig in, dig in—*heave*—

at last our bow sat pointing south. Time-trials:
edge to the racecourse starting-line. Blades poised.
"*Partez!*" 38 strokes a minute,
surging, burning, settle, surge, take it up—
"Seat three, you're late. Six, you're late, keep time!"
The cox's clapper clapped like a lone drum,
we skidded with the wind, lost Coach's voice,
churned one blistering power-ten at the end,
then sagging, past the stands. Waves smacked our blades.
The dirty orange finish-line flags flap-flapped.
What could we do for Jean? Nothing. Nothing!
She was the first. "Follow!" the cox was crying,

"Two miles to home! Stay together now,
together!" Our oars left purling circles
that blended, blended; blended; began to fade.

Buying the Farm

Crossing over—
will we be standing at a dory's prow,
clouds cooperating grandly in the background,
profiles like captains charting the Passage,
new moon, ice floes, capes?

Pass away
like an unlucky dynasty
or a craze for snuff bottles,
our lives no thicker than a snowflake?

A little folding of the hands to sleep—
straw hat tipped over my nose,
I'm dozing to the lilac's inquisitive wrens;
you, your spade still beside you,
sprawl, just starting to snore.

It's curtains for us,
clasping hands behind the dusty, still-swaying swag—
at last these doublets can come off,
the swipes of rouge and sideburns, then we'll stroll
to greet the flashing city with our true faces.

Let's sleep with the fish,
—yellow tangs flocking like suns,
eels with Sid Caesar eyes
easing into a Romanesque coral-arch.

It's the end of the line,
the train nudges its way to the platform's edge,
we're the only two in the graffiti-swirled car
softshoeing down the gum-gobbed aisle.

And yes, let's buy the farm—
the loft's tucked full of hay,
the combines are waiting,
here is your morning basket of fresh eggs.

As I Was Saying

Blotched undercarpet (no carpet) the hue of lead.
A pilfered coaster
welded to a sill.
Sooty cupboards. One dented
plastic bear rigid with honey.
Nightlong *scritch-scratching*—an anxious mouse
cowering in the crumb pan of his toaster.
The back door bore a Zorro-slash of mustard.

Oh, how sweetly he sang when he wanted
to borrow your money!
While you scurried for work,
he toppled his latest pickups into your bed.

A hundred lists you etched: How I Can Improve.
So what did you think—that was love?
Why didn't you do what I said?

Slit open his mattress, insert two stinking trout,
tip last week's beer over his speakers
and light out.

4 BILL GASTON
An excerpt from the novel *The Order of Good Cheer* (summer 2008)

Champlain: Juin, 1607

At table, alone, Samuel eyes the steaming birds without hunger, when the sentry calls a warning.

Bonneville the cook had just moments ago brought in and deposited the meat platter angrily, perhaps because he knows he needs must deliver it again, reheated, once Poutrincourt and the other nobles return. All day they've been off in the longboat in the headwaters of the bay, exploring salt marsh that might be diked and drained. A wind has risen to fight their return, and Samuel hopes this is the lone reason they are late.

He nudges a bird breast with a knuckle. The flesh does not give. Perhaps it wasn't anger on the cook's face—perhaps Bonneville is embarrassed by his own fare. Samuel eyes the platter of five duck. That is, he tries to think of this as duck, though the thin black bill suggests less a mallard than a kind of seabird. His tongue knows it, too; their taste is more of salt reeds than of flesh, and everyone is tired of it. Samuel can smell nutmeg rising from the pooled yellow fat, and also garlic, but no cook's magic helps. And one must wonder why the heads have been left on. These birds are not game, this is not the after-hunt, one's trophies displayed on the platter. These birds can be netted and broken to death by children, and are barely food. Smelling them, Samuel almost yearns—almost—for the salt beef and biscuit they ate every day of the crossing voyage, the smell and memory of which makes the floor pitch and move with swell. The common men eat it still.

He pinches up a bird by the beak, lets it drop, stiff-necked. He takes his knife and taps a black bill. It glistens well; its shape is not unlike the curled thrust of a talon, the kind that adorns necklaces worn by the great sagamores to the west. He must remember to snap these bills off and collect them in his pouch, for a necklace of his own, a bit of craft he might fill some hours with, to complete and save and take back to France next summer and give to...whom?

Praying for appetite, Samuel hoists a dripping creature whole and takes a bite of skin. Bonneville won't want him eating his bird cold, when it tastes all the worse.

The sentry's bellow has brought Poutrincourt's boy—who is one of several in this colony who can be smelled before he is heard—to stand pungently at his side to tell him there is a lone savage at the gate.

"Is he old?"

"Sir, I do not know that."

"Please, quick, find if he is old."

The young man walks rather than runs. Samuel wonders if the boy's risked impudence is due to Samuel's rougher clothes—he lacks finery, but that is his choice–or because he is the lone noble who hasn't a servant—even the priest has one. The boy would have run if Poutrincourt were here, and though Samuel will say nothing of it he guesses that before winter is out this boy will be lashed. Samuel also finds the boy's red waist sash somehow impudent. Nor does he care for the up-tilt of the boy's nose, which allows a constant view into his nostrils—though Samuel knows one should strive to love whatever of God's designs a man is born with.

He has heard only that the sagamore is impossibly old, and that one of his names is Membertou. Membertou is the reason Samuel stayed behind today, and yesterday, and the whole week previous, the sagamore having sent word that he would soon come. Samuel hopes that Membertou is who it is. If only to get this waiting over.

Samuel finds the Micmac tongue twisted and mystical and often senseless, but of all the men and nobles he is the most able at it and so it is his duty to stay and make first contact with the sagamore. Indeed, Poutrincourt made formal request that he do this, possibly suspecting Samuel's regret. For though Samuel knows their words he is less at ease with their ways—their false smiles, the bluster and sometimes interminably long speeches about unlikely and vainglorious deeds. Samuel is a mapmaker. He is a mapmaker who belongs at sea and who on land is made edgy at the very thought of anyone else in the longboat without him, face into the breeze, discovering even so much as another expanse of mud and clams. They should have left behind the lawyer Lescarbot, who could trick out the sagamore's trust with those sly winks and soft little pinches to the elbow.

The odorous boy barely pokes his head in the door to tell him, "The savage is old. No weapon. Not very large, but tall."

So it is Membertou, and it is the day Samuel has both wished for and dreaded, this meeting that would mark, truly, the meeting of France with New France. Poutrincourt has expressed some worry about their welcome by the savages, for no one had yet even seen this sagamore, not even off in the trees amongst the earlier scatter of savages; first the men, peering out, then more emboldened, standing in calm postures with weapons in view, and later the women, and then also children, who laughed and sometimes bent to aim their bums.

Samuel finishes chewing and rises. He plucks a serviette to wipe his chin in case of bird grease—though some savages will veritably enshine themselves with it, with grease of any kind, in these parts preferring, apparently, bear fat. He wonders why Membertou is alone. Up the Canada River in Hochelaga, Samuel met more than one great sagamore, and none of them, not even those of lesser rank, ever appeared without entourage, braves to fetch things and to yell at. Not so unlike the French military.

The air of the courtyard is fresh as he strides through. The westerly has some scowl to it, and it will rain by tomorrow. Samuel sees that the cook has wedged open the door to his hot kitchen and, inside, Bonneville stands on tiptoes to peer out his vent, toward the gate. One door down, the smithy's clanging and rending has likewise stopped. Samuel wonders if Membertou is truly over one hundred and, if so, how well he walks.

At the barred double door, Poutrincourt's boy leaps away from the Judas hole and stands aside. Samuel hesitates and, feeling watched by the boy, says, inexplicably, *"Oui."* He clears his throat and stoops to peer through the hole. No one stands without. There, empty, lies the field of fresh black stumps running down to the beach and the choppy waters of the bay. To either side, more stumps, and then the dark forest. But there at the beach he spies the thin grubby beak of a Micmac canoe, aground where the longboat normally rests. But no savage, no old sagamore, no Membertou.

Now, an inch from his eye, rises the top of a head and some dirty, greasy hair. No top-knot, no part or braids—it is hair made by the wind and also, so it appears, by sleep. Now a forehead, though not that of an old man. Now eyebrows, grey and fine and glistening with grease, two narrow pelts trod upon by snails.

Still in his prank, the savage continues rising to the hole slowly, very slowly, delaying the show of his eyes.

Now the eyes do come, and both they and the skin around them are deeply those of an old man. Performing his duty, Samuel regards Membertou's eyes bravely, setting himself the task not to look away first. For these indeed are the eyes of New France. They have risen full centre in the Judas hole and they widen in surprise at seeing Samuel's own. When they calm, Samuel sees the smile in them and understands that the surprise was actually feigned, was mirroring his own expression. Membertou's eyes hold their humour but Samuel sees something more behind, a quality eager and strong, though he cannot put a word to it. If wisdom's gleam and curiosity's lust could marry, it would be that.

In a tongue Samuel must tilt his head to know, the sagamore Membertou lisps softly, "I smell duck."

5 PATRICK BROWN

An excerpt from the nonfiction book *Butterfly Mind: A Journalist's Life in China* (summer 2008)

Chapter Three

"Workers of the world, unite!"
    —Karl Marx

The demonstrations had begun on April 16, 1989, in response to the death of the former Communist Party leader Hu Yaobang, who had collapsed from a heart attack during a Politburo meeting the day before. He had kept his Politburo seat when he lost his position as General Secretary of the Communist party over the handling of previous student demonstrations in 1987. He was generally supposed to have been in favour of reform, so his death was an ideal opportunity for raising that issue again.

As on previous occasions, paying respects to a dead leader provided the pretext for criticizing, obliquely or directly, the conduct of live ones, but this time conditions were ripe for a prolonged crisis. Paralysis at the top prevented the quick decisive response that would have nipped the protests in the bud. At the same time, people really were angry about the corruption and hypocrisy of the party.

Another important factor was the impending visit of the Soviet leader, Mikhail Gorbachev. On the one hand, his efforts to reform the Soviet Union could provide a focus for anyone in

China who was thinking that change was needed in China, too. And on the other hand, Gorbachev would be accompanied by large numbers of journalists and their cameras. Anything that happened would be guaranteed a great deal of world media attention. Gorbachev's visit to the Great Hall of the People signaled the end to more than a quarter of a century of hostility between Beijing and Moscow. Had it taken place earlier, the rapprochement would have had great strategic importance, but with the Cold War over, the spontaneous combustion taking place on the streets outside was much more compelling.

I had been asked in mid-April to get ready to go to Beijing to reinforce the small bureau there for the visit, and I applied for a visa just as the student demonstrations began. For two weeks I waited anxiously, convinced, as usual, that the project was not going to work out. Since I had stopped drinking eighteen months before, there seemed to be a section of my brain devoted to fulltime chatter about every conceivable thing that might go wrong. This could be a valuable asset when things actually did go wrong because whatever happened, I had probably already given some thought to how to deal with it. Much of the time, though, my fears were unfounded, and it was extremely tiring to be in constant state of anxiety. I was afraid that the protests would be over before I could get to see them, or that the embassy would stop issuing visas to shut down international coverage. I was delighted and relieved to be given a visa at the beginning of May.

News organizations did not ignore the Gorbachev visit completely, but like the rest of the pack, I found the protests far more interesting. My script from the day Gorbachev and the Chinese supreme leader Deng Xiao Ping sat down for a banquet reveals how badly I misread the event. My account of the day was flat-out wrong.

I made much of the image of the younger Gorbachev grappling vigorously, if clumsily, with his chopsticks while Deng Xiao Ping feebly used his to transport the odd morsel with trembling hands to his tortoise-like face. I used the pictures as an extended metaphor for their relative strengths, and probable futures, writing about Gorbachev as a confident reformer at the height of his powers, and Deng as a feeble old man in the twilight of his.

As it turned out, of course, Gorbachev and the Soviet Union would be gone in a couple of years, while Deng was about to assert his grip on China through the ruthless use of military force, then follow that up by launching a second economic revolution at the beginning of 1992 and remaining the unchallenged supreme leader of the country until his death in 1997.

Outside the Great Hall, the clamour for less corruption and more openness had struck a chord that resonated with vast numbers of Chinese. They shared a widely held view that young people now had the audacity to voice out loud: namely, that officials who preached socialist austerity for everyone else had grown shockingly rich themselves. The mood was one of support for young idealists who dared say in public what many had been saying in private during a decade of economic reform. People thought the party should come clean in more ways than one. "Sell your Mercedes and Pay the National Debt!" was a popular slogan.

More honest information was an important part of what people were asking for. On April 26, *The People's Daily* had published an editorial denouncing the protests as counter-revolutionary. The next day, the protestors were back in larger numbers and with renewed vigour, screaming one of the dullest slogans I've ever heard: "Retract the *People's Daily* editorial of April 26!" During many attempts to talk the students back into their campuses, it was officially acknowledged that they had made good points, ones that the Party and government should address. Deng Xiao Ping himself said that not a hair on the students' heads would be harmed.

Student activism was not entirely new to China, and a convenient anniversary presented itself on May 4, a red-letter day for the Communist Party as well as for reform-minded Chinese. It was a landmark in China's struggle to reverse the nineteenth-century depredations of the Western powers. On May 4, 1919, students had begun large demonstrations in front of the Tiananmen Gate in protest against the results of the Versailles Conference on issues arising from the First World War. The students had been outraged by the humiliating news that the conference had decided to award the German "concession" in Shandong to Japan instead of returning it to Chinese sovereignty.

Seventy years later, students marched to the Tiananmen gate knowing the anniversary would afford them a degree of tolerance and license. It was obvious to all Chinese, but not to me at the time, that the same tolerance would not be accorded to rebellious peasants or workers. When the students were approached by the handful of workers who thought the time was ripe for the establishment of a free trade union, the students refused even to permit the workers to join the main protest on Tiananmen Square. Instead, they allowed the workers to settle into a small ghetto on the Northwest corner of the square.

It was there I ran into Han Dongfang, the spokesman for the Beijing Autonomous Workers Union, whose headquarters was a tent pitched on the fringes of the student occupation. He has a wonderfully persuasive, rich, deep voice, and an unshakeable conviction that his cause is just and will one day prevail. I remember thinking when I first heard him speak that he would have a marvelous presence on radio.

Han Dongfang was an electrician who had worked for the railway, travelling round the country maintaining refrigerated wagons. He was also a former soldier, and had served for three years in the prison service of the Peoples' Armed Police, a branch of the army. When he was eventually detained, one of his prison guards recognized him from having served in the same unit.

Han Dongfang was not a natural rebel or dissident. Even his name testifies to his parents' communist conformity. Dongfang, meaning the East, is taken from the Maoist anthem, "The East is Red." He had volunteered for the army and had later applied several times for membership in the Communist Party, but was turned down. He says he was finally disillusioned with the system after witnessing protestors being beaten up by police during the earlier student demonstrations in Beijing in 1987. He gives the impression that if only the party had lived up to its promise of brotherhood, equality, and a better life for workers and peasants, he would still be working on the railway today.

Han Dongfang says he and "about fifty or a hundred" others formed the Beijing Workers Autonomous Union a few hours after Premier Li Peng declared martial law on May 19, 1989. They held elections for a five-person committee and chose Han Dongfang as spokesman. It was one of those moments that change a person's life forever.

Meanwhile, the students' inspired tactic of a hunger strike coupled with public resentment over the clumsy declaration of Martial Law provoked even bigger demonstrations. People from all walks of life were now turning out to support the students.

Tiananmen Square itself is supposed to hold at least a million people. During one of the big turnouts after Martial Law was declared, I walked from the square for seven kilometers, along the wide boulevard to the television station, pushing through crowds of people jammed shoulder to shoulder all the way. It's estimated that, at their height, at least three million people took part in the demonstrations. Walking along the overpass that crosses Beijing's second ring road, I saw it was clogged with trucks and buses bringing people into the centre of the city, brandishing banners and flags, blowing horns, and banging drums and cymbals. The cavalcade included large numbers of ordinary workers waving banners echoing the students' slogans, and others announcing the name of the factory or work unit to which they belonged. It was as if truckloads of delegates were going to some gigantic convention, or as if the annual outings of hundreds and hundreds of factories and offices were all heading for a picnic at the same place at the same. People seemed to be enjoying every minute of the escape from routine drudgery, laughing, cracking jokes, and making a deafening racket as they went. Ordinary citizens far outnumbered the students. Workers from countless factories, and employees of big downtown hotels and many government organizations, showed up for what felt like an enormous street party.

Without doubt, there was a great deal of admiration and support for the students and sympathy for their demands, but Chinese friends who were there remember *qihong*, the Beijing impulse to join a boisterous crowd to see what's going on, as a major motivation too. But hardly anyone among the millions who went down to the square was interested in joining the Beijing Workers Autonomous Union. Its membership never got much beyond double figures. "When we approached them, asking if they wanted to join our organization, they would step back, saying they were just there to support the students, and they didn't want complications," Han Dongfang says. "This was partly a hangover from the Cultural Revolution, when being part of a counter-revolutionary organization was far worse than being declared a counter-revolutionary individual, so people would take part as individuals, and not take responsibility."

One of the few things I got exactly right during this first visit to China was an on-camera "stand-up" I did in the square on May 24. A giant plaster replica of the Statue of Liberty, which art students had made, hauled onto the square, and artfully renamed "The Goddess of Democracy," was now the focus of protests. Loudspeakers were blaring Beethoven's setting of Schiller's "Ode to Joy" from the last movement of the Ninth Symphony as a violent spring thunderstorm struck, lashing the banners waving over the huge crowd into a frenzy. The storm cast an eerie light over an apocalyptic scene. Struggling to make myself heard over the noise, I said into the camera that the statue of an American icon in front of the Great Hall of the People was a provocation the authorities could not possibly tolerate, while warning of bloodshed if they tried to remove it by force.

I still feel regret when I recall what happened next.

6 SHANI MOOTOO

An excerpt from the novel *Viveka's Story* (Fall 2008)

Just before moving onward, you will be hit with a strong, sweet whiff of garlic, scallions, and ginger as they are sautéed, a street away, in peanut and sesame-seed oil. But you won't see Hing Wan Chinese Restaurant, the best this side of the oil refinery, as it is obscured behind the Town Hall, on the slope of land that falls toward the commercial centre below. Hing Wan's is where the aldermen, the mayor, and lawyers take their lunch, and where some of the doctors take theirs, too. Today you would find Dr. Mansingh there. He is in one of the several private rooms, at the back of the restaurant. He is, of course, not alone, but the staff here is discreet. Despite the distraction of the aroma, know that there is street-food higher up, exceptional and unusual food, near the gates of the Girls' School. You will want to sample that, to buy it from the vendor there, so have courage and steer the Promenade tour onward.

Behind speaker's corner is a large, shallow round pool, with a fountain at its centre, a bronze mess of scaly fish entwined, open mouths that once spouted water. But the fountain has not worked in years, and its pool is empty of water. The ceramic blue-tiled floor of it, however, is covered in a carpet of freshly fallen orange petals. There are benches around the fountain, and they are occupied by court-hearing attendees, and office clerks, and idlers. Nut vendors walk up and down the promenade, cream-colored canvas bags slung from their shoulders.

Their outstretched hands show off small brown-paper packages of unshelled peanuts. It is nearly the town's official lunchtime, and the air is becoming fragrant with the scent of foods from vendors' outdoor cooking and from jeeps parked near the Promenade's far end, from which hotdogs and hamburgers are already being sold. Huddled at the base of the tall stately trees are people who have staked claim on those meager spots, and who will ward off anyone who trespasses with shrieks of curses and lunges, armed with frail fists and fearsome body odours. Even the police leave these people alone. If you look closely, you will see sleeping figures in the densest sections of shrubbery planted by the town's gardeners, in clumps here and there. The scent of food rising up from all corners of the city at this time of day is a blessing.

Past the fountain is a towering bronze pedestal base, on top of which is a disproportionately smaller, pigeon-blessed statue of Mahatma Gandhi, loin-cloth clad and stepping briskly forward. He seems about to step off his base and into the air. Behind the Gandhi statue, in the centre of the tree-shaded promenade, is the biggest statue of all, a full and highly detailed bronze of Queen Victoria in ample skirt, every fold rendered, sporting crown and scepter, also streaked in pigeon droppings. Fading into the distance are more water features, none of which function, and more statues, of past governors, past mayors, and business benefactors of the town.

The high school attached to the convent has just recessed for lunch. The electronic wrought-iron gate grates, rumbles, and sputters as it slides open, and the girls, rowdy and excited, spill out. They head for the doubles vendor, who has been waiting for this very moment. When they cross the boundary line of the gate that separates the world of commodities and desires from that, supposedly, of learning and restraint, the girls seem, one by one, to take a vertiginous step, and there's an instant when they seem to misstep and falter, then land a little to the side or, illogically, too far forward. If one were to videotape their exit/entrance, and playback the moment in slow motion, one would see that what caused that odd blip in appearance and gait was a grabbing of the waistbands of skirts and smart flicks of the wrists to turn the waistbands under, once, twice, sometimes even three times, in order to shorten the skirts well above the knee, a movement studied and practiced until it is executed so swiftly that to the outsider there appears to have been a jump-cut in life. The collars of their white shirts are normally pinned tight at the neck with a brooch, but by the time the girls reach the food vendor, the house badges have been whipped off and necks exposed.

All morning, the vendor has been preparing for this lunch-time crush by frying batches of split-pea flour patties and heating up the large vat of curried channa that she carted from her home. Already buzzing around the vendor are the sixth-form students from the boys' college three streets away. They have come for the girls first, and the doubles as a kind of side order. Vashti Mansingh is here. So is Pria Castano, whose father's law office is at the top of the Promenade. And Felicia Clark, whose mother works as a clerk in the police station. Lloyd Gobin is here, too. His mother teaches at the convent but does not know that her son is here to meet one of her students. His father is the manager of the furniture and rug store in the town centre. He would see nothing wrong with his son being here, but would not contradict his wife's judgment. In any case, prefects from the girls' school have been stationed to make sure that the girls do not stray. So the rendezvous, orchestrated to look like little more than coincidental line-ups of boys and girls who happen to find themselves elbow to elbow with each other, last no more than ten minutes, that being too long, even so, for buying this quickly prepared street food, which the girls must take back behind the gates to consume. They take care not to be caught chatting or directly facing the boys or acting as if these meetings have been planned. But those ten minutes will be the stuff that keeps them from hearing anything that goes on in class that afternoon, and the stuff, too, of that evening's, that night's, confused and excited longings.

The vendor's helper, a girl, perhaps the vendor's daughter, takes care not to look into the eyes of the students, many of whom are older than she is. Vashti Mansingh knows better than to stand out there too long, or to get caught chatting with the boys, so she orders her doubles—the vendor pulls a yellow chickpea flour flap from a pile in a tea towel, and she already has a little square of grease-proof brown paper in the palm of the other hand, and she places the bara flat on top of that, then slaps its centre with tamarind paste, and in the cup she has made with the back of the paste's spoon she slaps a heaping tablespoon of curried channa, and then pulls another flap over that, and she folds the lot in two, and with a twist and flick of the paper's ends she has created one order in less than fifteen seconds—and Vashti pays the vendor's helper or daughter and heads back to the gate.

A bedraggled woman, who had been lying on the ground near some shrubs, leaps up and hobbles quickly to Vashti. Vashti hears her name whispered. She spins around and her heart begins to thunder. The woman appears to be old and haggard, but Vashti knows she is only a handful of years older than Vashti is. She is, in fact, the age of Viveka, Vashti's sister. She is thin, with the depleted meagerness of the alcoholic. Her long black hair is oily and clumped. She wears what was once a white shirt, a school shirt, from not too long ago, but it is yellowed and soiled, and the trousers she wears, men's trousers, are covered in dirt, dust, urine. They are several sizes too big for her, held high above her waist with a belt, and as if that were not enough, with a length of heavy rope. She is barefoot.

Vashti wants to pretend she can't see who has called her. She wants to pick up her pace and hurry across the street and back through the gates. And as much as she wants to do this, she wants, too, to go to this woman, stand with her and ask her if she can do anything for her. But she does not want to be seen by her friends, or anyone on the promenade, or even people who would be strangers to her; she doesn't want anyone to see her with this woman about whom rumors have spread far and wide. People have driven their cars here on a Sunday to see if they could spot her. She is said to give her body over to men, right here on the promenade, behind statues at night and in the bushes in the day, in exchange for a cigarette, or money to buy a flask of rum. It is much discussed. Vashti hears the talk, and in the moment, as she lets her eyes meet the woman's eyes, it is as if she, too, is saying these things: "But if she is doing this sort of thing, what they say about her can't be true then. It can't be so that she is a buller. If is woman she like how come she doing it with men? Well, maybe is not a bad thing, then. That might cure her. And from such a family, too. It is killing her parents. No wonder they put she out the house."

But Vashti knows this woman. Merle Bedi. She used to visit Viveka, and Vashti and Viveka would sit in the living room and listen to Merle play Beethoven on the piano. And Debussy. *Au Clair de La Lune.* Their favorite. And when Merle played, she forgot the world around her. Sound, but not only sound, for it seemed, too, as if some unearthly understanding of the meaning of every note arched through her body, filled her lungs, and weakened her. Watching her made you breathless. Her fingertips touched each key and the key gave itself up to her, as if it too had been waiting for her. Vashti and Viveka knew that Merle would be a great pianist one day. That is what Merle wanted. But her parents insisted that the piano came too easily to her, and for that reason it should be her passion, not her job. They insisted that, since she also did well in science, she was to study medicine. If only, Vashti finds her self wishing now, if only the other students, and the people staring as she walks slowly over to Merle, could know how brilliant and talented Merle is. Or was.

"Vashti, can you spare some money?"

Vashti is taken aback. She thinks Merle might have asked how she is. She instinctively holds out her brown-paper package of doubles. "No, but you can have this."

Now that she has stopped and faced Merle she wants to ask her something, to say something more, but her mind goes suddenly blank. Merle does not reach for the doubles, but says, "You don't have any money? I need some money."

Vashti says, "Sorry. I don't have any more on me," in such a soft voice that Merle does not hear and approaches closer.

Vashti steps back, shaking her head emphatically. Merle turns and limps off. Vashti hurries across the street, tears welling in her eyes. She turns, before going through, at the gate, but Merle has already disappeared.

7 LISA MOORE
An excerpt from a novel-in-progress (2009)

Harry hadn't looked out the window when he first took the room. The Chandler Hotel on 31st and Madison, and the curtains had been closed but the television was on and there was a peculiarly static shot of a cherry tree bending over a waterfall.

The shot had an almost imperceptible zoom, until a single flower filled the screen, and then a single petal, almost white. His mother had called on his cell and she was talking about weather and Christmas baking but the phone filled with static.

A droplet of water hung from the flower petal and it was full and began to tremble and then Harry could actually see the edge of the drop begin to tear away from the edge of the petal.

The butter, she'd said. While his mother spoke, the water droplet, magnified, had become a burning globe of pure radiance, white within white within white, filling the screen.

A roaring surf of noise mounted behind his mother's voice and whelmed it with hissing and wonky feedback but what he could still hear was the cadence of her speech. He could hear the texture of her voice and the idiosyncratic lilt, but the words were morphed. They lost whatever adherence they'd had to language and became just his mother, her essence diluted, emptied of content, a husk, a shadow.

Then he'd thought he heard his mother say Jane had called. Jane. He'd shaken the phone as if it were a saltshaker. He understood technology but there he was shaking the phone, knocking it against the heel of his hand, pointing it in different directions, toward the bed, toward the shower, toward the radiant drop on the television. And he lost her.

He tried to turn off the television but he couldn't find the remote. The buttons on the console didn't work and there was no remote. Jane had called his mother.

Harry's mother was making her poundcakes; she gave them out for Christmas, cherry cakes she wrapped in transparent red cellophane. She bunched up the cellophane at the top and tied it with silver ribbons. He could see her running the ribbon between her thumb and the blade of the scissors to make it curl.

He closed the wooden cabinet doors over the television and went to the bathroom to shave. He stood in the mirror and his face looked like a face that had slept on a plane. It was creased and young.

A hoarse, bubbling snore erupted from his bed. It was a private and unfeminine noise, guttural and glottal, full of snot and dreams. The woman in his bed was North Korean and he had not had sex with her. He had met her on a plane and two days later met her again, by mistake, by coincidence, at a disco he'd wandered into and she had thrown her purse at his head.

He had been at meetings and had wandered the city and though it was only late November it had become very cold overnight.

Jane had called him and he was supposed to send her money. The meeting and lunch with associates and he was supposed to find a bank but it was getting dark and he needed a coffee. He needed, always, a pause before he parted with money.

His fifteen-year-old daughter, Miranda, had taken a job riding around in a glass transport truck. She was in the back of the transport truck, which was a big glass box made to look like a beach, with sand and beach umbrellas and a soccer net and three men in swimsuits, and she was in a bikini and they smoothed sun-block on her back. Sometimes she read a beach book and the men crouched at her feet, out-of-work actors, the men, and she had quit high school and lied about her age. Harry was getting the story on a cranky cell phone between meetings. The transport truck was driven around cold dark cities all over the continent to advertising Caribbean vacations.

Jane had flown to Ottawa to bring her back. Jane. He needed a pause to think about Jane. It was very, very cold.

The guy selling fruit outside the Second Cup on Fifth Avenue was bent over against the wind and he wore gloves and the pears sat in tissue paper cups that fluttered in one direction and the other. There were crates of pears and apples and oranges in rows and the oranges caught the streetlight and were loudly orange.

Harry had walked around in the late afternoon, looking up from the sidewalk at the Empire State Building listening to Jane who was standing near a fountain, it sounded like, in a mall somewhere in Ottawa and he could hear the shushing of cash registers and piped in carols and she sounded weird and the Empire State Building seemed to slant back against the sky.

He ducked into the Second Cup and the staff wore earpieces and peaked caps and they marshaled the line so it moved and pointed to a clerk behind the counter and said: Inez is ready for you now. Or: Jasmine, at the end, is ready.

A woman asked if she could sit with Harry and she unzipped her jacket and turned toward the window and she fell in like a cake. She sighed so deeply that she seemed to sink into her coat and he asked if she was from New York. She said she had come in from New Jersey on business.

He told her he was Canadian and he was surprised to hear himself talk. It was getting darker outside and every time the door opened there was a gust of cold winter air. The Second Cup was playing a remix of Bob Marley. Harry was surprised by how lulled he felt. He felt he could confess things and the woman might confess and Bob Marley would preside.

They were getting ready for Christmas in New York and there was a fashion window with mannequins in red evening gowns and a gold fireplace and jewels and cream-coloured furniture and a pyramid of gold boxes with bows. The reflections of yellow cabs slid over the long full red gowns and the cabs were swallowed up in the voluminous satin folds of the skirts.

The woman who had sat beside him in the Second Cup said she channeled spirits for a living.

It's draining work, she said. She glanced over at the counter with the cream and milk and said she needed sugar and she was going to get some. But she narrowed her eyes and stayed very still.

I feel a vibe, she said. Coming from you.

Let me get the sugar for you, Harry said. What do you want, sugar?

I believe you've lost someone, she said. She had stood up and raised her finger. She was about to pronounce upon Harry and all that he was; an ambulance tore down the side street and for a moment the woman with her finger raised was washed red and distracted, perhaps she heard a call from a passing soul in the ambulance; Harry felt the continent sweep through him and he thought if he closed his eyes and opened them he would be in his mother's kitchen.

He thought of the men and women who had been sleeping on the plane, their mouths hanging open; the concentrated, hard-won abandon on their faces. But the woman abruptly clamped her mouth shut.

I'll just get the sugar, she said.

ABOUT THE AUTHORS

ATWOOD, MARGARET

Margaret Atwood is one of the world's preeminent novelists, and winner of the Booker Prize, the Giller Prize, and the Governor General's Literary Award, among many other honours. She is the author of more than twenty-five books. Included here are excerpts from her first major collection of poetry, *The Circle Game* (Contact Press, 1966; House of Anansi, 1967), which won the Governor General's Award for Poetry in 1966. The book was acquired by Dennis Lee for Anansi in 1967 and has been in print ever since. Also included here are essays from Atwood's nonfiction collections with Anansi, *Second Words: Selected Critical Essays* (1982) and *Moving Targets* (2004). The fifty essays in *Second Words* span twenty years and reveal Margaret Atwood's views on feminism, Canadian literature, the creative process, nationalism, sexism, as well as critical commentary on a number of influential writers. *Moving Targets: Writing with Intent 1982-2004* is the companion volume to *Second Words*, and includes political essays alongside pieces that delve into the rich back-story and diverse range of influences on her work. Atwood lives in Toronto.

BABSTOCK, KEN

Ken Babstock was born in Newfoundland and grew up in the Ottawa Valley. His poems have appeared in many Canadian journals and anthologies, and won gold at the 1997 National Magazine Awards. He also won the Milton Acorn People's Poetry Prize and the Atlantic Poetry Prize for his first collection *Mean* (1999). Babstock's second collection,

Days into Flatspin (2002), was a finalist for the Winterset Award. The excerpt here is from *Airstream Land Yacht* (2006), which the *Globe and Mail* called "the most important poetry book yet from any Canadian born in the 1970s or beyond." It won the 2007 Trillium Award and was a finalist for the Governor General's Award for Poetry, the Griffin Poetry Prize, and the Winterset Award. Babstock lives in Toronto.

BARTON, JOHN

John Barton is a three-time winner of the Archibald Lampman Award for Poetry and has also won the CBC Literary Competition in the poetry category. He lives in Ottawa, where for many years he co-edited *ARC: Canada's National poetry Magazine*. The excerpt here is from *Hypothesis* (2001), Barton's second collection with Anansi (after *Designs from the Interior*).

BEHRENS, PETER

Peter Behrens' stories and essays have appeared in *The Atlantic Monthly, Tin House, Saturday Night,* and *The National Post* and have been anthologized in *Best Canadian Stories* and *Best Canadian Essays*. He is the author of one collection of stories, *Night Driving* (Macmillan). The excerpt here is from Behrens' internationally acclaimed first novel, *The Law of Dreams* (2006), which won the 2006 Governor General's Award for Fiction and was a finalist for the Rogers Writers' Trust Fiction Prize, the Commonwealth Writers' Prize, the CBA Libris Award for Fiction Book of the Year, and the Amazon.ca/Books in Canada First Novel Award. Behrens was born in Montreal and lives on the coast of Maine with his wife and son.

bissett, bill

bill bissett garnered international attention in the 1960s as a preeminent figure of the counter-culture movement in Canada and the U.K. In 1964, he founded blewointment press, which published the works of bpNichol and Steve McCaffery, among others. Bissett has also published more than seventy books of his own poetry. A pioneer of sound,

visual, and performance poetry, bissett composes his poems as scripts
and has worked to extend the boundaries of language and visual image,
creating a synthesis of the two in his concrete poetry. The excerpt here
is from *Nobody owns th Earth* (1971). Bissett lives in Toronto.

BLAIS, MARIE-CLAIRE

Marie-Claire Blais has been a literary legend since the publication of her
first book, *Mad Shadows*, in 1959 when she was twenty years old. She has
written more than twenty-five books and is a three-time winner of the
Governor General's Literary Award. She has also won the Athanase-
David Prize, the Medicis Prize, the Molson Prize, the Writers' Trust
Matt Cohen Prize, and Guggenheim Fellowships. The excerpt here is
from *These Festive Nights* (1997), the first volume of her prize-winning
trilogy that has been acclaimed as one of the greatest undertakings in
modern Quebec fiction and "the *Divine Comedy* of our time" (*Le Devoir*).
Blais divides her time between Quebec and Florida.

BOWERING, GEORGE

George Bowering was born in Penticton, British Columbia, in 1935.
After serving as a photographer in the RCAF, Bowering attended the
University of British Columbia and started the influential magazine
TISH. Bowering has taught at the University of Calgary, University of
Western Ontario, and now teaches at Simon Fraser University in
Vancouver. Bowering is one of Canada's most prolific writers of
poetry, short stories, and novels, having published over forty titles.
He is also one of the most acclaimed and versatile, and has won the
Governor General's Literary Award in both the poetry and fiction cat-
egories. He was also a finalist for the 2004 Griffin Poetry Prize. The
excerpt here is from his GG-winning volume of poetry, *The Gangs of
Kosmos* (1969).

BROWN, PATRICK

Patrick Brown was educated in his native England at Cambridge, and
holds a Master's degree in social anthropology. Brown came to Canada

in 1970 and joined Radio-Canada International as a news editor. He went to Montreal to work for the local CBC radio station as a reporter in 1976 and became a national reporter two years later. Appointed to London in 1980, Brown covered the gamut of news from wars, revolutions, elections, and riots to royal weddings. Now based in Beijing and Bangkok, Brown specializes in CBC documentaries focusing on Asia. Brown's coverage from Cambodia on the impact of the Paris peace treaty earned him the 1993 Gemini Award for Best Reportage. He also received Geminis for his coverage of the war in Afghanistan in 1992 and again in 2002. The excerpt here is from his forthcoming nonfiction book, *Butterfly Mind* (2008), about life as a foreign correspondent in China and elsewhere. Patrick Brown lives in Beijing.

BUFFAM, SUZANNE

Suzanne Buffam's poetry has appeared in various journals in the United States and Canada, in the anthologies *Language Matters* (Oxford University Press), *Breathing Fire: Canada's New Poets* (Harbour Press), and *Breaking the Surface* (Sono Nis Press), and won the 1998 CBC Literary Prize for Poetry. A graduate of the Iowa Writers' Workshop and the Master's program in English at Concordia University, she is currently Visiting Poet at Columbia College, Chicago. The excerpt here is from *Past Imperfect* (2006), which won the Gerald Lampert Memorial Award. Buffam lives in Chicago.

CARRIER, ROCH

Roch Carrier was born in the small town of Sainte-Justine, Quebec, in 1937. He published his first book, *La Guerre, Yes Sir!* in 1968. Since then, he has continued to publish and has also served as secretary-general of the Theatre du Nouveau Monde in Montreal, Director of the Canada Council from 1994 to 1997, and was appointed National Librarian in October 1999. The excerpt here is from *The Hockey Sweater* (1979), a story so beloved that a piece of it is reprinted on the back of the Canadian five-dollar bill. Carrier lives in Ottawa and Montreal.

CHOMSKY, NOAM

Noam Chomsky is an internationally acclaimed linguistics scholar, author, and political radical. He was born in 1928 in Philadelphia, Pennsylvania, received his PhD in linguistics from the University of Pennsylvania and is currently a professor at the Massachusetts Institute of Technology. A self-proclaimed anarchist, Chomsky has established a skepticism towards authority characterized by political activism. He is the author of numerous influential books, including *Manufacturing Consent* and the book excerpted here, *Necessary Illusions* (the 1989 CBC Massey Lectures). Chomksy lives in Boston, Massachusetts.

CLARKE, AUSTIN

Austin Clarke is a Canadian novelist, essayist and short story writer who lives in Toronto, Ontario. Born in St. James, Barbados, in 1955 Clarke moved to Canada, where he attended the University of Toronto, became a reporter, joined the Canadian Broadcasting Corporation, and eventually became a freelance journalist. In 1998, he was made a Member of the Order of Canada. In 2002, he won the Giller Prize for his novel *The Polished Hoe*, and in 2003 he won the Commonwealth Writers Prize for the same book. The excerpt here is from his collection of stories *When He Was Young and Free He Used to Wear Silks* (1971). Clarke lives in Toronto.

CONNOLLY, KEVIN

Kevin Connolly is a Toronto poet, editor, and arts journalist. He was founding editor of the influential 1980s literary magazine *What!*, and his Pink Dog chapbook series published early work by many of the city's best young talents. Connolly's first collection of poems, *Asphalt Cigar* (Coach House, 1995), was nominated for the 1996 Gerald Lampert Memorial Award. His second collection, *Happyland* (ECW), was published to wide acclaim in 2002. The excerpt here is from his Trillium Award-winning collection *Drift* (2005).

CROSBIE, LYNN

Lynn Crosbie is a cultural critic and author of five collections of poetry, *Miss Pamela's Mercy, VillainElle, Pearl, Queen Rat,* and *LIAR,* and two acclaimed novels. She is also the editor of two acclaimed anthologies of feminist writing, a controversial book on murderer Paul Bernardo, called *Paul's Case,* and is a regular contributor to *The Globe and Mail.* The excerpt here is from *Queen Rat* (1998), which the *Toronto Star* praised for its "stringently surreal beauty and consummate kiss-my-ass class." Lynn Crosbie lives in Toronto.

DEWDNEY, CHRISTOPHER

Christopher Dewdney was born in London, Ontario, and is now a professor at York University. Dewdney's interest in the sciences can be seen in his substantial use of vocabulary and themes from physics, biology, and geology. He has published more than eleven books of poetry, including *Predators of Adoration* and *Radiant Inventory,* both of which were nominated for Governor General's Literary Awards. A first-prize winner of the CBC Literary Competition, Christopher Dewdney also received a Governor General's Literary Award nomination for the book excerpted here, *The Immaculate Perception* (1985). His most recent book of essays is the acclaimed *Acquainted with the Night* (2004). Dewdney lives in Toronto.

DOMANSKI, DON

Don Domanski is known for intense, beautiful poems that explore a dreamlike world, a surreal landscape of the heart and mind. His work has been featured in Margaret Atwood's *Oxford Book of Canadian Verse,* Dennis Lee's *The New Canadian Poets,* Ken Norris's *Canadian Poetry Now,* and other anthologies. He has published eight books of poetry, two of which (*Wolf Ladder,* 1991, and *Stations of the Left Hand,* 1994) were finalists for the Governor General's Literary Award for Poetry. In 1999, he won the Canadian Literary Award for Poetry. The excerpt here is from *Hammerstroke* (1986). Domanski lives in Halifax.

DREW, WAYLAND

Wayland Drew lived and taught in Port Perry and Bracebridge, Ontario. He is the author of twelve books, including *Superior: The Haunted Shore,* the science-fiction trilogy *The Erthring Cycle,* and the novel excerpted here, *The Wabeno Feast* (1973). He was awarded an honourary Doctorate of Letters from Trent University and a Lieutenant-Governor's Award. Drew died in December 1998.

ENGEL, MARIAN

Marian Engel was born in Toronto and educated at McMaster University and McGill University, where she wrote her Master's thesis on the English Canadian novel under the supervision of Hugh MacLennan. She taught briefly at McGill and at the University of Montana, married Howard Engel in 1962, and began to raise a family and pursue a writing career. Her first published novel, *No Clouds of Glory,* was published in 1968, quickly followed by the novel excerpted here, *The Honeyman Festival* (1970). Engel's most famous and controversial novel was *Bear* (1976), a tale of erotic love between a librarian and a bear which won the Governor General's Literary Award. She also wrote a number of children's books. In 1982, Engel was made an Officer of the Order of Canada. After her death in 1985, the Writer's Development Trust of Canada instituted the Marian Engel Award, which is presented annually to a woman writer in mid-career.

FERRON, JACQUES

Jacques Ferron was a doctor from the Gaspé, founder of the absurdist Rhinoceros Party, a negotiator between the government and the FLQ during the October Crisis, and a winner of the Governor General's Literary Award for Fiction. The excerpt here is from his *Selected Tales* (1984), translated by Betty Bednarski. Ferron died in 1985 at the age of sixty-four.

FRYE, NORTHROP

Northrop Frye was one of Canada's, and the world's, most distinguished and respected authorities on English literature. He was principal and chancellor of Victoria College, University of Toronto, and a Fellow of the Royal Society of Canada. Among his numerous books are the classics *Fearful Symmetry: A Study of William Blake, Anatomy of Criticism, The Great Code, Divisions on a Ground*, and *The Bush Garden*. The excerpt here is from Frye's beloved and bestselling CBC Massey Lectures, *The Educated Imagination* (1993). Northrop Frye died in 1991.

GASTON, BILL

Bill Gaston is the author of several acclaimed story collections and novels, including *Mount Appetite, The Good Body, Sointula*, and *Gargoyles* (2006). His story collection *Mount Appetite* was a finalist for the 2002 Scotiabank Giller Prize and the Ethel Wilson Fiction Prize. The novel *Sointula* was a finalist for the Ethel Wilson Fiction Prize and the City of Victoria Butler Prize, while *Gargoyles* was a finalist for the 2006 Governor General's Literary Award, the Ethel Wilson Fiction Prize, the City of Victoria Butler Prize, and winner of the ReLit Award. In 2002 Gaston was the inaugural winner of the Timothy Findley Award, presented by the Writers' Trust of Canada. The excerpt here is from his forthcoming novel, *The Order of Good Cheer* (2008). Gaston lives in British Columbia, where he teaches at the University of Victoria.

GIBSON, GRAEME

Graeme Gibson is the acclaimed author of *Five Legs, Communion, Perpetual Motion*, and *Gentleman Death*. He is a longtime cultural activist, and co-founder of the Writer's Union of Canada and the Writers' Trust. He is also past president of PEN Canada, the recipient of both the Harbourfront Festival Prize and the Toronto Arts Award, and is a Member of the Order of Canada. The excerpt here is from his influential and bestselling novel *Five Legs* (1969), which jumpstarted Anansi's fiction programme. Gibson lives in Toronto.

Ticknor, was released by Anansi in
ıs & Giroux in the United States, and
cerpt here is from Heti's astonishing
 collection *The Middle Stories* (2001),
Anansi in Canada and McSweeney's
] into German, French, Spanish, and
Trampoline Hall, a popular lecture
York, at which people speak on sub-
se. Heti lives in Toronto.

] in the Missouri Ozarks, moved to
American-Canadian citizenship. She
acclaimed books of poetry, memoir,
gation, which won the 1984 Governor
try; *Sitting in the Club Car Drinking*
a finalist for the 1986 Ethel Wilson
n Road Show, which was a finalist for
ovel Award; and *Enemy Women*, win-
st Fiction Prize. The excerpt here is
 poetry, *Waterloo Express* (1973). Jiles

 has published five novels, the last
in Canada by Anansi, as well as four
s of nonfiction. She has twice been
oung British Novelists and has won
nerset Maugham Award, the Encore
ttish Book of the Year Award. The
), which inspired *The London Review*
of prose." Kennedy lives in Glasgow,
creative writing at the University of
ning career in stand-up comedy.

GINSBERG, ALLEN

Allen Ginsberg was born in Newark, New Jersey in 1926. Known best for his long format poem, *Howl*, Ginsberg became one of the leading figures of the Beat Generation, dedicated to uninhibited self-expression. Ginsberg was involved in numerous political activities, including protests against the Vietnam War, and he spoke openly about issues such as free speech and gay rights. Among many other honours and accolades, in 1993 Ginsberg received the Chevalier des Arts et des Lettres (the Order of Arts and Letters) from the French Minister of Culture. The excerpt here is from *Airplane Dreams* (1968), one of Anansi's early international co-editions. Ginsberg died in 1997.

GODFREY, DAVID

David Godfrey, with Dennis Lee, co-founded House of Anansi Press in 1967. He was born in Winnipeg, Manitoba, educated at the University of Toronto, Iowa State University, and Stanford, and taught in Ghana for several years before teaching at U of T and then the University of Victoria in British Columbia. It was Godfrey's experience in Ghana that resulted in "Anansi" being named after a West African trickster spider-god. After Anansi, Godfrey went on to found another press, New Press, and also became a key partner at Press Porcépic. His novel *The New Ancestors* won the Governor General's Literary Award in 1970. The excerpt here is from *Death Goes Better with Coca-Cola* (1967). Godfrey now runs a small vineyard in the Cowichan Valley of British Columbia.

GRANT, GEORGE

George Grant was born in Toronto in 1918. He was a Canadian philosopher, teacher, and political commentator best known for his nationalism, political conservatism, comments on technology, Christian faith, and his conservative views on abortion. In 1981, he was made an Officer of the Order of Canada and was awarded the Royal Society of Canada's Pierre Chauveau Medal. He was also a Fellow of the Royal Society of Canada. The excerpt here is from his nonfiction book *Technology and*

Justice (1986), a searching exploration of the meaning of justice in a society dominated by technology, and a classic in Canadian thought. George Grant died in 1988.

GUNNARS, KRISTJANA

Krisjana Gunnars was born in 1948 in the Icelandic capitol Reykjavik. Drawing on her Nordic roots and related mythology, she has published numerous volumes of poetry and two novels, in addition to short stories, translations, critical studies, and selections of Icelandic writing. Her nonfiction book *Zero Hour* was a finalist for the 1991 Governor General's Literary Award. Gunnars has also edited a volume of critical essays on Canadian novelist Margaret Laurence. The excerpt here is from *Wake-Pick Poems* (1981). Gunnars taught creative writing at the University of Alberta from 1991 to 2004, and lives in Edmonton.

HAGE, RAWI

Rawi Hage was born in Beirut, Lebanon, and lived through nine years of the Lebanese civil war. He immigrated to Canada in 1992, and is an award-winning writer, visual artist, curator, and political commentator. His first novel, *DeNiro's Game* (2006), was a bestseller and a finalist for the Scotiabank Giller Prize, the Governor General's Literary Award, the Commonwealth Writers' Prize, and the Rogers Writers' Trust Fiction Prize. It also won the McAuslan First Book Prize and the Paragraphe Hugh MacLennan Prize for Fiction, was a *Globe and Mail* "Book of the Year," and has been sold to numerous international publishers and translated worldwide. The excerpt here is from Hage's forthcoming second novel, *Cockroach* (to be published in 2008). Hage lives in Montreal.

HÉBERT, ANNE

Anne Hébert was born in 1916 in Sainte-Catherine-de-Fossambault, a small village outside of Québec city. Her first volume of poetry, *Les Songes en équilibre*, appeared in 1942 to good critical response and was awarded the Prix David. Despite this success, the violence in her 1945 story "Le Torrent" and the darkness of her poetry collection *Le Tombeau*

was too disgusting. Heti's nove
2005 and published by Farrar, Str:
Editions Phebus in France. The e
and much-praised first book, he
which was published by House c
in the United States, and translat
Dutch. Heti is also the creator o
series based in Toronto and Nev
jects outside their areas of expert

JILES, PAULETTE

Paulette Jiles was born and raise
Canada in 1969, and retains dual
is the author of several critically
and fiction, including *Celestial Nav*
General's Literary Award for Po
Rum and Karma Kola, which was
Fiction Prize; *The Late Great Hum*
the 1986 Books in Canada First N
ner of the 2002 Rogers Writers Tr
from her stellar early collection (
lives in San Antonio, Texas.

KENNEDY, A.L.

The Scottish writer A.L. Kennec
two of which have been publishe
collections of stories and two bo
selected as one of *Granta*'s Best of
numerous prizes, including the Sc
Award, and the Saltire Society Sc
selection here is from *Paradise* (200
of Books to call Kennedy "a virtuos
Scotland, is a part-time lecturer in
St. Andrews, and also has a burge

GINSBERG, ALLEN

Allen Ginsberg was born in Newark, New Jersey in 1926. Known best for his long format poem, *Howl*, Ginsberg became one of the leading figures of the Beat Generation, dedicated to uninhibited self-expression. Ginsberg was involved in numerous political activities, including protests against the Vietnam War, and he spoke openly about issues such as free speech and gay rights. Among many other honours and accolades, in 1993 Ginsberg received the Chevalier des Arts et des Lettres (the Order of Arts and Letters) from the French Minister of Culture. The excerpt here is from *Airplane Dreams* (1968), one of Anansi's early international co-editions. Ginsberg died in 1997.

GODFREY, DAVID

David Godfrey, with Dennis Lee, co-founded House of Anansi Press in 1967. He was born in Winnipeg, Manitoba, educated at the University of Toronto, Iowa State University, and Stanford, and taught in Ghana for several years before teaching at U of T and then the University of Victoria in British Columbia. It was Godfrey's experience in Ghana that resulted in "Anansi" being named after a West African trickster spider-god. After Anansi, Godfrey went on to found another press, New Press, and also became a key partner at Press Porcépic. His novel *The New Ancestors* won the Governor General's Literary Award in 1970. The excerpt here is from *Death Goes Better with Coca-Cola* (1967). Godfrey now runs a small vineyard in the Cowichan Valley of British Columbia.

GRANT, GEORGE

George Grant was born in Toronto in 1918. He was a Canadian philosopher, teacher, and political commentator best known for his nationalism, political conservatism, comments on technology, Christian faith, and his conservative views on abortion. In 1981, he was made an Officer of the Order of Canada and was awarded the Royal Society of Canada's Pierre Chauveau Medal. He was also a Fellow of the Royal Society of Canada. The excerpt here is from his nonfiction book *Technology and*

Justice (1986), a searching exploration of the meaning of justice in a society dominated by technology, and a classic in Canadian thought. George Grant died in 1988.

GUNNARS, KRISTJANA

Krisjana Gunnars was born in 1948 in the Icelandic capitol Reykjavik. Drawing on her Nordic roots and related mythology, she has published numerous volumes of poetry and two novels, in addition to short stories, translations, critical studies, and selections of Icelandic writing. Her nonfiction book *Zero Hour* was a finalist for the 1991 Governor General's Literary Award. Gunnars has also edited a volume of critical essays on Canadian novelist Margaret Laurence. The excerpt here is from *Wake-Pick Poems* (1981). Gunnars taught creative writing at the University of Alberta from 1991 to 2004, and lives in Edmonton.

HAGE, RAWI

Rawi Hage was born in Beirut, Lebanon, and lived through nine years of the Lebanese civil war. He immigrated to Canada in 1992, and is an award-winning writer, visual artist, curator, and political commentator. His first novel, *DeNiro's Game* (2006), was a bestseller and a finalist for the Scotiabank Giller Prize, the Governor General's Literary Award, the Commonwealth Writers' Prize, and the Rogers Writers' Trust Fiction Prize. It also won the McAuslan First Book Prize and the Paragraphe Hugh MacLennan Prize for Fiction, was a *Globe and Mail* "Book of the Year," and has been sold to numerous international publishers and translated worldwide. The excerpt here is from Hage's forthcoming second novel, *Cockroach* (to be published in 2008). Hage lives in Montreal.

HÉBERT, ANNE

Anne Hébert was born in 1916 in Sainte-Catherine-de-Fossambault, a small village outside of Québec city. Her first volume of poetry, *Les Songes en équilibre,* appeared in 1942 to good critical response and was awarded the Prix David. Despite this success, the violence in her 1945 story "Le Torrent" and the darkness of her poetry collection *Le Tombeau des rois* caused Québec publishers to refuse to publish them. In 1954 Hébert used a grant from the Royal Society to continue her writing in Paris. From then until 1997, Paris became her home, but only three of her novels are set there. Her seven other novels, including *Kamouraska* (1970), *Les Enfants du sabbat* (1975), *Les Fous de Bassan* (1982), *Le Premier Jardin* (1988), *L'Enfant chargé de songes* (1992), and *Aurélien, Clara, Mademoiselle, et le lieutenant anglais* (1995) are rooted primarily in Québec. Over the course of her nearly sixty-year career, Anne Hébert won countless literary awards, including the Prix David, the Prix France-Canada and the Prix Duvernay, the Governor General's Literary Award in 1960, 1975, and 1992, the Molson Prize, and the Prix Fémina. The English translation of *Est-ce que je te derange?* (*Am I disturbing you?*; Anansi, 1999) was a finalist for the Giller Prize. The excerpt here is from Hébert's influential early novel *Kamarouska* (1973). Hébert died in January 2000.

HEIGHTON, STEVEN

Steven Heighton is the author of poetry (*The Ecstasy of Skeptics*; and *The Address Book*), two novels (*Afterlands*; and *The Shadow Boxer*, a bestseller), and two collections of stories (*Flight Paths of the Emperor*; and *On earth as it is*). His work is translated into nine languages, has been internationally anthologized, and has been nominated for the Governor General's Literary Award, the Trillium Award, a Pushcart Prize, the Journey Prize, and Britain's W.H. Smith Award. He has received the Gerald Lampert Award, The Petra Kenney Prize, the Air Canada Award, and gold medals for fiction and for poetry in the National Magazine Awards. The excerpt here is from his acclaimed poetry collection *The Ecstasy of Skeptics* (1994), which was a finalist for the Governor General's Literary Award. Heighton lives with his family in Kingston, Ontario.

HETI, SHEILA

Sheila Heti studied art history and philosophy at the University of Toronto, and playwriting at the National Theatre School, though she did not graduate from theatre school, leaving after her first year when her adaptation of Faust was pulled by teachers, who determined that it was too disgusting. Heti's novel, *Ticknor*, was released by Anansi in 2005 and published by Farrar, Straus & Giroux in the United States, and Editions Phebus in France. The excerpt here is from Heti's astonishing and much-praised first book, her collection *The Middle Stories* (2001), which was published by House of Anansi in Canada and McSweeney's in the United States, and translated into German, French, Spanish, and Dutch. Heti is also the creator of Trampoline Hall, a popular lecture series based in Toronto and New York, at which people speak on subjects outside their areas of expertise. Heti lives in Toronto.

JILES, PAULETTE

Paulette Jiles was born and raised in the Missouri Ozarks, moved to Canada in 1969, and retains dual American-Canadian citizenship. She is the author of several critically acclaimed books of poetry, memoir, and fiction, including *Celestial Navigation*, which won the 1984 Governor General's Literary Award for Poetry; *Sitting in the Club Car Drinking Rum and Karma Kola*, which was a finalist for the 1986 Ethel Wilson Fiction Prize; *The Late Great Human Road Show*, which was a finalist for the 1986 Books in Canada First Novel Award; and *Enemy Women*, winner of the 2002 Rogers Writers Trust Fiction Prize. The excerpt here is from her stellar early collection of poetry, *Waterloo Express* (1973). Jiles lives in San Antonio, Texas.

KENNEDY, A.L.

The Scottish writer A.L. Kennedy has published five novels, the last two of which have been published in Canada by Anansi, as well as four collections of stories and two books of nonfiction. She has twice been selected as one of *Granta's* Best of Young British Novelists and has won numerous prizes, including the Somerset Maugham Award, the Encore Award, and the Saltire Society Scottish Book of the Year Award. The selection here is from *Paradise* (2004), which inspired *The London Review of Books* to call Kennedy "a virtuoso of prose." Kennedy lives in Glasgow, Scotland, is a part-time lecturer in creative writing at the University of St. Andrews, and also has a burgeoning career in stand-up comedy.

Thomas King holds a PhD in English/American Studies from the University of Utah and has taught Native Studies at universities in Utah, California, Minnesota, and Alberta for the past twenty-five years. He is currently Associate Professor of English (teaching Native Literature and Creative Writing) at the University of Guelph. His widely acclaimed novels include *Medicine River; Green Grass, Running Water;* and *Truth and Bright Water*. King has been nominated for the Governor General's Literary Award as well as the Commonwealth Writer's Prize. He is the editor of *All My Relations: An Anthology of Contemporary Canadian Native Fiction* and co-editor of *The Native in Literature: Canadian and Comparative Perspectives*. He's also well-known as the creator and writer of the CBC radio series, *The Dead Dog Café*. The excerpt here is from King's popular and bestselling CBC Massey Lectures, *The Truth About Stories* (2003). Thomas King's father was Cherokee, his mother is Greek, and he is the first Massey lecturer of Native descent.

LADOO, HAROLD SONNY

Harold Sonny Ladoo was born and grew up in Trinidad. Like many writers of his generation from Trinidad, he went abroad, emigrating to Canada in 1968. The excerpt here is from Ladoo's extraordinary novel, *No Pain Like This Body* (1972), long recognized as a classic of Canadian and Caribbean writing. Shortly after its publication, on a visit home to Calcutta Settlement, Trinidad in 1973, Ladoo died an untimely and violent death. He was twenty-eight. Ladoo's novel *Yesterdays* appeared posthumously in 1974.

LANE, PATRICK

Patrick Lane was born in Nelson, British Columbia in 1939. The author of more than twenty books, he has been recognized by many writers and critics as one of the best poets of his generation. His poetry, short stories, criticism, and non-fiction have won many prizes over the past forty-five years, including The Governor-General's Literary Award for *Poems: New & Selected* in 1979, The Canadian Authors Association

Award for his *Selected Poems* in 1988, and in 1987, a "Nellie" award (Canada) and The National Radio Award (USA) for the best public radio program. The excerpt here is from *Beware the Months of Fire* (1974). Patrick Lane lives in village outside of Victoria, British Columbia, where he is adjunct professor in the Writing Department at the University of Victoria.

LEE, DENNIS

Dennis Lee was the co-founder, with David Godfrey, of Anansi in 1967 and was instrumental in acquiring and editing many of the iconic books published in the press' first decade. Lee has written twenty-one of his own books for adults and children. His children's poetry, including the classic *Alligator Pie*, is read around the world. Lee is also a noted essayist and song lyricist. Among many other honours, he was Toronto's first poet laureate from 2001 to 2004. The excerpts here are from his influential poetry collections *Civil Elegies* (1972), which won the Governor General's Literary Award, and *Un* (2003), which the *Globe and Mail* called "a hair-raising yikes of a book...[that also shows] a howling love for the world." Lee lives in Toronto.

MALLA, PASHA

Pasha Malla's fiction and non-fiction have appeared in a number of magazines, journals and anthologies, including *Hobart, Maisonneuve, Grain, Prism International, Fiddlehead, Prairie Fire, Matrix, McSweeney's* and *Journey Prize Stories 2005*. The excerpt here is from his forthcoming first book, a collection of stories to be published by Anansi in 2008. Malla lives in Toronto.

MANDEL, ELI

Eli Mandel was born in 1922 in Estevan, Saskatchewan. He was a major figure in Canadian prairie poetry, teaching many up-and-coming writers and helping to define the canon of Canadian poetry by editing numerous influential anthologies. His collection *An Idiot Joy* won the Governor General's Literary Award for poetry in 1968, the same year

Alden Nowlan won for *Bread, Wine and Salt*. The excerpt here is from *Crusoe* (1973). During his career, Mandel held positions at the University of Alberta, University of Victoria, University of Toronto, and York University. He died in Toronto in 1992.

MARLATT, DAPHNE

Daphne Marlatt was born in Melbourne, Australia, and grew up in Penang, Malaysia, until her family immigrated to Canada in 1951. Her poetry collections include *Steveston, How to Hug a Stone, Touch to My Tongue*, and *Salvage*. The excerpt here is from *Ana Historic* (1988) Marlatt's first novel, which was originally published by Coach House Press in Canada and The Women's Press in the U.K., before being re-released by Anansi. The French translation was published by Les Éditions du remue-ménage. In 2006, Marlatt was made a Member of the Order of Canada. She lives in Victoria, British Columbia.

MOORE, LISA

Lisa Moore is a graduate of the Nova Scotia College of Art and Design. Her story collection *Open* (Anansi, 2002) was a finalist for the Scotiabank Giller Prize and the Winterset Award, winner of the Canadian Authors Association Jubilee Award, and a national bestseller. The first excerpt here is from her novel *Alligator* (2005), which was a finalist for the Scotiabank Giller Prize, the Orange Broadband Prize, the IMPAC Dublin Literary Award, and the Thomas H. Raddall Prize for Fiction, won the Commonwealth Prize for Canada and the Caribbean, and was a *Globe and Mail* "Top 100" book and a national bestseller. It was also published to acclaim internationally and inspired Richard Ford to call Moore, "an astonishing writer." The second excerpt is from Moore's forthcoming novel (2009) with Anansi. Moore lives in St. John's, Newfoundland.

MOOTOO, SHANI

Shani Mootoo is a Trinidadian-Canadian writer and artist whose family has traversed the cultures of India, Ireland, England, Nepal, and Trinidad. She was raised in Trinidad and Tobago, and moved to Canada at the age of nineteen. Her first collection of short fiction, *Out on Main Street*, was published in 1993. Her debut novel, *Cereus Blooms at Night*, was released in 1999, published in fourteen countries, and became a finalist for the Giller Prize, the Ethel Wilson Fiction Prize, and the Chapters/Books in Canada First Novel Award. Mootoo's second novel, *He Drown She in the Sea*, was published in 2005 to international acclaim. The excerpt here is from Mootoo's forthcoming novel, *Viveka's Story* (2009). In addition to being a writer, Mootoo is a multimedia artist whose paintings, videos, and photos have been exhibited internationally. Mootoo lives in Toronto.

MORITZ, A.F.

A.F. Moritz has written more than ten books of poetry, and has won the Governor General's Literary Award, the Award in Literature of the American Academy of the Arts, and a Guggenheim Fellowship. He also won *Poetry* magazine's Bess Hokin Prize for 2004, for his poem "The Sentinel." The excerpt here is from *Night Street Repairs* (2005), which won the ReLit Award. Moritz lives in Toronto, where he teaches at the University of Toronto.

MOURE, ERÍN

Erín Moure is one of Canada's most eminent and respected poets, and a translator from French, Spanish, Galician, and Portuguese. Winner of the Governor General's Award for *Furious* and the Pat Lowther Memorial Award for *Domestic Fuel*, Moure has published twelve books of poetry, including *A Frame of the Book*, which was co-published in the U.S. by Sun and Moon Press, and three books of poetry in translation, including *Sheep's Vigil by a Fervent Person*, which was shortlisted for the 2002 Griffin Poetry Prize and the 2002 City of Toronto Book Prize. Her 2005 volume, *Little Theatres*, was a finalist for the Griffin Prize, the Governor General's Literary Award, and the Pat Lowther Award, and won the A.M. Klein Poetry Prize. The excerpt here is from her much-admired GG-winning volume, *Furious* (1988). Moure lives in Montreal.

ONDAATJE, MICHAEL

Michael Ondaatje was born in Sri Lanka, and came to Canada in 1962. He is the author of many internationally celebrated novels including his most recent, *Divisidero; Anil's Ghost*, winner of the 2000 Giller Prize, the Prix Médicis, and the Governor General's Award; *The English Patient*, winner of the Booker Prize and the Governor General's Award; *In the Skin of a Lion*, winner of the 1988 City of Toronto Book Award; and, *Coming Through Slaughter*, winner of the 1976 Books in Canada First Novel Award. In 1970, he won the Governor General's Literary Award for the book of poetry excerpted here, *The Collected Works of Billy the Kid* (1970). In 1988, Ondaatje was made an Officer of the Order of Canada and two years later became a Foreign Honorary Member of the American Academy of Arts and Letters. Ondaatje lives in Toronto.

PARTRIDGE, ELISE

Elise Partridge's *Fielder's Choice* (2002) was shortlisted for the Gerald Lampert Memorial Award for best first book of poems in Canada. The excerpt here is from her forthcoming second book, *Chameleon Hours* (2008), will be published simultaneously by Anansi and the University of Chicago Press. Her poetry has appeared in *The Fiddlehead, The New Quarterly, The Malahat Review, Poetry, The New Yorker, Poetry Ireland Review,* and elsewhere. She has taught literature and composition at several universities and currently lives in Vancouver, where she works as an editor and tutor.

PURDY, AL

Al Purdy was born in Wooler, Ontario. He served in the Royal Canadian Air Force during World War II. He received the Order of Canada in 1982, the Order of Ontario in 1987, and the Governor General's Literary Award twice, once in 1965 for his collection *The Cariboo Horses* and once in 1986 for his *Collected Poems*. The excerpt here is from *Poems for All the Annettes* (1973), which includes one of his most famous and beloved poems, "Quinte Hotel." Purdy died in April 2000.

REDHILL, MICHAEL

Michael Redhill is the author of four poetry collections, including *Light-crossing* and *Lake Nora Arms*. His first novel, *Martin Sloane*, was nominated for the 2001 Giller Prize. It also won the Books in Canada First Novel Award and the Commonwealth Writers' Prize (Canada and the Caribbean Region). Redhill's play *Building Jerusalem* was nominated for a Governor General's Award in 2001. His most recent novel, *Consolation*, published in 2006, won the City of Toronto Book Award and was longlisted for the Booker Prize. Redhill is also an editor of *Brick: A Literary Journal* and was an editor at Coach House Books. The excerpt here is from the critically acclaimed volume of poetry *Light-crossing* (2001). Michael Redhill lives and works in Toronto.

ROSENBLATT, JOE

Joe Rosenblatt was born in Toronto in 1933. In 1966 his first book, *The L.S.D. Leacock*, was published by Coach House Press. Since then, he has published more than a dozen books of poetry and fiction. His selected poems, *Top Soil*, won the Governor General's Literary Award. Another volume of selected poems, *Poetry Hotel*, won a B.C. Book Prize. His poems have appeared in numerous anthologies and periodicals across North America, and Rosenblatt has held several writer-in-residence positions in Canadian universities and libraries, as well as short-term writer-in-residence positions internationally. The excerpt here is from *Winter of the Luna Moth* (1968). For the past fifteen years, Rosenblatt has been living in Qualicum Beach on Vancouver Island.

SATIN, MARK

Mark Satin is a lawyer and editor of the online political periodical *Radical Middle Newsletter*. In the 1960s, Satin was co-founder and executive director of the Toronto Anti-Draft Programme, a draft-dodger assistance organization during the Vietnam War. The excerpt here is from Satin's book *Manual for Draft-Age Immigrants to Canada* (1968), which was an underground classic, and one of Anansi's bestselling books ever. Satin has served as advisor to Centrist Coalition, Reuniting America, Vasconcellos Project, and other U.S. activist organizations. He lives in the San Francisco Bay Area.

SAUL, JOHN RALSTON

John Ralston Saul is the author of the bestselling *Voltaire's Bastards*, *The Doubter's Companion*, *Reflections of a Siamese Twin*, and *On Equilibrium*. His other books include the novels *The Paradise Eater*, *The Next Best Thing*, and *The Birds of Prey*. He has received many national and international awards, most recently the Pablo Neruda International Presidential Medal of Honour from the Chilean government. The excerpt here is from his CBC Massey Lectures, *The Unconscious Civilization* (1995), which won the Governor General's Literary Award, as well as the Gordon Montador Award for "Best Canadian Book on Social Issues." In addition to his writing, Saul is co-chair of the Institute for Canadian Citizenship, and patron and former president of the Canadian Centre of International PEN. He is also Chair of the Advisory Board for the LaFontaine-Baldwin lecture series, Honorary Chair of the Project Advisors' Committee for Evergreen at the Brickworks, Distinguished Patron of the Canadian Academy of Independent Scholars, and Patron of PLAN (a cutting edge organization that works with people with disabilities), Engineers without Borders, and the Canadian Landmine Foundation. A Companion in the Order of Canada (1999), he is also Chevalier in the Ordre des Arts et des Lettres of France (1996). Saul lives in Toronto.

SHARPE, DAVID

David Sharpe is a short-story writer, poet, and teacher, whose work has appeared in many magazines and anthologies. His one nonfiction book is excerpted here: *Rochdale: The Runaway College* (1987). Sharpe has taught in the writing program at Brown University in Providence, Rhode Island, and also for many years in Toronto. He now lives in Athens, Ohio, where he teaches at Ohio University.

Award for Best Specialty Book of the Year. Her third book, *Lost August,* won the Pat Lowther Memorial Award. Spalding is a contributing editor to *Brick* magazine and was the editor of the 2003 *Griffin Poetry Prize Anthology.* She also co-edited the anthology *Lost Classics* with Michael Ondaatje, Michael Redhill, and Linda Spalding. Esta Spalding lives in Guelph.

TAYLOR, CHARLES

Charles Taylor is a Canadian philosopher who has made significant contributions to political philosophy, philosophy of social science, and the history of philosophy. He was educated at McGill University and at Balliol College, Oxford, where he studied under Isaiah Berlin and G.E.M. Anscombe. For many years he was Professor of Political Science and Philosophy at McGill University, where he is now professor emeritus. Taylor was a candidate for the New Democratic Party in Mount Royal on three occasions in the 1960s. He lost all three times, most famously in the 1965 election to future prime minister Pierre Trudeau. In 1995, Taylor was made a Companion of the Order of Canada. In 2000, he was made a Grand Officer of the National Order of Quebec. And in 2007, he was awarded the Templeton Prize, which includes a cash award of $1.5 million. Taylor's influential writings include *Sources of the Self: The Making of Modern Identity,* and the book excerpted here, Taylor's CBC Massey Lectures, *The Malaise of Modernity* (1991). Charles Taylor lives in Montreal.

THESEN, SHARON

Sharon Thesen has published seven much-admired books of poetry, three of which have been finalists for the Governor General's Literary Award. *A Pair of Scissors* (Anansi, 2000) won the Pat Lowther Award from the League of Canadian Poets. The excerpt here is from *The Good Bacteria* (2006), which was a finalist for the Governor General's Literary Award, the Pat Lowther Award, and the Dorothy Livesay Poetry Prize. Thesen lives in Lake Country, British Columbia, and teaches at Capilano College.

THOMPSON, JOHN

John Thompson was born in England in 1938 and taught for many years at Mount Allison University in Sackville, New Brunswick. He is the author of two slim and extraordinary volumes of poetry, *At the Edge of the Chopping There are No Secrets* (1973) and *Stilt Jack* (1978). Two posthumous works have also been published, *John Thompson: Collected Poems and Translations*, edited by Peter Sanger, and *I Dream Myself Into Being: Collected Poems*. Thompson died suddenly in 1976.

VANIER, JEAN

Jean Vanier is the son of former governor general Georges Vanier. He is the founder of L'Arche and Faith and Light, both international networks of communities for people with intellectual disabilities. He wrote his doctoral thesis on Aristotle and taught philosophy at the University of Toronto. In 1997, he received the Paul VI Prize for his work on behalf of human development and progress. The excerpt here is from his bestselling Anansi book, *Becoming Human* (1998). Jean Vanier lives in France.

WINTER, MICHAEL

Michael Winter was born in England and grew up in Newfoundland. He is the author of the "Gabriel English" novels *The Architects are Here*, published in the fall of 2007, and *This All Happened*, which won the 2000 Winterset Award and was nominated for the Rogers Writers Trust Fiction Prize. He has also written two story collections, *Creaking in Their Skins* and *One Last Good Look*. The excerpt here is from Winter's novel *The Big Why* (2005), which won the Drummer General's Award, was a finalist for the Trillium Book Award and the Thomas Head Raddall Fiction Prize, and was published internationally. Winter divides his time between St. John's and Toronto.

WRIGHT, RONALD

Ronald Wright is an acclaimed novelist, historian, and essayist who has won awards in all three genres and is published in more than a dozen languages. His nonfiction books include the bestsellers *Time Among the Maya* and *Stolen Continents*, which won the Gordon Montador Award and was chosen a book of the year by the *Independent* and *The Sunday Times*. His novel *A Scientific Romance* won Britain's David Higham Prize for Fiction and was chosen a book of the year by *The Globe and Mail*. The excerpt here is from Wright's CBA Libris Award-winning CBC Massey Lectures, *A Short History of Progress* (2004), which has been on the bestseller lists since the year of its publication and has been widely published internationally. Wright lives in British Columbia.

WYATT, RACHEL

Writer and playwright Rachel Wyatt was born in England in 1929 and has lived in Canada since 1957. She began her career as a non-fiction writer for magazines and newspapers and then wrote prolifically for radio and television, most often for the CBC and BBC. Wyatt has written four novels; successful stage plays, including *Chairs and Tables* and *Crackpot*; and short stories, including the collection *The Day Marlene Dietrich Died* (1996). Wyatt was Director of the Writing Program at the Banff Centre for the Arts during the 1990s and has appeared at writer's conferences across Canada and internationally. She won the CBC Literary Competition Drama Award in 1982. In 2002, she was awarded the Order of Canada, and in 2003 she received the Queen's Jubilee Medal.

INDEX OF AUTHORS

INDEX OF BOOKS